The Kikuchi Diary

The Kikuchi Diary

Chronicle from an American Concentration Camp

The Tanforan Journals of CHARLES KIKUCHI

Edited by JOHN MODELL

University of Illinois Press

Urbana and Chicago

Illini Books edition, 1993

Manufactured in the United States of America

P 5 4 3 2 1

This book is printed on acid-free paper.

Library of Congress Cataloging-in-Publication Data

Kikuchi, Charles.
    The Kikuchi diary : chronicle from an American concentration camp
    : the Tanforan journals of Charles Kikuchi / edited by and with an
    introduction by John Modell. — Illini books ed.
        p.   cm.
    ISBN 0-252-06283-3 (pb)
    1. Tanforan Assembly Center (San Bruno, California) 2. Japanese
Americans—Evacuation and relocation, 1942–1945. 3. Japanese
Americans—California—Diaries. 4. Kikuchi, Charles—Diaries.
I. Modell, John. II. Title
D769.8.A6K54 1993
940.53′1779469—dc20   92–17297
                                                                   CIP

To DOROTHY SWAINE THOMAS, our teacher,
whose vigorous humanity has enlightened
both diarist and editor

Contents

Preface   ix

Introduction   1

A Note on the Editing   40

The Kikuchi Diary   42

Preface

Being invited to reflect upon an earlier piece of one's own scholarship at twenty years' remove is, of course, pleasing. But the reflections startle one: how much has changed!

When the late Dorothy Swaine Thomas introduced me to the diary notes of Charles Kikuchi in 1970, I had just completed my doctoral study of Japanese Americans in Los Angeles, which took them from the beginnings of the community to their removal from their homes in 1942. My age was very nearly that of the diarist at the time he composed the document I would edit.

To a young historian like me, reading the sparkling, insightful diary notes and then meeting Charlie in his New York townhouse (he had some years before made a *very* fortunate real estate transaction, as he explained to me with typically ironic self-dismissal) was a joy and a challenge. How has the placid, middle-aged man in the living room emerged from the extremely individualistic, almost detached, young man who wrote so well of his evacuation and that of his family and people from their homes to a horse track? To my mind, something of the central theme of the Japanese American experience was contained in the biography of this man, which I sought to explore in my introduction to the edited *Diary*, published in 1973.

This reissue of the *Diary* appears at a historical moment that heightens its pertinence. In the past twenty years, the Sansei— the third generation of Japanese Americans—have come to maturity in an era in which public protest of discrimination against racially defined minorities is far more the norm than when their parents became adults. Sansei scholars and community figures are asking demanding questions about the generally accommodative response of their parents' generation to the World War II "relocation," about both the uniformity of accommodation and its explanation. *The Kikuchi Diary*, by an atypical Nisei, is grist for this examination. That the United States government has finally set up a restitution program to pay cash damages to those whose lives it disrupted and whose property it dissipated in no way closes these questions for the Sansei, or for others interested in the nature of American democracy. And while the *Diary* sheds no light on the nature of white American prejudice against Japanese Americans, the recent and shocking reappearance of public abuse directed at Japanese Americans reminds not only Japanese Americans but all Americans that the national origin of ethnic groups may be remembered in other than benign ways. I have earlier argued that a surprising element of white American hostility toward Japanese immigrants and their descendants stemmed from anxiety about the competence and aggressiveness of the Japanese nation; many Americans currently harbor quite similar anxieties, and some have taken them out on Japanese Americans. Any contemporaneous account of the "relocation," however sardonic, may serve as a fruitful reminder today of the depth of prejudice.

In 1970, and, indeed, at least through the publication of a revised version of my dissertation in 1977,[1] I generally adhered to the euphemistic term — "relocation camps" — that the United States government had applied to the isolated, barbed-wire-bounded settlements to which Pacific Coast Americans of Japanese birth or descent had been removed. (Before construction on the camps was completed, their future inhabitants were moved into makeshift "assembly centers," like Tanforan, where *The*

---

[1] *The Economics and Politics of Racial Accommodation: The Japanese of Los Angeles, 1900–1942* (Urbana: University of Illinois Press, 1977).

Kikuchi Diary is set.) I kept to this terminology to emphasize the difference between the treatment of the Japanese Americans and the far crueler treatment suffered in concentration camps run by Japanese for American prisoners of war and by Nazi Germans for civilians of the wrong ancestry. My use of the term "concentration camp" as the subtitle to the *Diary* was meant to shock. In the twenty years since I published the book, the shock has more than worn off, and the euphemism has come to embarrass me. (Indeed, American historians generally have become less prone to accept governmental definitions as presumptively accurate.)

I was myself middle aged when, in 1988, Charles Kikuchi died. Characteristically, Charlie died in action, becoming acutely ill while participating in the International March for Peace from Odessa to Kiev, dying shortly after an emergency return home. The man never lost his vibrant idealism, which coexisted somehow with the gentle cynicism that so obviously pervades the *Diary*. To my great regret, I never came to know him much better than I did in the early 1970s. Mainly, we exchanged annual letters updating one another on our activities, mine relentlessly professional, Charlie's often oriented to observing the life around him while assisting his wife in her highly acclaimed dance career. Thinking about the man after hearing of his death, I realized that Charlie has meant more to me than I ever imagined he would, not because of his ethnicity, but because of his ability to be uncomplicatedly, contentedly, openly *there*—no excuses, no disguises—whatever the situation. I hope readers can find traces of this in his *Diary*, quite apart from the more specifically historical significance of the document.

My interest in writing my dissertation about Japanese Americans had been in ethnicity. In the late 1960s, when I wrote, a sociologically informed community study of the American ethnic community was a somewhat unusual venture. Although I shifted my scholarly focus away from ethnicity after the publication of the revision of my dissertation and then of a second, and far more structuralist, treatment of ethnicity that considered the

Japanese Americans as a test case of some theoretical proposi-
tions,[2] ethnicity has become a major issue among American
historians. But in the last twenty years far more sophisticated
approaches to the topic have emerged.

My 1973 introduction to *The Kikuchi Diary* presumes ethnicity
virtually as a given in a situation. Charlie is discussed as choosing
whether to renounce or embrace his Japanese American ethnicity. Oddly, in my reading today of Kikuchi's diary text, it is
his *nationality* as an American that seems forced and problematic,
not his ethnicity as a Japanese American. Current scholarship,
taking its cues in part from analyses of class and of gender that
treat consciousness as a problematic and not as a given, starts
from a considerably more social-constructionist perspective upon
ethnicity (and nationality) than I assumed two decades ago. As
I look back on my Introduction to the *Diary*, I am pleased with
my instincts for leading me to a character who so obviously
could not be seen in simple assimilation/resistance terms. But
my instinct at that time also was to psychologize my account,
rather than to view and analyze Charles Kikuchi as an active
maker of his own self, and as a culture-broker and a culture-
maker, for producing the diary notes on order for a large,
university-based research project. Surely Charlie's participant-
observer role, however creative, carries interpretive complexi-
ties that those who read the text today will seek. A historian
today, I think, would be far more likely to pay close attention
to the circumstances under which Charles Kikuchi produced the
notes and to the readers that he imagined would read them. I
think the text has the depth to bear such a demanding reading.

The dramatic events that framed Charlie's early-1942 reflections, of course, defined *The Kikuchi Diary* as a uniquely Japanese
American phenomenon, and so I presented it. Among American
ethnic groups, however, Japanese Americans are not alone in
the special defining resonance that World War II has for them.
And just as World War II has had varied and complex meanings
to different American groups, so, too, has racism and the impact

---

[2] Edna Bonacich and John Modell, *The Economic Basis of Ethnic Solidarity* (Berkeley: University of California Press, 1980).

of the many cultural and political nationalisms that our century has seen. I would hope that, were I to come to this document fresh, I would be alert and responsive to a wider context, a more comparative framework, than when I first encountered it.

As I emerged into the American historical profession, I found myself sometimes described as an Asian American historian. I always rejected this designation as inaccurate because I knew very little about the experience of other Asians in America besides the Japanese and as an unfortunate clustering in any case. I was not, and am not, persuaded that there is such a thing as Asian American history. Groups so disparate in background and experience as the Chinese, Japanese, Indians, Filipinos, Koreans, Vietnamese, and Hmong in the United States just do not have all that much of a common history. And even if to some extent they do, the experience of Japanese people in the United States probably bears at least as close a comparison to that of Eastern European Jews and of Greeks as to that of Koreans. Although immigration and ethnicity, a field defined by common concerns, makes an appropriate specialization for historians of the United States, I see no such commanding logic for Asian American history.

Close readers of my 1973 introduction will note two sub-themes that are surprisingly unremarked in the context of current concerns. Charlie Kikuchi was a victim of *child abuse* (a phrase I probably did not know in 1973), exiled from his parents' home because his father's physical battery of him could not otherwise be stayed. From one perspective the *Diary* is the account of the path toward reconciliation with family of a battered child whose resilience was sufficient to allow him to return to his family, no longer his parents' dependent although hardly a fully independent adult either, in view of the constraints of the relocation. The second disregarded subtheme is gender: Charles Kikuchi, in his mid-twenties, had a strong interest in women, to some extent as sexual objects and his is very much a diary of a young man. And although Charlie intentionally suppressed much material he gathered on sexual patterns in the camp, the *Diary* is loaded with observations, many with a charming 1940s sound to them, about young men and women thrown together in very close quarters under very great stress. So far as I can remember, I really paid no special attention to such intriguing passages as that of May 25, in which family fun, transvestism, and ethnic ambivalence all mix. "The gals have a new fad of wearing jeans now and Alice, Emiko, and Bette [Charles' sisters] were trying ours out. . . . Emiko started a fashion show by putting on our clothes, so Jack put on Emi's shorts and brassiere and mimics their gestures before the mirror, while I did a Charlie Chan strut with her skirt. We laughed so much I bet our neighbors think we are crazy."

Texts deepen, I think, as we ask new questions of them. I'm very pleased that *The Kikuchi Diary* will see new light.

John Modell
1992

The Kikuchi Diary

Introduction

The removal from the Pacific Coast states of some 110,000 persons of Japanese birth or ancestry between March and mid-August, 1942, was by design indiscriminate. Indeed, the Supreme Court decision upholding the right of the military to treat American citizens of Japanese ancestry much as though they were enemy aliens specifically cited the purported difficulty of distinguishing loyal from disloyal "Japanese," the category of loyalty overriding that of citizenship.

> The adoption by Government, in the crisis of war and of threatened invasion, of measures for the public safety, based upon the recognition of facts and circumstances which indicate that a group of one national extraction may menace that safety more than others, is not wholly beyond the limits of the Constitution and is not to be condemned merely because in other and in most circumstances racial distinctions are irrelevant. . . . Whatever view we may entertain regarding the loyalty to this country of the citizens of Japanese ancestry, we cannot reject as unfounded the judgment of the military authorities and of Congress that there were disloyal members of that population, whose number and strength could not be precisely and quickly ascertained. We cannot say that the warmaking branches of the Government did not have ground for believing that in a critical hour such persons could not readily be isolated and separately dealt with.[1]

1 *Hirabayashi* v. *U.S.*, 320 U.S. 81 (1943); order of the quotation slightly rearranged.

For those thus summarily evacuated and incarcerated, none was more suffused with loyalty to America than Charles Kikuchi, twenty-six years old at the time, born in Vallejo, California, and a resident of Berkeley. "If we are ever going to prove our Americanism, this is the time," he wrote in his diary on the day of Pearl Harbor, adding on the following day, "I don't have any doubts about where I stand even if I am worried about what happens to us." More dramatically, he appended a section to a class paper dated December 12, 1941:

> But, where does the Nisei [2] stand in this picture? This is the question that will often be asked, and the Nisei must be prepared to demonstrate with their undivided loyalty. No longer can they waveringly sit upon the fence. . . . Instead of utter disorganization I believe that they will stand firm in their fundamental beliefs. Instead of chaos, this is the time for constructive action. The Nisei believe that now is the time to prove their loyalty is something more than mere surface words. This crisis is their opportunity. . . . They do not weep for self pity. They want to act for America, terribly. The question is, "Will they be given a chance!"

Half a year later Kikuchi even hoped that the government might provide "Caucasian leadership" needed for "a successful Americanization program."

Such feelings were widespread among both Nisei and their parents. The group, however, was kept by law from returning to the coast until 1945. For some evacuees the "relocation" lasted a year or even two longer. These, victims of especially severe psychic scarring, remained resolutely in the relocation camps to which they had been taken. In some cases the camps had to be closed, the electricity and water shut off, before their victims could be induced to re-enter the larger society.

No such apparent wounds were suffered by Charles Kikuchi, whose departure for Chicago in mid-April, 1943, placed him

[2] Japanese American of U.S. birth. The immigrant generation is known as the Issei. Nisei who had been sent to Japan as youths for much of their schooling are known as Kibei. The generational pattern continues with the Sansei (third generation) and Yonsei (fourth generation).

among the earlier Nisei to leave the camps. Nor does Kikuchi's fierce loyalty—"Americanism," as he called it in the hollow-sounding terminology of the day—explain the interest of his diary for us, for simple loyalty was nearly universal in the American-born majority of evacuees. Although the patriotism of a complex man, imprisoned because of his race by his country, is one of the recurring themes of the document here published, it is by no means its only thread. Nor is the injustice of the mass relocation at issue here, although the diary provides further evidence of the fact if more evidence is required. Rather, the genius of Charles Kikuchi's diary, aside from its author's salty observations on the extraordinary turn his life took in 1942, is *ambivalence:* a peculiar discomfort and uncertainty about the strange and sometimes conflicting demands placed upon a gut individualist by friends, family, ethnic group, and country, and a nagging feeling that perhaps all these demands were justified. Such ambivalence, although more submerged in less complex persons, and at less trying times, was at the very heart of the experience of the Nisei. Such ambivalence, variously modulated by differing cultural and historical circumstances, is in fact one of the central experiences of many American ethnic groups. Sociologists half a century ago recognized this phenomenon as being a function of "marginality," the state of being at least partially *in* two groups but *of neither.*

Kikuchi's diary can profitably be read on at least three levels: as an insider's record of events in "America's concentration camps,"[3] as the daybook of a man who was no mere detached observer but for whom the camp experience was a psychic turning point, and as one strangely glowing example of the far wider phenomenon of ethnic ambivalence.

The Japanese emigration to the United States, like most emigration, had a strong economic motivation. Land was scarce in mountainous, densely populated Japan, and even a hard-

---

[3] This phrase was the title of a recent popularized account of the episode. Literally (and constitutionally), the phrase is entirely apt; in practice, the camps must be seen in the light of personalities which (not unlike Kikuchi's) matured and deepened under the formally rigid but practically rather mild strictures of camp life.

working population undergoing the beginnings of a massive transformation to an industrial and urban society could not, as it grew, find land enough to keep the population gainfully employed. Emigration to Hawaii—where young men, usually married, worked as plantation laborers—began on a large scale in 1884. Almost simultaneously the Congress of the United States shut off the migration of Chinese laborers to the United States on the ground that their entry "endangers the good order of certain localities." California vigilantism and anti-Orientalism, already well-established traditions, had scored a significant victory, one which would in several ways have a profound effect upon the Japanese Americans.

The 1890 Chinese population of the continental United States, about 107,000, barely exceeded that of 1880; the exclusion legislation, passed in 1882, was doing its work. By 1900 a substantial decrease had occurred. But at this time a new group, the Japanese, deemed at the time more appropriate resident aliens because less "degraded" by "coolie" traits, began to supply the balance. By 1910 there were 72,000 Japanese in the United States, a number just barely exceeding that of the Chinese. The Census Bureau issued a special report on Chinese and Japanese in the United States in that year; it is of note that in many tables the two groups were added together rather than treated separately. Like the Chinese, the Japanese were substantially concentrated in California. But unlike the earlier Chinese, who had constituted a quarter of the Golden State's foreign-born population in 1880 and nearly a tenth of its total population, the Japanese were numerically hardly more than a drop in the bucket of the growing California population. In 1920, when the number of Japanese immigrants in California reached a peak, there were over 50,000 of them, but this was less than 2 percent of the state's population.

The anti-Chinese tradition in California, and on the West Coast as a whole, nevertheless soon became an anti-Oriental tradition. James D. Phelan, mayor of San Francisco and later a U.S. senator, put it neatly in 1900: "The Japanese are starting the same tide of immigration which we thought we had checked [by the Chinese Exclusion Act] twenty years ago. . . . The Chinese and Japanese are not bona fide citizens. They are not the stuff of which American citizens can be made."

By 1907, agitation in California was sufficient to bring President Theodore Roosevelt to negotiate with Japan a quiet agreement by which emigrant passports would be denied to Japanese "laborers," except for those "who, in coming to the continent, seek to resume a formerly acquired domicile, to join a parent, wife, or children residing there, or to assume control of an already possessed interest in a farming enterprise in this country." The "coolie" image had thus again been invoked in order to rationalize the grounds for California anti-Orientalism.

	Total "Japanese" (all generations)	California "Japanese"	Percentage of U.S. "Japanese" in California	Total California Population	Percentage of California Population "Japanese"
1900	24,326	10,151	41.7	1,485,053	0.7
1910	72,157	41,356	57.3	2,377,549	1.7
1920	111,010	71,952	64.8	3,426,861	2.1
1930	138,834	97,456	70.2	5,677,251	1.7
1940	126,947	93,717	73.8	6,907,387	1.4

The Gentlemen's Agreement did not long satisfy those whose outcries against the Japanese immigrant had forced the action upon Roosevelt, for the stream of immigration, though changed in composition, was not stopped. Hardly a legislative session in California went by without discriminatory legislation being proposed, and some of it passed. But nothing availed. The battle was brought to the federal stage, for only here could immigration of the Japanese be halted altogether. California anti-Japanese, like U. S. Webb, longtime state attorney general, argued at some length and at an even greater remove from the facts of the situation about the need for a total ban on Japanese immigration. The Japanese are, he told Congress in 1924, the year in which this goal would in fact be achieved, "different in many respects": "They are different in color; different in ideals; different in race; different in ambitions; different in their theory of political economy and government. They speak a different language; they worship a different God. They have not in common with the Caucasian a single trait." "This is a Government of the white race," he argued; Congress agreed.

Yet even as Japanese immigration was being closed off, first by more stringent interpretation of the Gentlemen's Agreement and ultimately by an explicit exclusion section of the generally restrictive Immigration Act of 1924, the "Japanese," considered as a racial group—as indeed they were considered—continued to grow in the continental United States, at least until the depression of the 1930s.

	Total "Japanese"	Immigrants	American-Born
1900	24,326	24,057	269
1910	72,157	67,655	4,502
1920	111,010	81,338	29,672
1930	138,834	68,357	70,477
1940	126,947	47,305	79,642

In 1922 *Ozawa* v. *United States* had made it clear that although legally settled Japanese immigrants could remain, they could not gain American citizenship. Ozawa, a longtime resident of Berkeley, had argued that although since 1790 naturalization had been limited to "free white persons," except for the extension of this right during Reconstruction to "persons of African descent," [4] the authors of the 1790 legislation had not meant to exclude Japanese from naturalization but had really been concerned only with blacks and American Indians. The court admitted the plausibility of this reasoning but responded that even if true, "this should go no farther than to demonstrate

[4] It is interesting to note that even at the height of the Reconstruction period, when Senators Sumner and Trumbull argued for removing *all* racial qualifications for naturalization (since, as Trumbull declared, "the Chinaman . . . is infinitely above the African in intelligence, in manhood, and in every respect"), their proposal was solidly voted down. *In re Ah Yup*, 1 Fed. Cas. 223 (1878), judicially sealed the fate of Chinese naturalization, while Congress gratuitously added to the Chinese Exclusion Act, in the same year it was passed, a further law instructing all state and federal courts not to admit any Chinese to citizenship.

their lack of sufficient information to enable them to foresee precisely who would be excluded by that term." Rather, the court reasoned, "it is sufficient to ascertain whom they intended to include." Here the court, following "an almost unbroken line" of state and federal court cases, decided simply that the 1790 legislators had intended to include only persons "of what is popularly known as the Caucasian race" and that Ozawa was "clearly of a race which is not Caucasian [or African] and therefore belongs entirely outside the zone on the negative side." [5]

However, the Fourteenth Amendment to the U.S. Constitution explicitly granted the right of American citizenship to "all persons born or naturalized in the United States," without exception. Thus Charles Kikuchi, a Nisei, the son of Japanese immigrants, would be a citizen by right; his Issei parents could not be. Nor, for that matter, could even "Issei" who entered the country as infants: race, not culture, was the touchstone.

U. S. Webb, and those who thought as he did, had prevailed over the good-willed churchmen who saw an opportunity rather than a threat in the Japanese immigrant, and over those employers who still relied upon their labor. But Webb was shamefully mistaken about the qualities of the Japanese immigrant; and, if possible, he was even more wrong about the immigrants' children. From a very early date Japanese in this country had been orderly, economically shrewd, and on the whole quite successful in making a go of America, and had with great eagerness learned the language and adopted the customs of the country. Attendance at adult English-language classes, held under ethnic, religious, and state auspices, was substantial and, reportedly, enthusiastic; between 1900 and 1920 inability to speak English on the part of adult Japanese immigrants to America dropped from 62 percent to 15 percent; between 1920 and 1930 school attendance by Japanese Americans between the ages of five and twenty caught up to and passed that of native white Americans of native parentage. The one barrier that

[5] 260 U.S. 178 (1922).

could not be passed was that of race, a barrier affecting the Nisei as much as the Issei.

Yet by 1924 the anti-Japanese forces had accomplished all their proximate goals with the passage of the exclusion legislation, and little more could be done to consolidate the victory. The legally settled Japanese aliens already in the United States could by no stretch of the hostile imagination be forced to leave the country; the pain the immigration cutoff caused them, and the government of Japan, could not be felt or enjoyed by those whose actions were responsible for it. The psychological moment for further anti-Japanese action had passed, if indeed the 1924 act was not something of an anticlimax. The main heat of Pacific-state anti-Japanese feeling had been reached somewhat earlier, with the passage of legislative acts of economic harassment in California (1913 and 1920), Washington (1921), and Oregon (1923). These acts made the operation of agricultural enterprises more difficult for Japanese by limiting the right of "aliens ineligible to citizenship" to own farmland.

Despite occasional local harassments such as residential segregation or limitations on use of public facilities, despite occasional suggestions that the Nisei be somehow deprived of their citizenship, despite the obstinate refusal to grant even a token immigration quota to outraged Japan, the Japanese in America were left more or less alone for the decade and a half following the exclusion of 1924. In this period the first substantial numbers of Nisei attained their majority. The world most of them confronted was hard enough, but the Depression was as much, possibly more palpably, the cause of their hardship as was discrimination. Nisei life, especially in the major urban areas on the Pacific Coast, was intense, if ingrown. A panoply of age-based groupings attested to the vigor of their ethnic identity; so equally did the probing literature, much of it ephemeral, produced by the growing corps of talented Nisei. In these early efforts the question of the role of the Nisei in the larger society was a central concern. The "Nisei dilemma" was compounded of the economic successes of their parents' generation, the Depression, and the quiet acceptance by Americans of the racist ideology so well expressed by U. S. Webb. The Nisei had grown up to be American in culture, typical products of a pluralist society in this respect, but could not find their place in the general society, especially in the white-run economy. If the "Wanjies" baseball team—composed of members of the Los Angeles Nishi Hongwanji Buddhist Temple—playing in an all–Japanese American baseball league, was one symbol of the Nisei dilemma, the Japanese-run "Chinese" art stores on Grant Street in San Francisco (where, very briefly, Charles Kikuchi worked) were equally so.

Much of the gnawing ambiguity in Nisei life at this time can in fact be seen in terms of the occupational categories into which the success of the Issei in certain limited lines of enterprise—together with the Depression—seemed to be pushing them. Although the exact focus of the Issei economy had varied from place to place, since the immigrants had proven opportunistic in the best "American" sense, agriculture had in most places provided the Issei with their initial opportunity. From "squat labor" jobs in the fields, Issei who could accumulate a little money progressed to leases or (when and where possible) purchase of a few acres where capacity and training for intensive cultivation made an opening. Ultimately, the Japanese developed a rather substantial food-producing economy, which proliferated into food processing and retailing. By the 1930s, when the Depression struck the coast, Japanese were widely employing Mexicans and Filipinos, later arrivals no less the wrong color than they.

But the "Wanjies" played baseball, the Issei sent their sons and daughters to college, and large numbers of the citizen generation took little joy in the idea of following their parents' picky and highly demanding forms of enterprise—especially when this would force them to remain even longer under the seemingly outmoded tutelage of their alien parents. In Los Angeles, where Nisei were forced by lack of other opportunity to work in the fruit-and-vegetable stands so commonly run by their parents, the most nearly dramatic evidence of the Nisei dilemma was an unsuccessful effort to unionize the perpetually grumbling Nisei fruit-stand workers.[6] Elsewhere Nisei fought their battle for identity even more quietly, and with no more palpable success.

Pearl Harbor and its aftermath provided a thoroughly unexpected denouement to the inconclusive debate. One Issei recalled during the war that before relocation his generation "used to talk among ourselves and say that if war ever came with Japan, the Government might do something to us. But we didn't think our children would be touched." As war came, Kikuchi and his peers thought of stopgap measures which might rescue what they anticipated would be a ticklish problem in public relations. When Pearl Harbor was attacked, in fact, a "bull session" was taking place among Kikuchi and his Nisei friends about "the particular hardships which the Nisei group would face because they had not taken a firm stand on the dispute between this country and Japan. . . . All of us remarked that we would be very willing to fight against Japan in case of a war." [7] The prewar Nisei debate had been leisurely, its participants, Kikuchi wrote just after Pearl Harbor, "limited by their pseudo-cultural clubs of escapism." Subsequent events, imposed from the outside, would move with a speed and decisiveness that would, for some, be shattering.

Like himself, Charles Kikuchi's father had been a rebel. Of rather good family background in Japan, the elder Kikuchi, twenty-six years old in 1900, enrolled in the American Navy as a cook. (At that time, and for a substantial period subsequently, the U.S. Navy favored Orientals for menial positions at sea.) The move, stemming from resentment against his family which would later be translated into resentment against the Japanese way of life, was to be permanent. After being mustered out honorably, the senior Kikuchi remained in America, taking a variety of jobs until he settled down in a little barbershop in Vallejo, near the Mare Island Naval Station. According to his

---

[6] John Modell, "Class or Ethnic Solidarity: The Japanese American Company Union," *Pacific Historical Review*, XXXVIII (1969), 193–206.

[7] From a typescript retrospective piece written by Kikuchi in 1945 entitled "Covering 1940 to Relocation."

son, the choice of location had two motives: one was to be near American sailors, who might (and for a period did) offer the veteran a well-paying clientele; the other was to keep himself isolated from other Japanese. In 1940 the Kikuchis were one of seven families of Japanese birth or origin in Vallejo.

By 1913 Kikuchi found himself in a position to take a bride. Since the vast majority of the Japanese immigration to the United States before that date had been of men, Kikuchi—whose contact with Japanese in America was in any case limited, but who was certainly in no position to take a white bride and was probably without inclination to marry one of any other race—arranged through an intermediary a marriage with a Japanese girl of excellent family. Wedded in a proxy ceremony, Mrs. Kikuchi arrived in San Francisco in 1913, expecting what the intermediary had promised: a husband who had tapped some of the great wealth of America. When she arrived with her new husband at the Kikuchi barbershop, a shack-like structure, there began the not untypical existence for the "picture bride." She struggled to find the resolution to live out her destined role in unfamiliar surroundings, apart from the social buttressing of her kin in Japan, and in circumstances far different from those she had expected.

The tension inherent in the situation bore heavily on both of the senior Kikuchis, driving the husband to drink and the wife to threats of divorce. Charles, the eldest son and thus the crucial offspring in traditional Japanese culture, was to feel the tensions most acutely. An eight-year-old could hardly have recognized these roots when one day his teacher came home with him to discuss his language problem with his parents: no English was spoken in the Kikuchi home, and Charles's schoolwork had suffered. Louis Adamic's 1940 account of the episode is based on correspondence and discussion with young adult Charles. The father, Adamic wrote, had "nodded a few times and bowed Japanese-like" to the teacher, "and she left." [8] But

---

8 Adamic quotations from the pseudo-autobiographical account of Kikuchi, "American with a Japanese Face," in Louis Adamic, *From Many Lands* (New York, 1940).

Mr. Kikuchi brooded over the incident, was humiliated and irate that his first-born son had shamed him.

> As I whimpered[,] picking myself up after he had kicked me, his rage turned into sadistic passion, and he seized me. I was a disgrace to the race of Nippon! I was not his son, but only my mother's; and she was of the good-for-nothing upper classes. . . . I had not any Japanese virtue of any sort! In an attempt to remedy this lack, he hung me by the feet to the two-by-six rafters that cut the ceiling of the room in half, and whipped me with an old razor strop. I hung there, head down, for five or ten minutes.

From this day Charles could find little peace in his parents' home. His father's rages, abetted by alcohol, continued. Both parents discussed putting Charles up for adoption but could not agree where or how. Finally, after something like a year of this excruciating regimen, the Kikuchis agreed to place their son in a Salvation Army home, usually but not exclusively for orphans. For the next decade Kikuchi would lead the life of an orphan at the home, developing there the mental qualities which life after such extreme trauma demanded. As Kikuchi recalls, he grew up in rather rough but basically humane surroundings, a self-motivated but entirely "regular" guy. Behind these qualities Kikuchi has guarded the deeper recesses of his psyche; of these, the present diary at best reveals fleeting images, for by 1942 his defenses were well set.

Part and parcel of Kikuchi's new role as orphan-but-not-really-orphan was an ambiguous position with respect to his ethnicity. Kikuchi talks of the Salvation Army home as a place in which background (understandably) was not important; there was a boys' code of behavior that was reasonably explicit and which bore no relationship to family. (Kikuchi, for example, became quite a fine fighter, especially given his small size. It is doubly interesting that his small stature became an embarrassment to Kikuchi not when he had to fight to win respect but when, later, he came into social contact with Caucasian girls.) And the orphanage group was racially thoroughly heterogeneous. Kikuchi was the only Japanese American in the home, but there were a few Chinese. Taunts, although rare, were occasionally thrown at Kikuchi for being a "Jap." The home was still California, even though not in an area inhabited by other Japanese. One imagines that the taunts continued, maybe increased a bit, when Kikuchi attended the town high school while still living at the home.

But the taunts did not bother, at least in his memory did not seem to have bothered, Kikuchi. Why not? The explanation, I suspect, is in many ways similar to the explanation for many of Kikuchi's subsequent exploits and attitudes. As long as Kikuchi was the *only* "Jap," his ethnic qualities—presumably mainly physical—may have been something to make fun of, but they did not type him as a *member of the group*. As an individual Kikuchi could stand on his merits, could adapt to his milieu, for his mental and physical resources were plenteous: he could fit in, even though a "Jap." But the Japanese American community as a whole, or even the Nisei portion of it, had neither the resources nor the inclination so to adapt. The entire adult career of Charles Kikuchi has been one in which the impulse to stand off from the group (but without denying that he is a "Jap," which would be both untrue and cowardly) has been at war with the fascination and real affection he has both for the Japanese American family that at least temporarily nurtured him and, to a lesser extent, for the Japanese American group as a whole. The working out of this ambivalence in the confused context of the early relocation is, as I have indicated, the genius of his diary.

Charles, at any rate, could rightly account himself a "success" when he left the orphanage at age eighteen, a graduate of the local high school. He had been a leader, had achieved as much scholastic success as he had wished, and no doubt felt himself prepared to face a larger world. Leaving the home, he headed for San Francisco, attracted there for no deeper reason than its being the big city of the region in which he had grown up. The facts that his parents lived in the Bay Area or that a large Oriental community existed there were, if present at all, not prominent among his thoughts.

At once the Depression and his identification with a despised minority were brought home to Kikuchi. His status was made known to him, not atypically, by a white barber (a nice irony!) who refused him service on the ground that "we don't cut any Jap's hair, see? This is an American establishment." That a high school graduate with no connections and a Japanese face had little to hope for in the San Francisco job market of 1934 took somewhat longer for Kikuchi to learn but was no less painful a discovery. Upon Charles Kikuchi had caved in at once the dual facts of Nisei life with which, in some manner, most of those of his age and race had learned to live. Untutored in adopting the patient role common to the majority of Nisei, Kikuchi had to discover his own way. The first year after his arrival in San Francisco saw Kikuchi take two major but distinctly reluctant and tentative steps in the direction of embracing the fate seemingly his by virtue of genetics: he visited his parents in Vallejo, and he finally accepted employment in the stereotypical Japanese American position of houseboy. These junctures were as dramatic turning points for Kikuchi's sense of ethnicity as was the wartime relocation.

The Adamic version of Kikuchi's first encounter with his parents carries splendidly the drama of the incident.

> My mother recognized me at once, with a little gasp. She was very still a few seconds, looking at me. Then she closed her eyes and smiled as though she had been expecting me. Three months before, through the lawyer, she had received a notice from the institution that I had left for San Francisco.
>
> There were several youngsters in the room, my brothers and sisters. At first I barely saw them. They all stared at me, and whispered excitedly.
>
> My father shuffled into the backroom from the shop. He said something in Japanese, perhaps inquiring what was going on, who I was, and what I wanted. He did not recognize me, partly because his eyes did not immediately become adjusted to the

darkness of the room. I saw him clearly. He wore Japanese slippers over bare feet. He was only a shadow of the figure he had been ten years before. He was much smaller than I. Like a gnome.

When informed who I was, he folded his arms and his head dropped on his sunken chest, and he began to talk in a jumble of Japanese and English. I gathered that he thought I hated him. Finally he sat on the edge of one of the three beds that crowded the room, and, clutching a brass knob, asked me to forgive him for his mistreatment of me. . . . I felt dreadful over this, but managed to pat him on the shoulder and take his hand, which was weak and small and cold. Then he folded up on the bed and cried.

Though invited, through his siblings as interpreters, to move in with his family, Charles kept his distance, living in San Francisco. But he made visits at several-month intervals and grew to a greater mutual understanding with his parents.

In rejecting his parents' offer to return to their home, Kikuchi was choosing to continue to risk the abysmal Nisei job situation, already discovered in the brief period since he had left the home. In the winter of 1934–35 necessity forced Kikuchi to the decision he had dreaded to make to take the houseboy job that would permit him to attain his larger objective, a college education. In the fall term of 1935 Kikuchi enrolled at San Francisco State College, a commuter school far less prestigious than the nearby University of California at Berkeley and far less favored by the Nisei. At the same time he was working himself into a most unusual relationship with his employer.

The terms of his houseboy employment were those prevailing in the area as a whole: room and board, plus a small sum of money, in exchange for an average of five or so hours of menial work a day. Kikuchi recalls that when he signed on, he was told by his new employers, in perfectly conventional fashion, that he should "consider himself one of the family." Although Charles knew that the invitation was not meant literally, he chose to treat it as though it were: houseboy jobs were relatively plentiful, and the mental trick of denying his servile status permitted him to withstand the severe humiliation such work otherwise would have meant for him. A year passed before Kikuchi was able to convince his employers that he, as an honorary member of the family, ought not be required to wear the white coat of the houseboy except for special occasions. It took somewhat longer to be permitted to ride along with his boss in the front seat of the family car, and somewhat longer still before he would be invited in at propitious moments to chat and argue with house guests. Over time, Kikuchi converted his employers from typical California contempt for Japanese Americans to a far more enlightened position. Moreover, as Kikuchi remembers it, "living in that household was significant to me because . . . I began to develop [there] more and more identification with Americanism, so that it was not just an intellectual attitude, but an exposure to a way of life that I sort of accepted even though I was resentful of the so-called servant role (which was not really a servant role)." [9] In short, Kikuchi learned from this second strange "family" connection the middle-class values of hard work and material success. "I didn't get that in my own home; I didn't get that in the orphanage."

Kikuchi held his houseboy position for all four years of his college career, although throughout the period he concealed from his classmates the fact that he worked as a houseboy, as he also concealed most of his inner life. At "State" Kikuchi was withdrawn for his first two years but later found a somewhat perverse pleasure in becoming a student leader of sorts. His first big break, in his junior year, came through a favor he had done for some "campus queens" who sat near him in a philosophy course.

> They were so busy with their college social life that they were in danger of failing the course. So I devised a system—the exams were true-false and multiple choice (true-false, remember, in Philosophy!)—raise this foot, it's true, raise the other foot, it's false. And these girls sat there and they told the foot-

[9] Materials from Kikuchi otherwise unattributed are from interviews conducted by myself during 1970.

ball players . . . in the back row. . . . They all passed, and I got my usual A in the course anyway. And this did more than all else to break the ice, and then they all joined the small International Relations Club, as a reward.

Small indeed was the club when Kikuchi joined it, his only formal campus activity other than study, largely as a silent protest against the clannishness of the various ethnic groups on campus, especially the Nisei. Kikuchi was president of the club when he aroused the interest of the campus queens and the football players; for a year "it was the biggest club on campus."

To a degree, then, Kikuchi had been able to confront the problem of being a Nisei, at least insofar as his then current definition of the problem as being essentially *self*-segregation on the part of the Nisei was correct. Kikuchi had been shocked when he recognized in the Japanese American community of San Francisco the perpetuation of the intergenerational clash to which he subconsciously attributed his ejection from his family, as well as the subversion of the American dream he had learned at the orphanage. Knowing the costs so well, he could not afford to accept the temporary comfort that immersion in the ethnic community offered. To reject it outright, however, was impossible. The job situation remained bleak, however malleable Kikuchi's present employer, and the fact of race could not forever be denied, however strong the desire. While still a young man, Kikuchi recalled some of the internal conflict engendered by his decision not to entangle himself at this time.

I felt that economically I would be better off if I did not have a Japanese face. . . . Several times I talked [about possible jobs after graduation] to my professor at college, and she suggested jokingly that the problem might be solved by having an operation on my eyelids to eliminate the slant-eye effect. She said I could pass as a southern European if that were done. I took this quite seriously, and I even investigated several plastic surgeons to see if it could be done, but I gave up the idea when I was told that it would cost around $50.[10]

[10] "Covering 1940 to Relocation."

The concern about a job was serious, even if this particular suggestion was not. Just as Kikuchi was graduating from college, so were many hundreds of other West Coast Nisei, a number no doubt swollen by those who might otherwise have stopped their formal education after high school but who through no fault of their own could find no jobs. All were thrown onto a job market in which there were but two common openings for all Nisei, even those with college education: work in a Japanese or Japanese American business (as Kikuchi would do briefly) or work as a domestic. In anticipation of this problem Kikuchi had attempted to direct his course of study at college to a possible opening to the kind of white-collar job where his race might not be a great hindrance. His solution, a major in history in order to find a job teaching Far Eastern history in high school, was not an inspired one, in that no Japanese Americans were ever appointed to teaching positions in California public schools.

Upon graduation from San Francisco State in 1939, Kikuchi entered upon a year-and-a-half period which he has termed "disorganization." The term may or may not apply clinically, but from the point of view of Kikuchi's education, taken in the broadest sense, it is clear that the period was one in which he was playing the participant-observer in a possibly unconscious effort to discover the limitations of race and ethnicity in California. Toward the end of the period, it should be added, Kikuchi began once again to pursue formal education, not entirely divorced from his "disorganized" activities: he entered the School of Social Welfare, University of California at Berkeley. The intensity with which Kikuchi lived life during the interval between graduation from college and the outbreak of the war is the more remarkable when one remembers that during this period he was also, from time to time, hunting jobs and, further, did a creditable job of surveying the Nisei job situation for the National Youth Administration, one part-time job he was able to find.

Kikuchi explored two "fringes" of Japanese American life at this time. In contact with them, he forged further the stubbornly anti-authoritarian elements of his character which would be so apparent in his diary.

Of these, the first was the "Yamato Garage Gang," as Kikuchi called the group, in essence a largely Japanese American corner-boy group not unlike the contemporaneous Norton Street Italian American group in Boston described by William Foote Whyte in *Street Corner Society*. Like Whyte's Nortons, the Yamatos were young adults, usually out of work and beyond the point where they were looking for work very actively, usually unmarried, and on the whole contemptuous of the organized activities set out for people their age by social workers and other agencies of proper society. Devoted mainly to gambling, mischief, whoring, and especially to talking about these exploits, the Yamatos provided Kikuchi with casual, undemanding amusement. Beyond talk and mischief, the Yamatos had a further attraction for Kikuchi: they were (unlike the Nortons) to some extent an ethnically mixed group, including Chinese and southern Europeans as well as Japanese. For the Yamato gang members, the family could no longer contain the energies of young manhood that the occupational life did not satisfy. In the absence of jobs, spouses, and agencies of "propriety," as Kikuchi discovered, the barriers of "segregation" could at least temporarily crumble. The Yamatos, however, provided only weekend distraction. Eventually, in any case, Kikuchi decided that they were "maladjusted individuals" and far too lacking in purpose to satisfy his tastes. "I just sort of drifted away." Interestingly, Kikuchi resided in Berkeley during this period, across the bay, even at those times in which he was in frequent contact with the gang.

Kikuchi was also exploring ethnicity after his own fashion when he worked at the exhausting and unremunerative job of migrant agricultural worker in central California in the summer of 1940. At this time, lacking anything more definite to do, Kikuchi set out to earn a bit of money during the summer by joining the migratory workers in the fields, as many a California student, Anglo as well as minority, had and would. For two months, Kikuchi recalled, he and a friend "almost broke our backs pulling celery stalks out of the ground with our bare hands for 25 cents an hour. There were many times that I wanted to quit because I rebelled at the thought of being exploited like this, especially by a Japanese foreman. It seemed to me that these Japanese farmers were inhuman in their attitudes toward the workers and their only interest was to get as much out of them as possible."

The work crew was composed of Japanese and Filipinos, between whom hostility grew to the point where virtual segregation, except when working, seemed the only way to preserve order. Kikuchi, however, took advantage of the opportunity to get to know a Filipino next to whom he happened to work. He discovered distinct parallels between the situations of the two colored groups, despite the fact that for most persons of both races hostility was prescribed: Japanese farmers worked their Filipinos no less hard and with scarcely more understanding than their own white employers had worked them a few decades earlier. So distracted was Kikuchi by his conversations with his Filipino friend that he failed to notice what was going on about him in the packing shed where they were at work. "The first thing I knew about it was when this 12-inch knife came swishing through the air, cutting the tip of my nose. . . . A general riot was about to burst loose when Manuel jumped to my protection." The Japanese workers demanded that all the Filipinos be fired; the Filipinos reciprocated in kind. "After that, the Japanese and Filipino workers kept their distance, but I continued to go to Manuel and talk to him. The Japanese workers did not like this very much, and they said that I was betraying them, so they insisted I move out of their bunkhouse. I found a place in Manuel's bunkhouse and for the remainder of the season I worked with a Filipino crew." [11] It was entirely typical of Kikuchi.

Kikuchi recalls that at this point, and for the first time, he developed a sense of vocation: he hoped to become a social worker because he had seen "at first hand how these workers were exploited. . . . I felt that in this way I could work upon

[11] *Ibid.*

minority problems." Kikuchi also involved himself in sporadic efforts to organize the minority workers. He recalls the effort as having been doomed to failure from the start by a glaring inequality in resources between the organizers and the employers; eventually, he reports, he was "bought off" by wages a nickel an hour higher than others received.

Kikuchi, it seems, was freed to consider "ethnicity," even as a problem, only when the notion of "class" was laid across it, when ethnicity was shown to have a more universal relevance than the "segregated" sense most Nisei seemed to feel. It is not insignificant that the oppressor in the specific instance that involved Kikuchi in ethnic relations as a problem was an Issei employer, or that Kikuchi chose to spend most of the summer in the Filipino bunkhouse.

In a more conventional sense, too, Kikuchi was studying Japanese Americans when he was employed by the National Youth Administration to study the job market for Nisei. Kikuchi's final report, dated 1941, reveals its author's uncomprehending attitude toward the immigrant generation: "The older people have immobile features of the so-called 'dead pans,' whereas the Nisei are capable of and do display a great variety of emotions facially. Their sense of humor is better developed and frequently they are capable of great spontaneity in public which is shocking to the first generation." His outlook upon the Nisei employment situation further suggests the limitations on and some of the costs of pluralism without equality of opportunity. (The passage might equally well be drawn from the reflections of many contemporaneous Nisei; the attitudes revealed were quite common.) "Many of them [Nisei] may become totally disillusioned with the failure to find work and not realize that economic factors are equally as important as discrimination. The growing tendency of the Nisei to blame discrimination for all their problems may eventually result in this group becoming useless members of our society."

Kikuchi, it would seem, was no stranger to self-loathing. Compare the above analysis to a fictionalized piece he had written in the same year, entitled "Joe Nisei Looks for a Job."

Here the author exclaims in the voice of the narrator, with italics for emphasis: *"It's such a vicious circle: Can't get work without experience. Can't get experience because you're a Jap. And who would hire a Jap?"*

Having found no satisfactory answer to the question, however rhetorical it was in context, Kikuchi nevertheless pursued his vocational plans, applying to several graduate schools of social work for scholarship aid, working at odd jobs in the meantime, hoping to save some money. So unsuccessful was he in these plans that for a while he contemplated working his way east, an area of less discrimination but in which Kikuchi, like most Nisei, had little interest, in order to attend some university there. An offer of a fellowship at Berkeley finally arrived, however, and was eagerly accepted. Kikuchi began work toward a certificate in social work. Despite the interruption caused by Pearl Harbor, he was awarded it in 1942. At school Kikuchi wrote a class paper on campus Nisei, which—though he concluded that "the Nisei have lost all perspective on just what being an American really means as they so indiscriminately accept American symbols"—moves toward a more sympathetic as well as a more comprehending attitude toward the Nisei dilemma.

> The immediate barriers . . . of the outside society have contributed chiefly to the serious Nisei personality disorganization. The factor of race and discrimination evolving out of the American caste and class society has a direct bearing on these Nisei maladjustments. Adopting the American symbols of status, the Nisei are now faced with the question that perhaps this pattern of opportunity he learned in school is not for him. . . . It is hard for them to reconcile democracy with prejudice and the fact that they can't go to certain bowling alleys, barber shops, swimming pools, and hotels. . . . Torn between two cultures, the Nisei finds no place or security in either.

Contributing to Kikuchi's maturation, no doubt, was his first substantial contact with Nisei who were able to transcend by critical intelligence some of the parochial traits he had discovered in most of them. "Radicals," they were often called at Berkeley, although Kikuchi's diary entry of December 7, 1941, should serve more than adequately to remind the reader of the vast distance between 1941 and later Berkeley radicalism. It was these "radicals," most of them now occupying (as is Kikuchi) positions of responsibility in the general community, who introduced Kikuchi to the intellectual value of "marginality." The Nisei, or so it was argued, could gain from his discomfort a perspective on the broader workings of the society which contained but did not integrate "whites" and "Japanese." Typically, the Nisei intellectual was engaged in the study of sociology—concerned with yet abstracted somewhat from the solution to the dilemmas perplexing America—rather than social work, which was less concerned with knowledge, more with methods. No doubt some of Kikuchi's friends saw his persistence in social work an odd choice, but Kikuchi would stand out by his individualism in any crowd. He stood out, too, by "disorganized" tendencies he joyously imported to the Nisei "radicals." Rooming with a number of them in 1941 in Berkeley under minimal conditions of housing and food, Kikuchi would on occasion conduct raids to stock the larder. The high point of this petty theft, he recalls with pleasure, was an uninvited tour he made of the fraternity houses at Stanford on the day of the big football game with Cal.

The "radicals" and Kikuchi in his individualistic way maintained a very substantial distance in 1941 from the most nearly representative Nisei organization, the Japanese American Citizens League. The league, a federation with many local branches, was from its inception in the 1920s led by Nisei who, while maintaining firmly the citizen/alien distinction that divided them from their parents, had a stake in maintaining the ethnic community intact and (in effect) in justifying it to the white majority. Typically led by the more successful business and professional men, the league had really just begun to gain a substantial rank-and-file following when the war broke out, thrusting the Citizens League suddenly into the position of spokesman for the Japanese American community as a whole.

While protesting the relocation, the JACL pledged complete cooperation with the authorities and bravely stuck to this often embarrassing position throughout. Kikuchi and the "radicals" had always felt put off by the uncompromising and somewhat unadventurous emphasis of the JACL upon propriety; during the war (as the diary at several junctures indicates) they felt the league's position abject. Since the war the acceptance of Japanese Americans by the majority community has, of course, brought widespread applause for the JACL's wartime position, and the group has flourished as never before. Kikuchi, though, has kept his distance, along with a good number of dissenting types. In this, as in many matters, Kikuchi's point of view has been principled, possibly impractical, certainly untypical, and thoroughly idiosyncratic.

In 1941 the sociologically minded Nisei intellectuals spoke at length with Kikuchi about the acuteness of his observation and the quality of his prose. Among the contacts he made through them was with Dorothy Swaine Thomas, a sociologist at Berkeley and the wife of W. I. Thomas, a pioneer American sociologist who had a particular interest in the personal document as a resource for research. Dorothy Thomas quite apparently saw in Kikuchi the combination of "marginality" and intelligence that would make of him a splendid recorder of the meaning of important aspects of ethnicity. Thomas was eventually to recruit Kikuchi for the Japanese Evacuation and Relocation Study (along with several others of his group at Berkeley). But convincing Kikuchi of the value of his work along this line was harder than convincing him to keep the diary of which the present volume is an abridgment. To undertake the task, Kikuchi had had the encouragement of his Nisei intellectual friends; after he began it, his work seemed to him inferior to that of his smart and competitive peers.

Somehow neither before nor during the war could Kikuchi feel comfortable in the role of self-conscious ethnic: he never could clarify for his own mind what he felt about "his" people or about his family; and he thought his diaristic efforts were not sociological enough, despite encouragement from both Dorothy and W. I. Thomas. "I am continuing along on the diary," he wrote Dorothy Thomas in September, 1942, "and that certainly is nothing. . . . I feel inadequate when I think of the reams of material which your other observers are no doubt sending in." Hardly more impressed by his work in retrospect, he recalled in 1970 that "I never thought of doing my diaries as more than a kind of source material for myself." Kikuchi's position on the JERS project grew as the fascination of the project directors with his diary became more confirmed. By the end of the war Kikuchi had not only observed in Tanforan Assembly Center and Gila Relocation Center but had worked as a full-time researcher from 1943, collecting life histories of Nisei relocatees in Chicago. Ultimately, the life histories were incorporated into a volume of the JERS series of books.

The Kikuchi diary, which its author referred to as "nothing," was at the very least a prodigious amount of writing, usually the result of an hour or more of concentrated composition daily, late at night. His entire wartime diary, covering from early 1942 to mid-1945 when he entered the Army ("there are no other Nisei in our company," he wrote to Dorothy Thomas on USO stationery in August, 1945, "so I guess I won't be able to get any notes on them"), contains a vast number of pages and reveals an indefatigable observer and recorder. His Tanforan diary alone, from which the present volume is taken, covers only four months but, unedited and unannotated, would require about three times as many pages as in the edited form. The diaristic habit, perhaps not surprisingly, has stuck with Kikuchi, who to this day annually turns out a volume of roughly this size. (These, Kikuchi expects, others will never read. But he does not consider them basically private diaries either and insists that, aside from a few easily expunged personal references, he would not be averse to showing any of the volumes to curious persons.) Kikuchi writes "because it helps me think through what I'm doing. It's a time of the morning [he now wrote in his office, before his fellow workers arrived] I'm thinking. . . . It's no effort to write things down. . . . Sometimes it helps me make personal decisions." The habit of contemporaneous reflection upon an active life, and an exceedingly rare openness, help make Kikuchi's wartime diaries of immense value. Because the shock of relocation was most apparent in the earliest months, and because the Tanforan experience was both condensed and comprehensible, the decision has been made to present here material only from the Tanforan diary.

Kikuchi's period of stay at Tanforan Assembly Center was a mere four months. Transferred to the Gila Relocation Center in Arizona, Kikuchi carried on with his active data-gathering on behalf of JERS and with keeping another diary volume. Here Kikuchi remained until he removed to Chicago in April, 1943, one of the earlier Nisei to take extended work leave from the relocation camps. Drafted into the Army just before Hiroshima, Kikuchi served a brief and not overly glorious military career —his anti-authoritarian inclinations finally boiling to the surface, having been contained in Tanforan and Gila—but left with an honorable discharge and returned to his social-work studies. This time Kikuchi enrolled at the New York School of Social Work and received his master of social work degree in 1947. His thesis, based on his resettlement studies in Chicago, reflects in many ways the quality of his thought at the time, the mixed feeling he had for his ethnic group and for what had been done to them. He noticed with special interest in the thesis the "extreme resettler sensitivity . . . basically a protest against the social forces which confused the group so traumatically during the migration to the middle-west." Yet Kikuchi's prognosis was a happy one, since "for most resettlers, the wide opportunities of working with Americans of different racial stock was a completely new experience . . . and on the whole, they adjusted in a positive manner to it." Likewise, Kikuchi today believes that "on the whole the Nisei group didn't get too damaged" by the relocation. "Generally, we probably gained as a result."

In so believing, Kikuchi is by no means alone. Even Roger Baldwin, the civil libertarian, believes that "some good came of the tragedy," although he calls the relocation "incredible" and

characterized by "the most austere conditions." [12] Audrie Gird-
ner and Anne Loftis in a full and balanced account conclude of
the relocation that "this extraordinary incarceration program
was carried out in a smooth, efficient, and on the whole, humane manner." [13] Many students of the Japanese American
group concur that the relocation helped effect a transfer of
power from the Issei to the Nisei that otherwise had seemed
difficult or impossible, and that in some manner the events of
1941–45 helped purge white America of its hostile attitudes
toward Japanese Americans. Examination of the more perti-
nent documents and secondary accounts of the relocation leads
to much this conclusion; readers are referred to the Suggestions
for Further Reading.

In its relocation program the government revealed from start
to finish an intense confusion of purpose about just what it
was doing; but nowhere apparent within that confusion was
any desire to emulate Adolf Hitler or even the less relevant,
but to the Japanese American relocatees more threatening, example of the Japanese prisoner-of-war camps. Few, it would
seem, who were in a position to push through a policy of any
kind, took the Japanese relocation question seriously enough
to create more intense mischief than was created by the combination of a tradition of racism in California and neighboring
states, a bumbling and nervous military, and a local officialdom
ready and willing to translate the least signs of local antagonism
to the Japanese Americans into political pressure. The real vir-
tuosi of the relocation, the men who by their conviction and
energy were able to get the wheels turning, were in fact few
and not very highly placed. Roger Daniels's brilliant account
of the decision to relocate places the finger on Army Provost
Marshal General Allen W. Gullion, in charge of military polic-
ing, and his even more eager subordinate Karl R. Bendetsen,
chief of the Provost Marshal General's Aliens Division. That

12 "Introduction" to Allan R. Bosworth, *America's Concentration Camps* (New
York, 1967).
13 *The Great Betrayal* (New York, 1969).

such men could exert the leverage needed to bring Washington to violate the most basic civil liberties of a portion of the nation's citizenry is symptomatic both of how uninteresting the Japanese American question was to most people in early wartime Washington and of how slender a reed the Constitution can be rendered in time of national crisis, when it is the rights of an unpopular, colored minority that need protecting.

If in retrospect the relocation is more a story of official fools than official knaves, and for the relocatees a story not without redeeming elements, at the time the moves leading up to the relocation were to Kikuchi, to the Nisei, and to their parents, exceedingly serious and threatening. To conclude, on the basis of hindsight, that Kikuchi's early, nervous diary references to "concentration camps" were farfetched is to rob the event of the evacuation of its consistently indeterminate quality for those involved. Just as certainly, to conclude, on the basis of constitutional scruples or what we now think we know about the racist possibilities inherent in American life, that the relocation was a disaster unmitigated by humor, human kindness, or even real benefit for those relocated is to falsify the complexity of the historical event. Kikuchi's account of Tanforan, by virtue both of its diaristic qualities and of the ability of the man to tolerate ambiguity, provides us with a needed kind of account—not *balanced,* but *mixed.* Uncertainty, rumor, changes in expectation and hope: these characterize the narrative of Japanese American life from 1941 to 1945.

Within one day of the Japanese attack on Pearl Harbor, the FBI had rounded up no fewer than 736 Japanese nationals in Hawaii and on the U.S. mainland and placed them in "temporary detention." [14] Although still more Japanese were picked up in the days that followed—men who belonged to Japanese

14 In addition to the original sources cited in the Suggestions for Further Reading, my account of the relocation for the most part follows Roger Daniels, *Concentration Camps USA* (New York, 1971). Also especially useful were Stetson Conn, "The Decision to Evacuate the Japanese from the Pacific Coast," in Kent Roberts Greenfield, ed., *Command Decisions* (New York, 1959); Morton Grodzins, *Americans Betrayed* (Chicago, 1949); and John Modell, "The Japanese of Los Angeles: A Study in Growth and Accommodation, 1900–1946" (unpublished Ph.D. dissertation, Columbia University, 1969).

groups which seemed to have a military tinge, or who were known for their donations to Japan in her war with China, or who merely were the natural leaders of a community thought to be of highly uncertain loyalty—the FBI's actions affected only aliens and, however inappropriate the criteria employed, were *selective*. Attorney General Francis Biddle, under whose authority the FBI operated, assured the shaken Japanese American community that "at no time . . . will the government engage in wholesale condemnation of any alien group." And for a period it did not.

But the "Yellow Peril," the fear of subversion or conquest from Asia, was a well-worn path in the minds of many Americans, especially on the Pacific Coast. And pressures were beginning to develop for just such a mass evacuation as Biddle said would not occur. On December 15 Secretary of the Navy Frank Knox, back from an examination of Pearl Harbor, told (entirely falsely) of the massive role of Hawaiian Japanese in aiding the enemy in perpetrating the Day of Infamy, playing down thereby the realistically great responsibility of American military bungling. On December 19, General J. L. De Witt, commander of the Fourth Army, with responsibility for the defense of the western states, a jittery general quite pliable to the opinions of staff and community, urged the War Department that his task would be facilitated by a wholesale evacuation to points inland of all adult enemy aliens (including Japanese). De Witt hoped that perhaps the Nisei, a majority of whom were minors, would for the most part move inland "voluntarily" with their parents.

With De Witt showing such promising signs, Gullion and Bendetsen in late December began to press for more drastic steps. But while De Witt could be brought around, the Justice Department was sterner in its defense of the rights of the populace and, into mid-February, refused to give its cachet to a massive relocation of American citizens. But Justice did not make its representations as strongly as it might have. On February 11 the issue was settled, and by no less a personage than President Franklin D. Roosevelt, who on that day gave the War

Department a go-ahead, reminding them that "military necessity" must justify any action and admonishing them to "be as reasonable as you can." [15]

But by this date, Roosevelt had presumably heard much about "military necessity" from even less trustworthy sources than General De Witt, for in late January voices from California and the coast, till then remarkably quiet, began exigently protesting the continued presence of the Japanese in their midst. One study of California newspaper discussion of the local "Japanese" has shown that although interest in the subject was high for about the first week after Pearl Harbor, it then hardly made the front pages, and unfavorable references to the Japanese Americans were only about twice as common as favorable ones. Interest thereafter dropped rapidly and only in the last week of January picked up, now mixed with numerous demands for relocation. At this time stories about the Japanese were splashed widely on front pages, and unfavorable references outweighed favorable ones by over forty to one.[16] And so it was until the evacuation began. Local politicians, even some with records of humanitarianism or at least neutrality toward minorities, began to worry about Pearl Harbor–like fiascoes and to rationalize about the removal of the menace.

In Los Angeles, for instance, the first thought of the efficient chief administrative officer of the County Board of Supervisors, Wayne Allen, was that "doubtless, public opinion will reduce the amount of trade with these people." The solution was not (how could it be?) official assurances about the reliability of the local Japanese; rather, it was relief. This, however, would overtax local resources and therefore called for a national solution. When the supervisors acceded to Allen's logic, they put their concern in the form of a resolution calling upon the federal government to find a solution. Their reasons were twofold: the "need of some means of public support" for the Japanese and the "potentially dangerous fifth column enemy." The potential referred to was explained by human nature, since men "are

[15] Quoted in Daniels, *Concentration Camps USA,* 65.
[16] Computed from Grodzins, *Americans Betrayed,* 390.

prone to revert to original or native allegiance in periods of stress or emotion." The resolution, published late in January, suggested that transportation of Japanese aliens inland would solve both the economic and the security problems.

Indeed it would, but workings within the federal government were to bring about the relocation of aliens and citizens alike. (After all, as General De Witt noted, citizen minors bereft of their parents would also be a public burden and, if blood is thicker than water, a public menace as well.) The problem, in fact, moved stepwise toward the final decision over more than a month's time. The process was one of extinguishing the hesitancy of General De Witt and weakening the influence of the Justice Department.

On January 29, 1942, the Justice Department had readily agreed to a modest Army recommendation for the exclusion of enemy aliens from eighty-six strategic zones within De Witt's command. Only some 3,000 Japanese (plus 4,000 Italian and German Americans) were affected, a number far too small to satisfy opinion now surging in California and elsewhere. Three days later Justice and Army were in heated discussion regarding the narrowness of the limitations posed by the January 29 agreement, Gullion petulantly asking Biddle whether "if the Army, the men on the ground, determine it as a military necessity to move citizens, Jap citizens, . . . you won't help us."[17] The "man on the ground"—General De Witt—was thus thrust into increasing prominence by Gullion; by long-distance phone Bendetsen strengthened his determination to call for a total evacuation, as did also pressure from Governor Culbert Olson and other California officials, working both directly and through public opinion. The February 11 carte blanche handed to the War Department by the president placed De Witt in a leading position to define military necessity. Assistant Secretary of War John J. McCloy, the civilian official of the War Department most actively interested in the Japanese question, was also a convert to the total-evacuation position, and he, too, was buttressed by various expressions of Pacific Coast anxiety about

[17] Quoted in Daniels, *Concentration Camps USA,* 55.

and hostility to the local Japanese. The specificity of this anxiety—directed against the Japanese rather than the Italians or Germans—and its racist rather than nativist quality—it was directed against citizens of America as well as of Japan—had had its effect. The Justice Department, overpowered, reluctantly agreed to the Army's evacuation plans. The new acting consensus within the administration was formalized on February 19 by Executive Order No. 9066, authorizing the War Department to do its will; and War transmitted the authority to General De Witt.

Just what De Witt would do with this authority, of course, was unclear to the public, as it seemingly was to De Witt himself. On March 2 De Witt's Public Proclamation No. 1 declared the western portion of the Pacific states a "military area" from which *all* Japanese, citizens and aliens, would have to evacuate. A press release accompanying the proclamation suggested that if Japanese voluntarily relocated inland, they would be allowed to remain without further official harassment. Nine days later De Witt established the Wartime Civil Control Administration, "to provide for the evacuation of all persons of Japanese ancestry . . . with a minimum of economic and social dislocation, a minimum use of military personnel and maximum speed; and initially to employ all appropriate means to encourage voluntary migration."

Although mass evacuation was decided upon on the basis of military necessity, many within the military did not wish to devote the personnel needed to coordinate a forced mass migration. The difficulties of the task they had begun became even more apparent as the early "voluntary" migration began to arouse hostility in neighboring western states, where, it appeared, the Japanese Americans were no more welcome than on the coast. The undirected migration, therefore, was quickly abandoned in favor of a directed movement into specified "relocation centers," to be established at government cost and maintained by a civilian agency. This agency, the War Relocation Authority, was established by executive order on March 18, to "provide for the relocation of such [non-"voluntary" evacuated] persons in appropriate places, provide for their needs in such a manner as may be appropriate, and supervise their activities." On the heels of this order Congress passed an act making violation of Army security measures under Executive Order 9066 a federal offense. The Army organized a "voluntary" movement of some 2,100 Los Angeles Japanese Americans to a temporary "reception center" then under construction in Inyo County, California, and De Witt declared a curfew for all Japanese within the military zone.

The turmoil of the "voluntary evacuation" period was transformed into a different but no less confused situation when, on March 27, General De Witt's Public Proclamation No. 4 forbade further voluntary movement of Japanese Americans from the area they had three weeks previously been urged to leave. Few had yet moved. Although the March 27 announcement contained no further instructions, the situation was a foreboding one for the coastal Japanese.

Two days later the first of a series of "exclusion orders" from De Witt's office, ordering all racial Japanese residents in several areas (and ultimately in the entire Pacific tier of states) into temporary assembly centers, took effect. The language was terse: "Pursuant to the provisions of Civilian Exclusion Order No. _____, . . . all persons of Japanese ancestry, both alien and non-alien [*sic*], will be evacuated from the above area by _____. . . . A responsible member of each family, preferably the head of the family, or the person in whose name most of the property is held, and each individual living alone, will report to the Civil Control Station to receive further instructions."

The assembly centers were set up wherever large public facilities with substantial shelter and access to water and electricity could be commandeered for the purpose. A majority of the assembly centers were fairgrounds or, like Tanforan and Santa Anita, the two largest, racetracks. From the assembly centers evacuees would be transferred to more substantial barracks —styled "relocation centers" and under WRA control—as soon as these could be constructed. The director of the Army agency which had charge of the assembly centers described the distinctions between them and the relocation centers in an April, 1942, memo to his counterpart at the WRA:

> Assembly centers are not designed to provide suitable semi-permanent housing and other facilities. They are temporary in nature. Their facilities are transitory only. They are made necessary because of the time required to select relocation sites. Their objective is to meet the demand of military necessity and to avoid any retarding effect caused by relocation site selection. . . . [The need for] speedy acquisition and construction of relocation centers . . . cannot be overemphasized in view of the essential characteristics of assembly centers.

Evacuee life for Charles Kikuchi thus began in hastily converted stable 10, stall 5, at Tanforan, near San Bruno, south of San Francisco. Charles had decided to relocate as part of his parents' household in order to help the aging couple in a time of unprecedented stress. The Kikuchis were but one of 2,043 families or single individuals who were to live at Tanforan in the 169 days of its existence as an assembly center—a much longer period of use, incidentally, than was initially expected. When Kikuchi arrived with his parents in early May, some 3,000 residents were already there. The numbers packed into the racetrack reached nearly 8,000 at its maximum. Army statisticians calculated that 1,104,575 man-days were passed during this time, that 64 births and 22 deaths occurred, and that 59 arrests were made by internal camp police. Virtually all of the 7,824 evacuees who at one time or another were in Tanforan came from the San Francisco Bay Area. Kikuchi, when he left Tanforan for the Gila River (Arizona) Relocation Center (on special assignment by the JERS), was one of but 39 camp residents so to move. No fewer than 7,673, or almost the entire camp, were transferred to the relocation center in central Utah, where many waited out the war.

Ten relocation centers were established, all but two (both in Arkansas) in sparsely populated regions of the West. Before Tule Lake (California) Relocation Center had closed its gates in March, 1946—the last residents exceedingly reluctant to leave—human drama on a large scale had been produced, drama far more thematic than any Kikuchi saw in his four months at Tanforan. Space permits the slightest of accounts here, but three interrelated themes deserve mention: the "loyalty" question; the WRA segregation program, which led for many to an eventual renunciation of American citizenship; and the often ignored resistance to WRA policy by camp residents.

The WRA was an unusual agency in that it approached its task with a distaste born of a sense that the rights of many were being sadly interfered with, since they (typically) believed from the beginning that at least *eight in ten* Nisei were thoroughly trustworthy. Accordingly, the WRA adopted as its central function the clearing of the loyal Nisei for jobs or schooling off the Pacific Coast and the preparation of public opinion to receive them and, after the war, their parents. This policy dictated that the Japanese Americans be shown to be the most trustworthy of citizens, the truest of the true. And, in early 1943, it dictated eager cooperation with an Army move to establish, first, a volunteer all-Nisei combat team and later to extend the usual draft eligibility to the Nisei. In the midst of the apprehensive stir the announcement of this decision caused in the camps, a WRA questionnaire regarding leave clearance was circulated. Two questions inquired into loyalty. The first asked (and, irrelevantly, asked of women and the aged) whether each relocatee would accept combat duty "wherever ordered." The second asked (and offensively to the Nisei, who were American citizens) whether they would forswear all forms of allegiance and obedience to the Japanese emperor.

Thousands answered No to each of the loyalty questions, despite WRA pressure to prevent this outcome. To the declarants, the No's meant a variety of things, of course. Equally important, the No responses shattered the WRA's hopes of a quiet solution to the Japanese problem, a solution by way of paying with a smile the price apparently demanded by white society. To salvage the position of the declaredly "loyal" evacuees, and to protect its own flank from a public opinion ever ready to accuse it of "coddling" its charges, the agency settled on a policy of segregating "disloyals" in Tule Lake Relocation Center. When the necessary transfers were completed, Tule Lake seethed with dissident voices, some primarily infuriated at American stupidity and viciousness, others in fact now more loyal to Japan than to America, still others just confused. Aspects of Japanese culture which Issei had been forbidden to perform in other camps appeared at Tule, and even stylized military exercises. And over time, the same kind of confusion and botched communication and suspiciousness that led over 18,000 to segregate themselves at Tule Lake led almost half of these to apply for postwar shipment to Japan. Of these, many thousands were Nisei who renounced their citizenship, a procedure made possible by a law passed by an obliging Congress in 1944. Most who finally lost their citizenship, although formally merely suffering the consequences of their own decision, were far more accurately victims of a unique sequence of events at the end of which personal accountability for "willed" acts seems neither just nor merciful.

Some, though, maintained a limited and clear-headed form of resistance which demands notice because the WRA's bland view of the cheerful Japanese relocatees predominates in the literature.[18] At Heart Mountain (Wyoming) Relocation Center the resistance focused on the refusal of substantial numbers of Nisei to submit to Selective Service procedures, even though by their own professions loyal.[19] The draft resisters were far from passive. They enlisted a white lawyer in their behalf and published their side of the picture in a Denver newspaper run by Japanese Americans who, not having dwelled within the Pacific Coast relocation area, were on the outside and free. When in May, 1944, no fewer than sixty-three Heart Mountain Nisei were indicted for draft resistance, the nation had its largest mass draft-resistance trial. The sixty-three, as also twenty-two

[18] The leading exception is Daniels, *Concentration Camps USA*, in which Chapter 6 describes the resistance and assesses its significance.
[19] Some resisted, but only some. An earlier generation found the very successful Nisei fighting men more appropriate and commendable. Heroism of this more conventional kind was also more common.

more in later trials, were found guilty. "If they are truly loyal American citizens," the judge held, their clear duty is to serve. A later generation may think differently.

Only months later, however, "loyalty" again was at the center of a judicial decision, and this one, *Ex parte Endo,* effectively brought the relocation to its end.[20] In *Endo* the Supreme Court ruled that because "a person who is concededly loyal presents no problem of espionage or sabotage," the WRA could no longer hold those against whom no charge of disloyalty could be brought. On January 2, 1945, the Pacific Coast was opened again to Japanese Americans. Only the segregants and re-nunciants remained as WRA problems, and those psychically unable to enter the outside world. The WRA did what it could on slender resources to reincorporate the Japanese Americans into their communities, and trusted that their pride and strength would serve once again to make them useful members of the community. It did, and has.

For Charles Kikuchi, Tanforan, and Gila Relocation Center after it, were to be his strongest immersions in the life of the Japanese American family and the Japanese American community. The family duties, which Kikuchi took on so self-consciously by relocating with his parents and siblings to Tanforan and Gila, were passed on to his siblings after he left Gila for Chicago. His study of Japanese Americans, pursued at the behest of JERS, ended with his entry into the Army. He moved to New York City after the war, disdaining to follow most California Nisei back to their state of birth. After attaining his master's degree, he began work as a clinical social worker in a Veterans' Administration hospital, from which he will soon be retiring.

A few old friends from the prewar Nisei community happen to be in New York: Kikuchi neither shuns nor especially seeks their company. He insists that he is no authority on Japanese Americans and is wryly amused at his recently initiated do-it-yourself project of a "Japanese room" in his Manhattan brownstone, complete with appropriate decor, mats on the

20 323 U.S. 283 (1944).

floor, and a shoes-off policy. "Once there is no stigma," he says, speaking of his hopes for racial harmony in America, "then why can't you have an integrated society. . . . And if you want to have [ethnic] religion, food, so what? . . . You know, the Uncle Tom label? I don't see it as an Uncle Tom label. . . . If my experience is closer to the majority culture, then that's the way I ought to live. . . . [But] I wouldn't deny my own children some exposure to the cultural background that they had." His feelings, in short, are both optimistic and ambivalent. Kikuchi married Yuriko Amemiya, a modern dancer from California, in 1946 and has a teenage son and a daughter in her early twenties, now dancing professionally in her mother's new company. The family is biologically Japanese, but its ethnicity, as a sociological entity, is so tenuous that one hesitates to use the term. They maintain only sporadic contact with the siblings Kikuchi first learned to know at Tanforan.

If Kikuchi is different from most Nisei, his ability to secure a professional position, so long denied the Nisei, is happily common. The education of the prewar Nisei was not, by and large, wasted. By the time the war was over, overt anti-Japanese discrimination had abated tremendously, even in California. The racial anxieties that were once turned toward the Oriental had a new focus in the black man, who constituted an important stream of wartime and postwar migration to the cities of the Pacific Coast. Nevertheless, the Japanese Americans have not chosen to blend into the "Anglo" background on the coast. Although residential segregation has lessened, identifiable Japanese American communities remain, some of them quite middle-class in job and life style. The events of the war are not, probably ought not to be, so quickly forgotten.

The Nisei who most heavily bear these mental scars in but few cases were actively vocal in their own behalf, but one hears that in comfortably all-Nisei settings anti-white mutterings are not unknown. However common this may be among the Nisei, until very recently the maturing third generation, the Sansei, have been largely ignorant of the virulent prewar discrimination and far from sophisticated in their understanding of the relocation. They are clearly "assimilated" according to pattern, or were, until analogies between themselves and blacks were brought to their attention by the black and student revolts of the late 1960s. A "Yellow Power" movement currently exists, dedicated to ethnic self-awareness. But one suspects that the dominant pattern among the Sansei is still strongly assimilative. And it is most certain that the rarest of patterns is the ambivalent, amused, but distant curiosity of Charles Kikuchi.

A Note on the Editing

To preserve the special flavor of the diary, and to communicate to the reader of this edition the vigor of the young diarist's life, I have followed the policy of preserving wherever possible the structure of Kikuchi's paragraphs and of the entries as a whole. I have almost never made deletions in sentences or between sentences; where I have, ellipses are inserted in the usual way. The sequence of paragraphs within an entry has never been changed, but where paragraphs have been deleted (except when they fell at the beginning or end of a daily entry) I have indicated the deletion by line ellipses. I have changed obvious spelling errors and insignificant grammatical slips, and I have spelled out abbreviations.

The most intuitive element of editorial policy has been the choice of *content* of material to include. Overall, I would say that the diary as here printed represents the largest part both of Kikuchi's personal reflections and of his more trenchant or historically significant observations about camp life. The *affect* of the full document (which is to be placed in the Bancroft Library, University of California at Berkeley), I should say, is not greatly different from the present version, except for the substantially greater inclusion there of affectless reportage. What I have removed is for the most part reports of the workings of the camp administration and in-depth studies of evacuees who otherwise were not a part of Kikuchi's personal life. The document has thus been somewhat altered from its original status as primarily a piece of social reportage to what is basically a personal document. These categories, of course, are matters of degree rather than of kind; Kikuchi was chosen as a JERS informant precisely because his idiosyncracy and liveliness made his writing straddle the distinction. Yet the reader should remember that in his early, insecure days as a diarist, Kikuchi himself made the distinction, even going to the point of keeping a "personal" diary in addition to his public one, "one which nobody ever got to look at" and which he destroyed. "It was about sexual patterns and I didn't want to identify anyone or run this kind of a risk and I didn't think at that time that it had any value to the Study" (Kikuchi to Modell, April 15, 1971).

The names of persons mentioned in the edited text who seem to me to have neither historical importance nor special importance to the young Kikuchi himself either have been given pseudonyms (where it has seemed necessary in order that the reader may be able to identify them from one mention to the next) or have been identified by initials only. (In some cases the original diary includes only initials.) The only names abbreviated are Japanese; to distinguish them, Caucasian names are always given in full, even if pseudonymous.

I would like to acknowledge the earlier efforts of Donald P. Kent and Barbara K. Fitts in editing and annotating Kikuchi's wartime journals. Although the present edition has an entirely different aim from their earlier project, their work was of interest and use.

The Kikuchi Diary

December 7, 1941, Berkeley, California

Pearl Harbor. We are at war! Jesus Christ, the Japs bombed
Hawaii and the entire fleet has been sunk. I just can't believe
it. I don't know what in the hell is going to happen to us, but
we will all be called into the Army right away. Wang [1] says he
has to do a report, but he is so stunned that he does not know
what he is doing. He is worried about his relatives as the radio
says there are riots in Los Angeles, and they think it is sabotage. I can't believe that any Nisei would do anything like that,
but it could be some of the Kibei [2] spies. I don't know what
is going to happen to us, but I just can't think of it.

I think of the Japs coming to bomb us, but I will go and
fight even if I think I am a coward and I don't believe in wars
but this time it has to be. I am selfish about it. I think not of
California and America, but I wonder what is going to happen
to the Nisei and to our parents. They may lock up the aliens.
How can one think of the future? We are behind the eightball,
and that question for the California Nisei "Whither Nisei?"
[is] so true. The next five years will determine the future of the
Nisei. They are now at the crossroads. Will they be able to
take it or will they go under? If we are ever going to prove our

1 Wang: Warren Tsuneishi, a friend of Kikuchi's.
2 Nisei is the Japanese term, commonly used by Japanese Americans, for the
children of the immigrants, the latter being known as Issei. The Kibei, also referred to, are Nisei who received much of their education in Japan.

Americanism, this is the time. The Anti-Jap feeling is bound
to rise to hysterical heights, and it is most likely that the Nisei
will be included as Japs. I wanted to go to San Francisco tonight, but Pierre [3] says I am crazy. He says it's best we stick on
campus. In any event, we can't remain on the fence, and a positive approach must be taken if we are to have a place in fulfilling the Promise of America. I think the U.S. is in danger
of going Fascist too, or maybe Socialist. Those Nisei progressives think it will be Socialists, but the Sacramento crowd sure
sound like Fascists. "These are the days which try men's souls."
I don't know what to think or do. Everybody is in a daze.
Maybe I should do my report on the Nisei daze. Everybody on
campus is in the same boat, and they will clear us all off to the
Army and no more time for college for anyone.

December 8, 1941, Berkeley

"Tolerance is not enough." I was very upset yesterday as we are
in a war now. I am afraid that there will be violence and it is
a hell of a mess. I should have confidence in the democratic
procedures, but I'm worried that we might take a page from
Hitler's methods and do something drastic towards the Issei. I
hope not. I don't give a damn what happens to me, but I would
be very disillusioned if the democratic process broke down. It's
a mess, but every draft age fellow probably feels the same as I.

Nobody can predict the future and things do look bad, but I
just feel we will win the war and I will survive nicely as things
do turn out for the best. I'm not pressing my luck any, since it
won't get any worse. I have to speak to the U.S. students today
as Pierre is in Nisei campus politics and he thinks I am a good
loyal American. I think that is a joke, but it is true in a way.
I don't have any doubts about where I stand even if I am worried about what happens to us. I guess this is what I will have
to say. God, I was excited yesterday. Now I feel more normal,
but less afraid, to hell with everything attitude, whistling in the
dark. We shall see. Maybe I'll go to San Francisco tonight and

3 Pierre: Kenny Murase, another friend.

chase girls. Wang says chase the girls for tomorrow we die, and he tries to act like he is a man about town, but he is a virgin and he really wants me to take him when Angelo [4] and I go to Chinatown to chase girls.

The Yamato garage guys [5] don't even know I am back in college, as I am just a bum to them and I refuse to take Wang and Pierre over there and corrupt them. Their friend, Jim Sakoda, is a Kibei, and he is more worried than any of us; but he says Kibei are loyal. Having bull sessions is so meaningless now. It's action which counts, no more words. FDR says Pearl Harbor will be a day of infamy. Last fall I tried to get into the Army, but now I want to be a student, as it is going to be hell in the Army.

December 9, 1941, Berkeley

Holy Christ! San Francisco last night was like nothing I ever saw before and everybody was saying that the Japs are going to get it in the ass. I ran into Jimmy Hong up on Grant Avenue, and he says I'm not allowed to screw Chinese girls anymore. Angelo, too, he says, because he is a Wop. Jimmy was kidding; and he will give me some kind of a badge which says that I am a Chinese as he says some of the Japanese boys from U. C. got beat up. I didn't hear anything about that. Kenny told me it was true when I got back, and he said that all of the students are going to be restricted to campus. A lot of them want to get the hell out of here and go home, but I don't know what good that will do. I don't know what good it will be to stay here.

Kenny has a friend, Shibs,[6] who is full of wild stories. I don't know where he gets them. He says Bill is spying for the Navy or the FBI. I don't believe that; but I guess the FBI do have guys on the campus. They have picked up some suspicious Japanese

[4] Angelo Badello, who was engaged to Kikuchi's sister Alice. (They never married.)

[5] The Yamato Garage Gang is discussed in the Introduction.

[6] Shibs: Tamotsu Shibutani, also known as Tom.

already. I saw Alice [7] and she is worried about Pop, because we live so close to Mare Island and she thinks that Jack should go over and tell the Mayor that Pop was in the U.S. Navy. I think Pop would praise Japan; but he is not going to blow up anything. It may be dangerous for him in the barber shop with all those Mare Island guys coming in. I told Alice to tell Mom to have Pop's Navy discharge framed and put on the wall next to the barber license and take that Buddha statue the hell out of there. Alice says the Army should put me in charge of patriotism because I am suspicious of my own father. I did not mean it that way; but it is true, I don't trust the Issei. If just one of them sabotaged something, what hell there would be to pay. Mrs. Edwards [8] seems very calm about the whole thing, I must say. She told me to study hard and become an officer in the Navy. What a laugh! The Navy would not even let me be a messboy. Jack says it's going to be bad, and he wants to go East to study medicine; but he can't walk out on the family like that.

December 10, 1941, Berkeley

The Japs are running wild all over Asia, and they may wind up this war before we get a fleet back there. I heard that some of the battleships are on the way back, so maybe I'll go over to Mare Island and see. There is some question that college may end for the term as nobody is studying. I went to San Francisco again and everybody is in a daze in Jap Town and all sorts of wild rumors are going around they are going to lock up the Issei. If they are spies, I don't see anything wrong with that.

7 The Kikuchi family included eight siblings. Charles was, of course, the eldest son, having been preceded by one sister, Mariko (who relocated voluntarily to Chicago before the family entered Tanforan). Charles was followed by John, Alice, Emiko, Bette, Tom, and Miyako. The four oldest children had moved out of the Kikuchi family before relocation but, as did Charles, elected to be relocated with their parents' family group.

8 A pseudonym. Kikuchi chauffeured Dr. Edwards up the coast to British Columbia the previous summer and retained friendly relations with the family. The Edwards family had employed Alice as a domestic servant before the relocation.

That's war. Wang and the guys have a bull session every night, and they are going to organize the Nisei progressives on campus to make a statement to the *Daily Cal.* I am for that. Kenny and I are supposed to work on this letter, but I will let Kenny do the writing and I'll pretend that I'm giving him the idea. He is a hell of a good writer. Wang can write too, but he has an inferiority complex. He keeps pestering me to take him to San Francisco to a whorehouse because he says he may get drafted into the Army and be sent off to war; and he does not want to die a virgin. Kenny gets sore when we talk like that because he is a Christian deep down and very pure in heart, and he thinks that we should keep our minds on the war and think progressive thoughts. He says I am a bad influence on the guys in the house because I go chase girls every night; and he disapproves of my fooling around with M. T. because he thinks campus Nisei girls don't fool around. He should ask Bob K. about that! Anyhow, all this running around and not studying is a diversion because none of us know what in the hell it is all about, or what is going to happen. I feel like a condemned man who wants to be a glutton before they lead him to the gas chamber. Kenny and his friend Shibs think that we have to be intellectuals and lead the Issei. I don't see how we can do that if we are in the Army. Germany is now in the war and things are never going to be like it was before.

December 19, 1941, Berkeley

All kinds of rumors and I am worried. There is no way to have a normal life, and I can't be a student anymore. But I don't want to leave the campus. Talked to Shibs and he says there will be a report on the Nisei on campus and that we should all write up everything that happens. I don't think I would be very good at it; but I might give it a trial. All the so-called intellectuals like Shibs, Kenny, and Jimmy Sakoda say that we should document everything. They are so cold and impersonal, and I don't know what good that will do if any violence starts.

There have been houses stoned in Placer County, [California,] and some of the newspapers are raising hell and making all kinds of wild statements about even the Nisei. Kenny showed me a lot of clippings, and it is very dangerous. Yet, I feel that we are so helpless. Who in the hell is going to worry about the Nisei when we are at war? Maybe the thing to do is to get into the Army. Wang says they will need the Nisei for interpreters. That's one thing I won't qualify for. I think that the Nisei should forget all things Japanese and not attract that kind of attention to ourselves. We must wave the old flag like the very first patriot. I think the Nisei are loyal, but we may be too short for the Army, and I refuse to be a messboy. There is a lot of hysteria going on. Went to Vallejo and the family does not know what to do. All kinds of restrictions coming in. I don't know what to say to them, as I really don't feel I am a part of the family. Jack will have to be the one. Mariko is talking of going East as the hysteria against Japs gets stronger. She says that the Japs are going to invade California; and she is convinced of it, and she says she is going to get a Chinese card too. She asked me to get a few more from Jimmy Hong for the family. I don't think things are that bad.

Berkeley, California
March 1, 1942

Dear Mariko,[9]

Received your card this morning and was glad to hear that you are gradually getting things under control. However, I'm not quite clear on some of the things which you mentioned. If

9 The previous entries were parts of a diary Kikuchi kept before arrangements with Dorothy Thomas were worked out, and they represent the only surviving entries dated before April 20, 1942. "Most of the pre-[evacuation] diary was stolen, lost, confiscated, disappeared except for those brief entries. Too bad!" (Kikuchi to John Modell, April 15, 1971). The present entry and the following one are excerpts from letters written by Kikuchi in Berkeley to his sister Mariko, the second after she had voluntarily relocated to Chicago. They transmit some sense of the widespread confusion which preceded the relatively tranquil monotony of life in the camp.

I understand clearly, the present plan is to send Mom and Pop to San Francisco, while you carry on the home there. I assume then that this is being done with the object of letting the kids get through school for this semester. That was my object, also, but may I throw another matter in for consideration? We have to realize this problem from the standpoints of our parents also and not be too arbitrary in any decision. You will probably realize that psychologically this is going to affect them to a great degree. In time of such a crisis, they will naturally have to have something to hang onto. This means the children. I was talking to Dr. Cassidy, the Head of our Social Welfare Department, to-day, and he pointed out the implications which such a move may develop. He doesn't think that such a thing would be the wisest move because this means the breaking up of the home and it is in such times that family unity is needed the most. However, I don't know exactly all of the details yet, so that I really can't jump to any conclusions. Could you please enlighten me as to the details?

.   .   .   .

The real reason why I went to see Dr. Cassidy was to drop out of school, but after talking it over with him, I have decided that perhaps it will be better for me to finish the next two and one-half months out and get my credential. Dr. Cassidy was quite frank in telling me that my chances for getting a social work position were nil, but in the post-war period there would be a very good chance for me. Anyway, I know you will understand this viewpoint. However, if things do get serious, I will drop out. I will try to get home this weekend to talk things over with you. I've been doing a little investigating around for possible resources, and I am sure that you and the rest of us can arrive at a workable plan for the immediate present.

Now what about the barber shop? Do you plan to remain there or were you thinking of moving to another place in Vallejo? I strongly doubt if we could get a cheaper place and perhaps you could talk with the landlady and see whether she

would reduce the rent a little although this is not likely. I know
that you are keeping a close touch with the Federal Security
Agency so that you will be informed on all the latest developments. They plan to keep the whole thing independent of the
Relief Program.

Berkeley
April 9, 1942

Dear Mariko,

Glad to hear that you are in good hands. How are the job
possibilities coming along? I think Alice is going to send your
drawing along shortly. I was home today and things are in a
madhouse stage. It's quite likely that evacuation will take place
in a matter of days. About 700 people have already gone to the
Assembly Center in Santa Anita (move over Seabiscuit!) and
the Federal Security Agency told me today that they expect to
have the Bay Area cleared out immediately. They sent me a
telegram asking me to take a job on the evacuation work as a
social worker, but I turned it down since I am so set on com-
pleting my training and obtaining my certificate. I hope to have
this completed in a couple of weeks. The job was only temporary, and I am sure that others will be coming up.

We are having quite a problem figuring out just what to take.
There is still so much junk around and you know how the
Japanese like to hang on to old things. Anyway, we will have to
store a lot of it, since they will not allow us to take more than
the barest of necessities. I do not know whether I will go down
with the family yet or not. I may follow after them, since
Berkeley will not be evacuated until after San Francisco.

Tommy and Miyako are all excited about the "vacation";
Alice confused; Jack calm; Emiko still thinking about the boys
and the clothes she has to take; and Mom and Pop not worrying too much as they think that I have a special "in" with the
government—just because I arranged to get the Federal check!

.   .   .   .

Curfew law works hardships on social life if you obey it, but you know Chas. I have a Chinese Student Club card, and it says "Shar Lee" on it for identification. A cop stopped me the other night and I showed him the card. Then he asked me my American name and I said Harry, because I am hairy, and he apologized for mistaking me for a Jap, and I said it was okay since we all had to sacrifice, and so to home I went.

.   .   .   .

I don't know what my present and future plans will be. Hardly feel like continuing at school at a time like this when so much is going on, but will go if nothing else turns up. Besides, I don't relish the idea of picking fruit again. However, I'm pretty optimistic and think that there will be many opportunities arising in the relocation work. Quite a few of the kids I know are working for the government now.

Don't mind the sloppy letter as I am rushed. I am trying to finish up my research papers before leaving. When this is completed, most of the hard work for the year will be over and the certificate practically in my hands. Probably will get the usual grades, since I have them all fooled, or something. All of the school authorities and my friends have been swell in this whole affair and sometimes I wonder where all this anti-Jap hatred is coming from. Of course, in times like this with so much at stake, people are bound to get a little hysterical and do things that they would not do under more rational considerations. Then the Japanese [Americans] really don't appreciate all that has been done for them because they don't get the information. However, you can be assured that they will be taken care of in a very humane manner with the Social Security Board [*sic*—a misunderstanding] handling the resettlement. So it's up to people like you who have gone out to prove to other Americans that we are Americans too (even if we have yellow fever faces!). It's hard on the old people, but for the Nisei it can be made an opportunity if they don't start getting to feel sorry for themselves and develop a persecutionist attitude. What are the Yabos like in Chicago? Do they have buck teeth, horn rimmed glasses, and *dai-kon ashii* too? [10]

S. F. Japanese Town certainly looks like a ghost town. All the stores are closed and the windows are bare except for a mass of "evacuation sale" signs. The junk dealers are having a roman holiday, since they can have their cake and eat it too. It works like this! They buy cheap from the Japanese leaving and sell dearly to the Okies coming in for defense work. Result, good profit. Lots of kids getting married off on the theory that they have to protect their vested interest when and if morals get loose in camp, but I don't think there is much danger of that happening, although the rowdier bunches will probably get rowdier for a while if they have nothing to do.

April 30, 1942, Berkeley

Today is the day that we are going to get kicked out of Berkeley. It certainly is degrading. I am down here in the control station [11] and I have nothing to do so I am jotting down these notes! The Army Lieutenant over there doesn't want any of the photographers to take pictures of these miserable people waiting for the Greyhound bus because he thinks that the American public might get a sympathetic attitude towards them.

I'm supposed to see my family at Tanforan as Jack told me to give the same family number. I wonder how it is going to be living with them as I haven't done this for years and years? I should have gone over to San Francisco and evacuated with them, but I had a last final to take. I understand that we are going to live in the horse stalls. I hope that the Army has the courtesy to remove the manure first.

[10] Kikuchi refers here to an interesting and common form of group self-hate on the part of the Japanese Americans. The buck-teeth-and-glasses was so much a white American stereotype of Japanese *in Japan* that it caused the Nisei little pain. But the *dai-kon ashii* (legs shaped like Japanese white radishes) referred to a characteristic of the Japanese American physique of which large numbers of young Nisei women felt shame, since by American standards short and thick legs failed the test of comparison to movie stars'.

[11] The Army authorities established control stations as collecting points for Japanese Americans awaiting evacuation to assembly centers.

This morning I went over to the bank to close my account and the bank teller whom I have never seen before solemnly shook my hand and he said, "Goodbye, have a nice time." I wonder if that isn't the attitude of the American people? They don't seem to be bitter against us, and I certainly don't think I am any different from them. That General De Witt certainly gripes my ass because he has been listening to the Associated Farmers [12] too much.

Oh, oh, there goes a "thing" in slacks and she is taking pictures of that old Issei lady with a baby. She says she is the official photographer, but I think she ought to leave these people alone. The Nisei around here don't seem to be so sad. They look like they are going on a vacation. They are all gathered around the bulletin board to find out the exact date of their departure. "When are you leaving?" they are saying to one another. Some of those old Issei men must have gone on a binge last night because they smell like *sake*.

Mitch just came over to tell us that I was going on the last bus out of Berkeley with him. Oh, how lucky I am! The Red Cross lady just told me that she would send a truck after my baggage and she wants the phone number. I never had a phone in that dump on Haste Street.

I have a queer sensation and it doesn't seem real. There are smiling faces all around me and there are long faces and gloomy faces too. All kinds of Japanese and Caucasian faces around this place. Soon they will be neurotic cases. Wang thinks that he has an empty feeling in his stomach and I told him to go get a hamburger upstairs because the Church people are handing out free food. I guess this is a major catastrophe so I guess we deserve some free concessions.

The Church people around here seem so nice and full of consideration saying, "Can we store your things?" "Do you need clothes?" "Sank you," the Issei smile even now though they are leaving with hearts full of sorrow. But the Nisei

[12] The Associated Farmers was a trade association of generally well-off California farmers; it had actively urged the relocation of the Japanese (who were in many instances competitors of theirs).

around here seem pretty bold and their manners are brazen. They are demanding service. I guess they are taking advantage of their college educations after all. "The Japs are leaving, hurrah, hurrah!" some little kids are yelling down the street but everybody ignores them. Well, I have to go up to the campus and get the results of my last exam and will barely be able to make it back here in time for the last bus. God, what a prospect to look forward to living among all those Japs!

May 3, 1942   Sunday

The whole family pitched in to build our new home at Tanforan. We raided the Clubhouse [13] and tore off the linoleum from the bar table and put it on our floor so that it now looks rather homelike. Takeshi [Tom] works pretty hard for a little guy and makes himself useful, but the gals are not so useful. They'd rather wander around looking for the boys. However, they pitched in and helped clean up the new messhall so that we could have our meals there instead of walking all the way over to the clubhouse. It's about 11:00 now and everyone has gone to bed. You can hear the voices all the way down the barracks —everything sounds so clear. Tom just stepped out to water his "victory garden." The community spirit is picking up rapidly and everyone seems willing to pitch in. They had a meeting tonight to get volunteers for cooks and waiters at the new messhall and this was done without difficulty. Rules were also made for each barracks such as radio off at 10:00 and not too many lights so that the fuse would not get overloaded.

We have only been here three days, but it already seems like weeks. Everyone here has fallen into the regular routine, without any difficult adjustments except Pop who was a problem child this morning. He got mad because he was not getting the proper food [14] so he went off by himself and got lost.

There are still many problems to be solved such as heating,

[13] The reader will need to recall, here and elsewhere, that Tanforan had until quite recently been operated as a racetrack, and had been "converted" to residential use only hastily.

[14] The elder Kikuchi required a special diet because of his diabetic condition.

cleaner dishes, more variety of foods, recreational, and other social problems but they will most likely be settled in time.

I saw a soldier in a tall guardhouse near the barbed wire fence and did not like it because it reminds me of a concentration camp. I am just wondering what the effects will be on the Japanese so cut off from the world like this. Within the confines of Tanforan our radios and papers are the only touch with reality. I hardly know how the war is going now, and it is so significant that the Allied forces win even though that will not mean that democracy will by any means be perfect or even justified. The whole post war period is going to be something terrific. Sometimes I feel like a foreigner in this camp hearing so much Japanese although our family uses English almost exclusively.

Taro [15] lives up in the Men's dormitory, the majority of whom are Issei, and he has a big American flag over his head for identification. I wonder what the Issei think of this. I haven't heard any talk about a "Japanese victory" although it must go on. You just can't change a group overnight, especially in the face of the fact that the Japanese have been so discriminated against in this state—witness the long history of anti-orientalism.

We are planning to get the paper underway as soon as possible. It is needed now as a "morale raiser" and also for the information service that it could render. With 4000 more people coming in next week, the confusion may grow greater.

From an individual standpoint our family has not lost anything. We have been drawn close together as a group and everyone seems cheerful enough. Jack is straining a bit because of Helen, I suppose, but he doesn't say too much. I tried to get him interested in the Medical Department here, but he was not too enthusiastic. He did show an interest in the library though. Tom and Miyako are having a grand vacation. I hope they do not delay in setting up an efficient school system—education is so important for the future.

15 Taro Katayama became editor of the *Tanforan Totalizer,* the camp newspaper on which Kikuchi would work.

May 4, 1942   Monday

There are such varied reactions to the whole thing: some are content and thankful; others gush "sank you" but are full of complaints within their own circles. Still others are bolder and come right out with it. We thought that we would not have any dinner tonight because the cooks went on a strike. They really are overworked—preparing 3000 meals. Then there have been considerable "personality difficulties." The battle for prestige here is terrific—everyone wants to be a somebody, it seems—any kind of work will do as long as they get the official badges that distinguish them. The waiters also joined the strike because they only have 1000 dishes to feed 3000 people and they really have to get them out in a rush. I saw one Issei dishwasher slap a Nisei girl because she complained that the cups were so dirty. Their nerves are on edge in the cooking division because they are the target for many complaints when it really is not their fault. They are going to open up the new messhalls for sure tomorrow so a great deal of the overload rush will be cut down. The electricians are also griped because they have to replace so many fuses. The wiring system in the stables is very poor and with all the extra lights needed, the system has broken down. Because of the cold, many of the people use cooking heaters to keep warm with. They brought in 50 kerosene heaters today for the aged, ill, and the babies, but this is by no means sufficient.

Oh, I sure could go for a hamburger now: the big juicy kind. I've eaten so much canned food the past week that it becomes tasteless. Many of the boys are worried about being fed saltpetre because they think it will ruin their manhood.

A contrasting reaction is the number of victory gardens that are being planted; these industrious Japanese! They just don't seem to know how to take it easy—they've worked so hard all of their lives that they just can't stand idleness—or waste. They are so concerned that water is not left running or that electricity is not being wasted. Today many of the smaller family units were asked to move to make room for the new evacuees and they certainly did squawk. Here they have their places all fixed up nice and cozy and then they have to start all over again. But they will take it without too much fuss. I wonder if it is because they feel thankful for any treatment that they get regardless of what it is or whether they still are full of unnecessary fears about how the government is going to treat them. Sometimes I get tired of hearing all these "sank you's" which certainly is not the real feeling in so many cases.

I ran across an interesting restroom today. Down by the stables there is an old restroom which says "Gents" on one side and "Colored Gents" on the other! I suppose it was for the use of the stable-boys. To think that such a thing is possible in California is surprising. I guess class lines and the eternal striving for status and prestige exist wherever you go, and we are still in need of a great deal of enlightenment.

About 20 of us met tonight to really get the Camp paper going because we really do need some source of information. Most of the group were represented and they are all behind the movement. Taro Katayama was elected Temporary Editor so that the policy setting will at least be liberal and outspoken. We plan to distribute the papers through the mail service. All the Nisei lads want to be postmen because they feel that it will be a good opportunity to get to know the girls. The postoffice, next to the Employment Department, is the most rushed place in camp right now. The Clerk there said he sold over 1500 one cent cards today and you should have seen the stack of mail that already has been received by the postoffice.

Some of the UC boys have a "U.C. Extension" sign posted up, but they don't seem to be doing much studying. They sit around and gab and listen to the records. One can't blame them for not studying at a time like this.

May 5, 1942   Tuesday

We got approval to go ahead with the paper and the boys are working hard in order to get the first issue out by Saturday; I'm supposed to write up the section on the employment situation in camp. The whole setup needs centralizing. There are too many conflicting orders about who is supposed to do the hiring, etc. A number of the Nisei are complaining that the S. F. gang is taking all the choice jobs and just working their friends in—a large part of which is true. It should be on the basis of merit because much of the skills and abilities are not being fully utilized. Mr. Greene,[16] the chief man under Lawson, does not seem to be a dynamic administrator and does not appear to me to be too good a person for such a responsible position.

.   .   .   .

Today I ran across the first Japan nationalist who reacted violently. He said that Japan "requested" that we be put into a concentration camp so that we have to do it for the sake of Japan. The man seemed pleasant and harmless enough at first, but when he started to talk on this subject, I was amazed to see the bitter look of hatred in his eyes and face. He asked us point-blank whether we were for Japan or America and we said "America" on the basis of our beliefs and education. He got extremely angry and pounded on the table while shouting that we Nisei were fools and that we had better stick by Japan because we could never be Americans; only "Ketos" [white men, literally, hairy people] could be Americans. Since we had Japanese faces we should be for Japan because she would always protect us and not treat us like dogs, etc. We argued for a while but apparently it is no use trying to reason with a person of this type who thinks emotionally. I get fearful of this attitude sometimes because it has been this very thing that makes Americanization so difficult, especially if there is a general tendency to get it from both sides. And I still am not convinced that it is impossible to educate the Issei, although the argument that we are in camp just like them and therefore not Americans is beginning to influence many Nisei. It's a good thing perhaps that

16 Greene served, Kikuchi recalls, as an employment officer throughout the entire existence of the Tanforan Assembly Center.

I don't understand Japanese because I am not exposed so much to this sort of talk. It makes me feel so uneasy and mad. It gripes me no end to think of being confined in the same place with these Japanists. If they could only realize that in spite of all their past mistreatments, they have not done so bad in America because of the democratic traditions—with its faults. It may be a sense of personal frustration which is projected to a hatred of all "Keto" and deep resentment towards America. I hope we are able to counteract this sort of thing among the young kids. Prof. Obata was in today and he was worried by this same thing —he is an Issei so there are many of them that live by the American way. He wants to direct a camp art class in order to raise the morale—this point needs to be stressed over and over.

.   .   .   .

The War goes on; men are killed, but this camp is not much aware of that. The Germans have not started the spring offensive although they are challenging the British fleet in the North Sea. Japan is still making gains and is about to cut the China lifeline in Burma, but the Allies are rapidly gaining power. I hope it is not too late.

May 6, 1942   Wednesday

Jack [Charles's brother John] and I were talking about the War. Sometimes, I wonder whether he really believes what he says or whether he is merely trying to get a rise out of me. He says a Japanese victory is the only solution to the Asiatic problem since the "Keto" will continue to exploit these people regardless of what we may claim about democracy. Could be. However, I said that under a democratic tradition there was more hope for the majority than under a militant nationalistic policy. And I wonder if he ever [would] "kow tow" to one of those officious "Japs" who has obtained a little power. Then a little later, he turns right around and condemns the lack of community spirit among the Japanese here and that he would not be able to adjust himself permanently to a Japanese community.

He wants to get the family settled and then go back east to school. Pop says brothers should not argue about the war.

.   .   .   .

Mario and Helen came to visit today and Jack sneaked them off to our stable, which is illegal. He told the M.P. that they were going to see "Mr. Johnson" in the Employment office, and the M.P. came in mad as anything looking for the Japanese with the varsity sweater. I told him that there were 4000 Japanese here and that he would have to give a better description. Later I sent one of our messenger boys down and told them to be "on alert." Helen flirted with the guard and so things turned out "ok."

Corregidor fell yesterday; overheard an Issei remark: "About time, no?" I feel so much like telling them off sometimes, but I guess this should be done in a more diplomatic way. To think that those soldiers are dying off like that, and then to have their efforts passed off like that. It makes me boil.

My first few days only make me feel like an American more, but that's something that you can't go "parading off." I just feel that way, I guess. It may be an overdefensive reaction, but I think it goes deeper than that. Mitch [17] and I are speaking only English to all applicants in the employment office as any large segregation of Japanese will easily drift into speaking only Japanese. It's very interesting to talk to the young Nisei that come in; they are so Americanized. I think that we should start some sort of discussion groups or something so that they won't lose contact with the outside influences. They are all fairly ambitious and think in terms of going on to school and then adjusting themselves here in the U.S. after the war. The more conservative ones invariably have fathers who were engaged in some business with Japan. I guess they get more of the "old country" influence from their parents.

.   .   .   .

17 Mitch Kunitani and his wife, Ann, were prominent Nisei liberals and close friends of Kikuchi's.

I feel like trying to join the Army also, but that's being heroic. I still can't decide whether I would be more useful doing service work among the Japanese here. I think I will be able to adjust myself easily enough although not knowing the language may be a handicap but not necessarily too big to overcome. At least I no longer feel apologetic about it. I guess it has been my emotional reactions against political Japan that have blocked my learning the language in the past few years.

Today they have started to put Nisei police to patrol the barracks and the messhall.[18] There have been several cases of theft reported and the kitchen has been raided a number of times. One woman reported a fur coat stolen, but she may have just lost it as I don't see why anyone would want a fur coat in a place like this. A more serious problem is the reported solicitations by Japanese prostitutes up in the single men's dormitory. The Army M.P. are on their trails and Nisei police have been stationed to intercept them if they show up at night. (And Mr. Greene thinks we don't need social workers!) This is not so bad; but if this sort of thing starts among the young Nisei, it will be very difficult to control. This camp has a sort of pioneer atmosphere about it and if the kids are left in idleness, trouble could easily develop. Already some of the so called "rowdy Nisei"[19] are shooting craps so that they can get money to spend in the canteen. The development of a well balanced recreational program will be a good influence. I sound like a moralist, but I am thinking more in terms of future social adjustments of the Japanese here, which will be difficult, and morale will have to be kept at a high level if we expect progress to be made.

May 7, 1942   Thursday

A new menace has entered our lives to make the pioneer conditions more uncomfortable. We are infested with tiny fleas that

[18] The administration hoped to reduce their problems in patrolling their charges by employing selected evacuees as part of the "internal police." White police were less frequently seen, although present—in addition, of course, to the military guards.

[19] Although on the whole an extremely law-abiding community, the Japanese Americans had by 1942 discovered the problems of juvenile and postjuvenile delinquency.

bite like hell. They must be horse fleas or something that come from the old stables. Gods, they certainly make life miserable.

.   .   .   .

One Issei came in today with his wife, daughter, and a young Kibei. He requested that we move this fellow from the grandstands into their apartment because he wants the boy to have a "trial marriage" with his daughter. I don't know how he ever roped the boy in; the daughter was really a sad case—one of these homely quiet Japanese types who looked and acted submissive. The request was not granted; told them that we could not do that because such things were not done in America. The man tried to play up to me by saying, "You have big education. Catch good job in Japan, no?" That settled it. Told him that I expected to stay here and, therefore, would have to do things the American way. He did not seem to catch on, so I put in the request for him and he left in a happy mood.

.   .   .   .

There are all different types of Japanese in camp. Many of the young Nisei are quite Americanized and have nice personalities. They smile easily and are not inhibited in their actions. They have taken things in stride and their sole concern is to meet the other sex, have dances so that they can jitterbug, get a job to make money for "cokes," and have fun in general. Many are using the evacuation to break away from the strict control of parental rule.

Other Nisei think more in terms of the future. They want to continue their education in some sort of "career" study and be successes. The background which they come from is very noticeable: their parents were better educated and had businesses. One Nisei girl was telling me today about how Grant Avenue [San Francisco] art goods stores were sold out. They used a lot of Nisei girls and those stores that were in control of Caucasian hands paid twice as much in salary as those owned by Japanese. Many of the shrewd Jewish businessmen bought the whole store out and they got a lot of old stock out of ware-

houses and sold them in the evacuation sale. They used the
Japanese stores as a front to unload this junk on the public.
The art goods stores, even Chinese, are having a difficult time
because they cannot get any more stock in from the Orient. I
asked the girl what her father expected to do after the war and
she said that he and his wife would probably be forced to leave
this country, but the girl expects to get married and stay here.

.   .   .   .

Made me feel sort of sorry for Pop tonight. He has his three
electric clippers hung up on the wall and Tom has built him a
barrel chair for the barber seat. It's a bit pathetic when he so
tenderly cleans off the clippers after using them; oiling, brush-
ing, and wrapping them up so carefully. He probably realizes
that he no longer controls the family group and rarely exerts
himself so that there is little family conflict as far as he is concerned. What a difference from about 15 years ago when I was
a kid. He used to be a perfect terror and dictator. I think most
of us have inherited this tendency to be dominant, except perhaps Alice. She is not too aggressive and she would perhaps
make some fellow a nice wife. She has worked hard for the past
four years and helped support the family so that now she is
more or less inclined to be a little queenish. Alice has never
gone beyond her high school level of friends and this is the type
that she goes around with now—nothing wrong in that, I suppose, but I do think that she should be more advanced than to
confine herself with Emiko's and Bette's "jitterbug" friends.

Emiko is very boy-conscious also and her idea of life right
now is good clothes, plenty of boy friends, and jitterbug music.
She will probably get over the stage soon. She gets along well
with the fellows and is capable of adjustments to any circumstances.

Bette is also getting at that age and sometimes she feels that
Jack and I don't approve of it so she hesitates a bit at times in
approving all of these light activities. She seems to be more responsible than the other two and she certainly has a clever sense
of humor. She, too, is getting boystruck. Right now, she worries

about her weight so that she makes Miyako or Tom walk around the track with her for the "exercise."

Mom is taking things in stride. I have a suspicion that she rather enjoys the whole thing. It certainly is a change from her former humdrum life. She dyed her hair today, and Pop made some comment that she shouldn't try to act so young. One thing about these stables is that it does cut down the amount of "nagging" because people can overhear everything that is said.

May 8, 1942   Friday

Terrific wind howling outside tonight again. Warren and Jimmy just left to go do their night patrolling. They ducked in here for a couple of hours to get out of the cold. Jack, myself, and those two got started on the war. We thought that it would be a good idea to put the U.S. flag up on the big pole up in the Grandstand in the morning for morale purposes, but decided to let the matter ride for a day or two since we heard that the Young Democrats [20] were considering the matter also. Any moves of this kind will cause criticism by the more conservative Nisei, but it is necessary and if doing such a thing is radical, then we are "pinks."

The question came up as to what were we fighting for. All of us were agreed that Fascism was not the answer, but there was a difference of opinions on whether an Allied victory would be any solution to the whole mess. Jimmy thinks that it offered the most potentialities and hope for the world. Would the solution include only the white races, or will we be in a position to tackle the problem of India, China, and the other millions of "exploited" peoples? If not, our efforts will not have accomplished their purposes. The problem is so immense that it staggers the imagination.

.   .   .   .

[20] The Young Democrats (YDs) were a group of politically aware Nisei, somewhat to the left of Kikuchi and most of his closest friends and considerably to the left of most Nisei. The group had been active in California politics for a few years and were in contact with similar organizations from other ethnic groups.

In regards to the Nisei, the reaction may be harmful if we do not continue to fight for the democratic way. We have to contribute to this process if we expect to share in it. From talks with many of the Nisei in camp, I have found out that most of the liberals show a fine degree of understanding of Democracy as a fight for equality and freedom which is yet to be attained. Their confidence in democracy has not been shaken since they realize that there are millions of other New Americans in this country who are with them in the struggle to achieve the potential ideals of this country. I think that the future advancement of the Nisei group will in large measure depend upon an increase in reinforcement of these beliefs. We can't afford to be passive because the prevalent idea appears to be one that we are guilty until proved innocent. Today's [San Francisco] *Chronicle* implied that all Nisei were disloyal and should be evacuated because two Nisei are now doing propaganda work for Japan over the radio. Isolated like we are in camp, the task will be doubly difficult to combat such things. I hope that the Nisei don't get in a "rut" while we are alienated from the larger American society. The days of the "little Tokyos" are past; from now on, we must constantly stress the fact that we look to Washington only. The Nisei who think that they have a future in Japan with a Japanese victory are only fooling themselves. They will be despised more than the Kibeis are here; in fact, the only hope for the future is America—come what may.

. . . .

The Grandstand is almost filled with single men and it probably is the most interesting place in camp. There are about 500 men in there and when they all take their shoes off, the odor that greets you is terrific. What a stench! They don't have any fresh air circulating around and the old clothes and closeness of body smells don't help out any. But the place is a study of varied activities. In one corner a sullen Kibei has built himself a little cube so that he can work on his master's thesis. Just down the aisle from him, an old Issei has set up a home made barber shop and he is doing a brisk business since this service has not yet been provided in camp. The place is full of home made clothes lines and they all hang their laundry by their beds where they can keep an eye on it. Little knots of Japanesy men cluster around the radios blaring the latest news and discussing the final Japanese victory. A brave Nisei occasionally opens his mouth and he is shouted down. But three American flags continue to hang upon the walls. Other single men sprawl out in their beds, smoking or playing Japanese cards. A few sleep with their mouths wide open, snoring like mad, which adds to the general confusion. Over in the far corner, there is a lone but seedy looking minister with a dirty collar, who sits so straight in his bed reading a Buddhist prayer book. Flies buzz around him, but he pays no attention. This room is about the most colorful place in camp, but I am afraid that those Isseis look to Tokyo rather than to Washington, D.C., for salvation.

.   .   .   .

Jack is studying nights for his finals so that he can get his credits and Miyako keeps him company by doing her typing lessons which Alice started her upon today. I have been trying to do a little reading, but don't seem to be able to get very far. My mind just doesn't seem to settle down. Perhaps I am bothered by "girl trouble." Mari [21] wrote today and she has been sent to Stockton to register the Japanese there. It doesn't look like she will get here until all the evacuation is completed. I guess I like her a lot because we are in the same kind of work and she is so Americanized and has a sort of personality that gets one. She makes friends so easily and I don't think she is particularly interested in me except "as a friend"—the old standby. One of these days I probably will fall for a Japanese girl, which will be mutual in reaction. She will have to be extremely Americanized, I guess, since this is the only kind of "Japanese" girl I seem to be attracted to. If I ever get one of those quiet submissive types, I am afraid that I would make her life miserable.

21 Mari (a pseudonym) was a Japanese American girl Kikuchi had known for several months before the relocation, having met her at the School of Social Welfare at Berkeley. She was hired to help families preparing to be evacuated.

I like people to fight back because then I respect them for it; whereas, a submissive person only draws my contempt.

.   .   .   .

Some of the Issei are sore because they think Mitch and I are too fresh because we don't speak Japanese to them [at the employment bureau] and act on a master and slave basis instead of frankly speaking man to man. It's all right to respect the client, but I think the time for "coddling" them passed after December 7. Most of them can understand and speak English, surprisingly enough, and they should be made to use it more. A lot of Nisei kids come in and mix their Japanese in with their English. Now that we are cut off from the Caucasian contacts, there will be a greater tendency to speak more and more Japanese unless we carefully guard against it. Someday these Nisei will once again go out into the greater American society and it is so important that they be able to speak English well—that's why education is so important. I still think it is a big mistake to evacuate *all* the Japanese. Segregation is the least desirable thing that could happen and it certainly is going to increase the problem of future social adjustments. How can we expect to develop Americanization when they are all put together with the stigma of disloyalty pointed at them? I am convinced that the Nisei could become good Americans, and will be, if they are not treated with such suspicion. The presence here of all those pro-Japan Issei certainly will not help things out any.

The house manager [22] of the men's barracks told some of the single Nisei up there not to speak English because the Issei did not like it. This kind of thing makes me boil; after all, we are in America. It's a good thing that we have a number of family units here or social disorganization would develop at a much faster rate. These parents more or less realize that the Nisei are

---

[22] House managers and block managers were evacuee officers, of either generation, whose authority was limited but whose prestige and influence rivaled that of the various representatives to the evacuee self-government organizations. Because of rules imposed by the authorities, the representatives were always U.S. citizens.

going through a difficult period and they keep quiet, except in a few cases where they just can't resist the "I told you so's." Pop and Mom rarely talk about the war; they seem to feel that we are of America and I just don't know how to figure them out. They may sincerely believe that Japan is in the right; but they have come to accept the democratic way and more or less live by it. It's a good thing that they are not rabid nationalists; I'm afraid that I would not be able to stand it. Our family probably is not typical because all of us are more outspoken and liberal in our ways—Alice is about the most conservative, or conventional, person in the family. A lot of the Nisei tell me that I'm different because I was reared in an American home, but I just can't see that. It encourages me to see the number of Nisei around here who really feel and live by the democratic way.

The Japanese are known for their politeness and honesty, but if they stay here long, they certainly will degenerate. Because of the inadequacy of facilities they take everything in sight. Some of the things they have done have been downright stupid—such as breaking up the coal bin for lumber and taking linoleum from the other stables. The manners will not improve either. I hate to think of seeing them eat in a restaurant after they eat in those messhalls for a year or so! They will be so coarse and vulgar; under frontier conditions, one could not expect to hope for any better. One Japanese woman remarked that the "honest" Japanese were no better than the Filipinos in this camp—they took everything!

.   .   .   .

I was up in the Grandstands and had a good view of the outside; maybe I was depressed, but a funny feeling of loneliness and of being out of place swept over me. Perhaps this was due to the fact that I walked through the men's dormitory where all those Japanese old men were jabbering away in their conversations about the war. These type of people should be evacuated, but why put all the innocent Nisei—99½%—in with them? This burns me up no end.

A funny thing happened today. A rumor has gone around among the JACL [23] "leaders" that a bunch of "pinks" are trying to control the newspaper and we had quite a time showing them that this was a community effort and for the benefit of the whole camp. I think the administration could have saved themselves from many problems if they had provided the setup as soon as we came in so that everyone could have the information instead of all these wild rumors that sweep the camp. These little cliques seem to persist yet and it is most difficult to overcome them. The Nisei who are more outspoken and liberal in their beliefs seem to be getting the disfavor of the more conservative ones. This is rather unfortunate because we should all be working together for the best future adjustments instead of breaking up into divergent interest groups.

.   .   .   .

Tom says that he writes a seven page typewritten report to Dr. Thomas every day; [24] I don't know how he finds so much to write about. He is afraid that they will get suspicious and censor his mail, but I think that he is over-dramatizing it a bit. J. Y. is also keeping notes as well as Warren. Hero is doing some water sketches and Prof. Obata is also making drawings. There is another wild looking thing who has been to Europe on an art scholarship, and she is doing a lot of sketches so that there should be quite a bit of material available for any future studies of this mess. I realized a long time ago that I can't write; it's too much of an effort on my part. I don't think I would like research so much because that is reflecting back on a thing after it has happened and I am more interested in being in the thick of things while it is going on with some social view of the future. Taro, Mari, N., and the kids in the social welfare department think that I can write, but that's not true. I don't seem to have enough perspective and insight or the ability to analyze a thing deeply enough. I am trying to do this journal, but I bet

23 The JACL—Japanese American Citizens League—is discussed in the Introduction.

24 Professor Dorothy Swaine Thomas of the JERS. "Tom" is Tamotsu Shibutani.

I don't keep it up; it's such a hodgepodge of miscellaneous notes.

I started out the day in a depressed sort of mood, but my faith in everything has been restored a bit with the news that the U.S. fleet has won a big sea victory over Japan (unconfirmed).[25] I just can't help identifying myself with America; I feel so much a part of it and I won't be rejected.

May 10, 1942   Sunday

Mom just said, "Me glad, come here, better than in Vallejo. No cook, just do laundry. I feel glad that all family together." Tom doesn't like it here. He thinks it "stinks." He doesn't go out to play much with the other kids but works hard around the house. As soon as he makes a few more friends he will probably enjoy it. Miyako likes it very much. The rest of us are beginning to feel restricted a bit. As far as I am concerned, I don't like the reasons why we were put here, but I am finding it interesting so far. I don't know how I will feel a month from now though. But I haven't got so much service in years. The girls make the beds and clean house; I don't have to do my laundry; Mom darns my socks and my shirts are ironed; I don't have to wash dishes and cook; in fact, I am getting all-around service without worrying about finances like I did when I went to school last term. I lived on about $25.00 a month budget and had to skimp like hell to make it; here I bet it costs the government a lot more per month for my upkeep. But then—all this still doesn't compensate for my liberty and freedom of movement from place to place. I see those big shining aluminum-bodied Army planes roaring through the skies overhead and I am conscious of the fact that a war is going on. What beauties they are! Too bad man has such a destructive nature. The more Americanized Nisei are finding adjustment a bit more difficult. They are more aware of the motives behind the evacuation and they can't take it so easily as some of the others. A few are not

[25] This was the Battle of the Coral Sea, in which the Japanese advance across the South Pacific was first halted.

tackling the problems in a healthy way. G.'s intense energy is devoted to leading a cause—the Nisei cause. He is compensating for frustrating situations by plunging away like a "bull in a China shop." To him the evacuation is a personal matter; he looks at it as a personal persecution, although he would vehemently deny this. Perhaps he feels that he must "serve" the Nisei cause because he is hostage to a sense of guilt and unworthiness. He feels very insecure and is fearful of the future, but cannot afford to admit it to anyone. It may be that he is seeking personal emotional peace because of this sense of insecurity. Will the neurotic tendencies increase among the Nisei as they come up more and more against these frustrating situations?

May 11, 1942   Monday

During the heaviest rush in mid-morning Mr. Greene called Mitch out and had a long talk with him. When he came back he told me that Greene told him to tell me that he did not wish me to work in the office for a while, because they had received complaints that we were too fresh and that we did not speak Japanese to the clients. But it is strange that Mr. Greene would not tell me himself. According to Mitch, the girls in the inner office were the ones to pass these complaints on to Mr. Greene. It seems that Mr. Greene does not like social workers. He told Mitch that the "U.C. Social Welfare" students have a bad reputation. So there must be some deeper reason for Mr. Greene's actions. I don't know the man, having only spoken to him slightly on a couple of occasions about the possibilities of a social welfare department—which he was definitely not receptive to. It can't be that he doesn't need extra help in the office, we had more applicants than we could handle. Naturally, I was resentful of the superficial reasons that were given without even having a chance to defend myself; in fact, I was plenty burned up. Why couldn't he have told me those things to my face? Mr. Greene stated that the Issei were not coming in to apply because we did not speak Japanese to them. But why coddle them?

If the solution is either Americanization or deportation, they must be made to realize that they are in America—not Japan. In the week that I have been working voluntarily, I had only one or two cases who could not understand English and they could all speak it in a way. If they had some definite policy about wages, etc., I am sure that they would come in and apply regardless of who was taking the interview.

And Mitch has been much more blunt and frank than I have, yet I am made the scapegoat for some unknown reason. Mr. Greene must have had some conflict with social workers in the past, otherwise why should he make such remarks about them to Mitch and Ann. He is not a profound man; this I can believe without prejudice. All he wants to do is to keep the Japanese busy and happy for the moment. He doesn't seem too concerned about the future. I was so mad that I had to go up to Taro's room and cool off a couple of hours. If I have a run-in with Mr. Greene now, I will be finished as far as this camp is concerned. Yet I cannot let this go by without defending myself. I had an appointment to see him this afternoon but he was too busy so I will see him tomorrow and find out what it is all about.

I am deeply disturbed about these events. I'm not trying to spy or anything; all I want to do is to be of service. But as things have gone, being an American is a handicap around here. Will I still have to continue bumping my head against a stone wall? Maybe I am not diplomatic enough, but I just can't stand kow-towing to a person just because he has a white face. I won't put myself in an inferior position for anyone. I wonder what Mr. Greene has against social workers. There doesn't seem to be any other reason for his actions because I haven't had but few contacts with him, and Mrs. E. of the placement division definitely dislikes Mitch because of his frankness. I certainly have cooperated with her. This morning she came out and started to speak to the Nisei in Japanese and Mitch remarked that they could understand English. She responded with a look that could have killed. I was an innocent bystander.

I wish I wasn't so set on being a social worker. By now I could have worked into something else here; but it's not what I want. I still think I could be of service in spite of not knowing Japanese, if only given a chance. I want to be doing something that has implications for the future. I thought Mari was stubborn in wanting a medical social worker job and nothing else, but now I can see her motivations. I feel the same way about this mess—for personal as well as social reasons. It gets to be a sort of frustrating thing and I still don't want to give up—why should I? I've been here only a week yet I can catch myself getting extremely anti-Japanese again. I'm being forced to live by Japanese ways and I rebel inwardly and outwardly. And I'm not the only one. I have noticed this same reaction among several of my progressive friends—one symptom of this is that they refuse to talk Japanese among themselves and they use the term "Japs" more often when they feel disgusted with the people. I hope this camp doesn't make us conform to the standard Japanese ways. But we may become disillusioned and maladjusted if we fight against it. I think the principles are worth fighting for and I, furthermore, do not have any other choice than Americanization. Ann suggests that I work into the Education department when it is organized. This may be one of the ways that I could be of use. I don't know.

.   .   .   .

Another police was put on to patrol the hospital because so many things such as thermometers have been stolen. A girl was taking a shower and somebody walked off with her bathrobe. Everyone is beginning to put locks on their doors. These things must indicate something, but it will take a sociologist to figure it out. An Issei and a Nisei got in a fight today because one claimed the other had stolen some lumber from him and the other did not like the idea of being called a thief and so he took a swing.

The Issei barracks busybody is going all around with a clipping of "Terry and the Pirates." He claims that the Japanese are insulted with these drawings of buck teeth. I think they are very realistic. The Issei man who is protesting has the biggest set of buck teeth that I have ever seen! Such is life.

There was a terrific rainstorm last night and we have had to wade through the "slush alleys" again. Everyone sinks up to the ankles in mud. Some trucks came in today with lumber to build new barracks, but the earth was so soft that the truck sank over the hubs and they had a hell of a time pulling it out. The Army certainly is rushing things. About half of the Japanese have already been evacuated from the restricted areas in this state. Manzanar, Santa Anita, and Tanforan will be the three biggest centers. Now that S. F. has been almost cleared the American Legion, the Native Sons of the Golden West, and the California Joint Immigration Committee [26] are filing charges that the Nisei should be disfranchised because we have obtained citizenship under false pretenses and that "we are loyal subjects of Japan" and therefore never should have been allowed to obtain citizenship. This sort of thing will gain momentum and we are not in a very advantageous position to combat it. I get fearful sometimes because this sort of hysteria will gain momentum. The S. F. Registrar has made a statement that we will be sent absentee ballots to which Mr. James Fisk of the Joint Immigration Committee protests greatly. Tomorrow I am going to carry a petition around to protest against their protests. I think that they are stabbing us in the back and that there should be a separate concentration camp for these so-called Americans. They are a lot more dangerous than the Japanese in the U.S. ever will or have been.

Listened to Maurice Evans and Judith Anderson tonight. What a gory murder play to listen to in the mood I was in! It's enough to depress anyone. It's a good thing that the family was cheerful when I came home. They had been to a movie or a dance so that they were not so bored with things. They certainly are a good influence upon me; I can't feel moody or depressed while around them. They seem so lively and full of pep that I

[26] The American Legion and the Native Sons of the Golden West (NSGW), the latter a voluntary association of persons born in California and wishing to glorify and protect their native state, had for over two decades been components of the California Joint Immigration Committee, whose sole purpose was to defend against the supposed menace posed by the Japanese immigrants and their offspring.

forget all these other things and just live for the moment. It gives one the courage to start afresh and figure out new ways to handle the day's problems. I still think that this camp is a most interesting place. I must get around and meet more people to talk to; there are so many different kinds. A little boy said to me today (when he saw one of those new army bombers overhead), "Gee, I bet they sure will give Tokyo hell!" I seconded the motion.

May 12, 1942   Tuesday

I had a talk with Mr. Greene today. He seemed rather nice, but he has a funny opinion of social workers. He said that in all of his years of experience, he never found one that was a good employment office worker and vice versa. This certainly does not seem to be much of a reason for his actions. He went on to say that he agreed with our policy of Americanization, but that they would resent it too much if we did not gradually get them used to it. I pointed out that 80% of the people here were Nisei according to Mr. Lawson's office and of the rest of the Issei group there were few that did not understand English of a sort. This can be explained by the fact that the [San Francisco] Bay Area Japanese have been largely a commercial group and also because of the large numbers of domestic workers who have had contacts with Caucasian people. Mr. Greene was very agreeable and he thought that perhaps he could find a place for me doing social work because "they did have social problems here." He suggested that I come in to see him in his new office in the morning and have another talk with him. D. H. is going into the office to handle the girl end of interviews. Mitch should be able to handle her easily enough. Now that things are clearing up, I can see that I can be of greater use in the field for which I was trained. As long as it is a service dealing with people, I don't care. The latest word is that we will be here from three to six months, if not longer. If this is so, then there is no use in gaining the disfavor of the administrators but attempt to work with and through them. I'm not so conceited as to think that I know everything: I know so very little and I haven't had the experience to analyze things perfectly by any means. Sometimes I feel confused, jittery, and scared of myself. We may even have a social upheaval or we may go completely Fascistic. Whichever way we turn, the world will no longer be the same pre-war world. For the Japanese and the Nisei, this is still only the beginning. We must be more definite in the Americanization policy. This is the only solution for us.

.   .   .   .

The Japanese certainly are a clean people. I never saw so much laundry out on the lines in all my life. Every day is wash-day. They also are clean in body. Every night they take a shower; it's quite a social event. And the stables are kept neat and clean, as well as the latrines. They don't have funny sex ideas and so sometimes the old women walk right into the men's room and proceed with their business, regardless of who is in there at the time. The old men don't mind it, but the Nisei boys flee in horror. One woman remarked that it made no difference because she was too old anyway. Ann's neighbors are more coarse. They are an old couple and their only topic of conversation seems to be about some form of excrement. The woman yells in a high voice about how she has to go to the can or else she says that she doesn't have to go because she did not drink so much water the day before. This goes on from morning until night. In contrast, the neighbors on the other side are a Buddhist priest and his wife. Every day he goes into his dull monotonous chant and keeps it up for hours. And we sit in Ann's room and talk about Americanizing the Japs. I wonder how they like it; they must overhear us.

May 13, 1942   Wednesday

C. A. thinks that we are in for great disillusionment after the war. He sees no hope for any solution to the racial problems and points out the Negro history since the Civil War as the prime example. Somehow he persists in drawing a close parallel

between the Negro and the Japanese problems; but I told him
that I did not believe that there was any comparison. If any
comparison was to be made, the Japanese in America are more
closely identified with the Jewish people. Fear of both groups
has arisen from economic competition and, unlike the Negro,
this motive has been stronger than any feeling of actual racial
inferiority, although I did not dismiss this as a possible element.
Then the Jewish people have a long cultural history based on a
faith; the same is true for the Japanese. Both groups are an
extremely sensitive and nervous people although the Japanese
may be able to cover up a bit better by his "stoic face." Then
there is a certain respect for a successful member of either
group, whereas the Negro is more often than not looked at with
contempt, etc. But C. A. believes that the strongest point for his
argument is the racial, and not the economic, basis. He cannot
see how this problem can be solved even by this war; it may
even be intensified if the masses of Asia ever rise.

May 14, 1942   Thursday

News of the wage scale for evacuees in the Assembly, reception,
and relocation centers was announced today by the government.
The scale announced is even lower than what was expected. Unskilled workers will get $8.00 a month; semi-skilled workers will
have $12.00 a month; and the professional and technical workers
will receive $16.00 a month. The reaction to this news was
varied. Many took the view that they would not have much use
for money anyway since there would be little to spend it on
around here. Skilled workers took it better than those who have
been doing the hard manual labor around here. People in the
messhall and the general laborers really work hard, putting in
way more than the required 44 hours a week. Some have already quit their jobs, feeling that it was not worth it. The Nisei
in the key positions felt that salary was not all-important and
some stated that they would even do the work voluntarily. This
is especially true in the recreational program where many Nisei
are pitching in and helping out in order to get the program

functioning. S. T. is a Phi Beta and has completed two graduate years at Boalt Hall [University of California] in law. I was helping him this morning conduct some games for little kids over in Messhall #9 and he feels that position and a badge are not important. He would much rather see more stress on organizational development with a definite policy in order to keep up the morale.

The wage scale is really not as low as it sounds. Besides room and Grade A army rations, free hospitalization, dental and medical care, and "necessary clothing" will be provided as well as all of the recreational activities—and our camp newspaper. Besides this each single person will be allowed up to $2.50 a month, a couple, $4.00, and a family up to $7.50 per month for other necessary toilet articles and other incidentals. No cash will be given; all payments to be made in scrip coupons which will only be good in these camps. It would perhaps have been better to give everyone a uniform wage; this would have eliminated some of this striving for external prestige. The amount is not so great anyway and at a time like this a greater stress should be placed upon cooperative effort rather than individual advancement. Almost all necessary things are provided anyhow or will be in the future, we hope. They even provide the camp with the best grade of toilet paper—the kind that costs 3 for 25¢! I bet the Japanese never had this before. And I am sure that many Japanese are eating better than they ever did at home. And there is not the eternal worrying over unpaid light and gas bills, etc. Yes, all this is fine, but—. It always ends in the endless rows of buts. Can these things compensate for individual freedom of movement? This bothers more Nisei than I who don't like the idea of being here as "suspected disloyal American citizens."

Typical Nisei humor: "Our aim is to keep the toilets clean; your aim will help!" I doubt if the Issei will catch on; they seem to be lacking in this light sense of humor. The men's latrines usually have enough Scott's tissue in it, but the women have a little difficulty because the young girls all walk off with it to use as Kleenex!

The first baby was born in camp last Monday. I wonder what it will be named. We got the news too late to headline it in the paper so had to box it in one corner. Taro certainly is having a headache with the paper. Everything has to be read and "ok-ed" by the front office. They are cautious to the nth degree. (By a consensus of opinion the paper was named the *Tanforan Totalizer,* a racing theme. I got a front page story on the postoffice, edited by Jimmy.) K. says that the administration is very sensitive about radicalism or unfavorable publicity; I think that he has pretty good information that a sample of the outgoing mail is censored, but I hardly think that this is true. There are bound to be mistakes made, but they shouldn't be afraid of that as long as they are sincere. W. H. and some others write directly to WRA with their complaints and they seem to think that they get immediate action. It would be much better if they were frank with the administration here and took their problems to them; I'm sure that they would give it consideration—if they had time. Notice was issued today that no notice could be placed on any bulletin board without an official "o.k." Reason??

May 15, 1942   Friday

The thing that I have feared is going to happen. The WCCA and WRA announced today that thousands of Japanese would be granted special furloughs to help bring in America's food crop under a rigorous "mutual protection plan." [27] Japanese will be enlisted in a day or so to go to Eastern Oregon to harvest the sugar beet crop, after the Army gives approval and a joint statement is signed by the government and the employer to maintain order and prevent violence. No Federal troops will be used for protection. The plan calls for prevailing wages and

27 Kikuchi here very perceptively recognized the conditions under which Japanese Americans were considered desirable in the western states: as controlled gang labor. It was because western states, through their governors, expressed their desire to have nothing to do with *voluntarily* evacuated Japanese moving from military areas on the coast that the Army adopted its mass forced relocation program.

local labor must not be competed against. All costs of transportation to and from the assembly center must be provided and it shall be on a voluntary basis. This is nothing more than a work corps. What about resettlement? I doubt whether much action will be placed upon it now. This means that although the Nisei will be able to make money, families will not be resettled on a permanent basis. And after the war, the Japanese may be permitted to come back into the restricted zones, but they will have to start over again. I just don't like the implications of the whole thing. What about the students? The Japanese must sign official forms to serve in the corps for the duration and agree to perform tasks assigned to them. There is no definite assurance on wages except the vague statement "going wages." Once signed up, it will be very difficult to do anything else but work as a farm laborer for the duration.

May 16, 1942   Saturday

Temperaments clashed tonight. I got Alice sore because I told her that she was too old to be chasing around with the young 18 and 19 year boys. They are more Emiko's age. I told Alice that she should get wider interests than dances and day to day activities. She rarely gives a thought to "why we are here, and from here where," and what we as Nisei could do. By this I did not mean that she should get moody or anything, but at least open her mind to other things. I didn't say it too diplomatically and she backfired with my lack of "cooperation" around the house, and all the laundry she does for me without appreciation, etc. But she just can't see the intangible things that I try to do and it's so hard to explain it. Like all "Japanese," industry is the spice of life [to Alice] and anyone that is not materially busy is a lazy person, etc. I'm more concerned with the wider issues involved in this evacuation and want to be of service along these lines rather than on an individual personal family basis. It's much more important than just being busy with the day to day activities, although these things have to be done by somebody. But Jack has been doing all the building, etc., he has a talent for sawing boards straight and I would only be in the way. But time spent on volunteer work on the paper and in the recreation department is just as important. I'm not the type of person who gushes thanks over every little consideration although I feel it within. Being silent or gruff about it is a sort of guilty conscience reaction, just like Jack used to complain for steak during the time the family was evacuated to S. F. from Vallejo. But that did not mean that he had no interest in the welfare of the family; he wasn't in a position to do much about it. But Alice never can see beyond the surface actions, and accordingly judges by that. It really is a suffering hero role although she would vehemently deny that. Even I get them—like tonight, perhaps, when I told her to leave my laundry alone and I would move up to the single Men's Grandstand if that would make her happier. Alice is really funny that way. She makes a fetish out of expecting thanks for everything done, even for Miyako. It's too extreme and it makes me react just the opposite even if I did feel thanks. Mariko has done a great deal for the family and she just takes it for granted that we appreciate it without making an issue out of it. I guess it's because Alice feels she is not being appreciated. She does work hard and it burns her up when anyone says that she neglects her duties. The whole point is: I get over-irritated because I don't think she is living up to her potentialities intellectually and so give vent to this feeling by criticizing her material actions.

.   .   .   .

Mariko would be a terrible misfit in this camp. She is too Americanized and independent. It's a good thing that she got out of domestic work for a while anyhow—perhaps permanently. In one day she decides that she doesn't want to go to camp; borrows $55 for a train ticket; packs and is off on the 8:30 train without knowing a soul or having a job on the other end. That takes guts. Fortunately she was taken in by Dr. Emmett, who is a very influential person.

May 17, 1942   Sunday

The importance of this Assembly Center is that some sort of organizational basis will be developed for self government, and it is not too important for us to perfect anything here, since our stay will be relatively limited in the camp. Some of the younger Nisei think that the Work Corps is a fine idea—if they get prevailing wages—and are anxious to do something as they are getting restless doing nothing here! Work opportunities will continue to be at the minimum here in this camp.

I might as well try to sign up in some way to go as a volunteer among the advance group. Social work is always needed but I wonder what the opportunities will be for me there? Perhaps I should stress the employment field more. Either would be acceptable to me because I could then have the chance to get at the center of things and watch it develop into something—or fall apart. Jack is definitely going to pull out and I don't know what Alice plans to do yet. I suppose that if I did leave first, some provisions can be made for the family to come to the same relocation area. The more I think about it, the more I become convinced that the family will not be a handicap but an asset. It is a stabilizing influence and will help to prevent individual degeneration. Whatever happens, our family can't lose.

.   .   .   .

Mom and Pop seem to enjoy people coming here to have fun because then they don't have to worry about what is going on. Pop even tried to jitterbug tonight and he was the hit of the evening. I was thinking tonight that the evacuation by itself has already in the past two weeks broken down some of the Japanese culture. Already some of the former causes for cultural conflict have become less intensified—with the Nisei holding the upper hand. We hold the advantage of numbers and the fact that we are citizens.

Many of the parents who would never let their daughters go to dances before do not object so strenuously now. They are slowly accepting the fact that their children cannot stay home night after night doing nothing without some sort of recreational release. Books are still a rarity. Consequently, the Thursday night talent show and the Saturday dances are jammed to capacity. There can no longer be conflict over the types of food served as everybody eats the same thing—with forks. We haven't had any Japanese food yet, thank God. The recreational program thus far has been pointed towards the Nisei and there is little for the older folks to do except go visiting.

The Nisei as a whole rejoice that they no longer have to attend Japanese language school.[28] This means that Japanese will be used less and less as the younger children grow up. A very few will be able to read and write it. And if these schools were a source of propaganda for Japan, they have now been eliminated. Thus, it is destined that Japanese will be used less and less among the Japanese here, and by the next generation it no longer will be a necessity to know it. Even among the Issei there will be a greater stress on speaking English so that they can continue to communicate with their children. It almost becomes a necessity. We are not getting any Japanese publications in camp so that even the Issei will be less exposed to the Japanese point of view. The only news they can get is from the newspaper (American), and the radio, which naturally will stress the American angle. Since short wave radios are not allowed, they can't receive any of the broadcasts from Japan.

.   .   .   .

The role of the Issei father in the family life has become less dominant because he no longer holds the economic purse strings. This will be true even after the war. Before, this has been the source of their power and it carried a lot of weight. The mother still has a role in the family life, because she still

28 The Japanese language schools, which young Nisei had more or less unwillingly attended after school at the insistence of their parents, were a prime subject for criticism by the enemies of the Japanese Americans. The complaint that emperor worship and Japanese nationalism were taught was nonsense. Most Nisei did attend at some time or other, but they learned only a little Japanese and a smattering of selected bits of old-country culture.

has to sew, do the laundry, and look after the welfare of her children. The only thing she doesn't have to do is cooking! But in general, the control and discipline of the parents have become loosened by the recent events. This may even be harmful if social disorganization develops at too fast a pace without suitable adjustments being made fast enough. But the family will more or less be held together because of the one dominant interest: what does the future hold in store for the Japanese in America? The Nisei consider themselves as Americans and if given a chance to demonstrate their loyalty, the trend will become stronger and stronger. The Issei will have no choice but to follow if they don't want to lose their families altogether.

May 18, 1942   Monday

Ann came over tonight. She witnessed an amusing scene on the way over. Some little boys were pointing at one of their pals and shouting, "He's not an American, he's not an American!" This picked up her interest so she went over and asked, "Why isn't he an American?" "Because," they replied, "he says he is a Jap!"

May 19, 1942   Tuesday

Taro and a few others are already thinking of going to Parker Dam [Relocation Center, Arizona] in the advance group to start the paper. They feel that this is only a transitional stage and there is too much red tape to do anything constructive. They do not have too high an opinion of the administration. Bob S. thinks that much more can be done in the relocation camp because it will be under the WRA administration and the top personnel will be more competent. Mr. [Richard] Neustadt, the head of the Western Division of the Federal Security Agency, was here today, and Mitch had a chance to speak a few moments with him. He has been asked to write about the condition here, and Mitch suggested that I do the same. Mr. Neustadt knows all about the JACL and the background of the leaders so that he is not fooled a bit by them. It will be up to the Nisei to make or break in the resettlement projects, and leadership is bound to arise out of this experience. One of the dangers of the whole thing is the prospect of isolation and segregation of the Japanese. If they are going to be cut off, there is a grave danger that they will be difficult. One sure thing is that resettlement away from the resettlement camps will break down a great deal of the past volunteer and forced segregation of the Japanese communities, since they will have to deal more and more with the greater American public. I still don't think there are enough capable leaders, and it is up to all of us to see that the job is not botched before they can be developed.

.   .   .   .

Somebody gave our block a Japanese name and put a sign up on the telephone post in Japanese with it so Tommy and I knocked it down. A couple of Kibei boys did not like it, so I told them that it was "Mr. Johnson's" orders. Tom tells them that nobody can read Jap around here anyway because we are all Americans. It's a good thing he is so Americanized. Even Miyako is this way—perhaps a bit too Americanized. And Emiko is full of self-confidence. She now has a full time job as one of the few private secretaries to the administrators who run the place. Bette works hard around the house, and she doesn't say much about Alice and Emiko working while she does the housework, but she probably feels a little left out. But she is young and she might as well have her time free.

May 20, 1942   *Wednesday*

I was lying in bed this morning—too lazy to arise—and listening to the radio telling about the dangers of B.O.; how wonderful it was to eat Wheaties; please smoke Chesterfields; and Ladies, wouldn't you like to have a cheap skunk fur coat? When the thought struck me: Here we are living at the end of an epoch in a great transitional stage and a great war in progress which will mean much to humanity, and yet most of us don't feel much differently. Even I feel this way at times. I can see and hear and read signs of the change all around me, but life seems to go along in its well-worn rut. Even the war is an event that one is deeply aware of yet so distant. The American public has not yet reacted fully to the significance of the whole catastrophe. We must be hard hit—directly—before this happens, and this will be soon. Maybe we are too human.

The world of tomorrow will be on a very different basis, but what? M. K. thinks that if Russia comes through, it will be the example for the world. Already its influence has covered a large section of the world among the less economically favored. Here in our community we will have some sort of social revolution, not necessarily violent, after the war. That is certain; but there is no way of predicting its form.

The term Communism holds an emotional block in our minds for most of us—except for the few (comparatively) converts. But aside from the "intellectual" ones, they, too, develop a one-sided approach and cannot see any other possibility. This verges on fanaticism, and I cannot accept such a dogmatic view.

Capitalism, in any event, is going to undergo radical change. Its basis is all wrong for our modern civilization. Instead of the greatest good for the greatest number, its doctrine is the greatest profit for the choice few. This is contradictory to our theory of Democracy. The two terms are neither identical or inseparable. Under democracy anything is possible and it does not necessarily advocate capitalism, which is a common fallacy.

May 21, 1942   Thursday

Ah! I must be degenerating. The fever of the poker game got me and I spent another eight useless hours to win $2.00. The boys ran out of money so they used stamps, and now I have a good stock on hand. I wanted to quit at 8 P.M., but was detained until 11:30. It must be in the blood. There's something fascinating about the game. You get to know the other fellows by the way they react. I think I'm the world's worst because I groan when I lose and I gloat when I win. J. T. is more calm—

he has a poker face—but his hands shake when he has a good hand. He lost heavily tonight so was feeling low. W. T. is the world's worst next to me. He hasn't won yet; I feel sorry for him, because we inveigle him into the game by telling him he will make up his past losses. He throws an emotional fit during the game which is worth the price of any show. L. Y. is a sociable sort of fellow; he plays more or less for the fun of it, because he is used to big games, but even he gets on edge when he is behind. R. M. is the same, only when he wins he tells us about the "big money" he made in Reno. S. K. is new. He was in Civil Service and he is a very likeable sort. He says he used to win a lot down at Monterey from the soldiers. He keeps fairly calm, but his bluffs won a number of games when we got scared off. The whole group is composed of college graduates so that it isn't exactly a game of loafers, etc. Our game was small stuff. Out in the Grandstands they were shooting for $125 table stakes. That money certainly looks tempting. All of us must have the gambling spirit within us. Only I get too curious and want to see the next card on hope—even when there is no chance. The only trouble is that I have won every time and it's hard to refuse them when they want me to play. As long as the stakes are cheap, I usually accommodate.

May 23, 1942   Saturday

Last night after I came home I heard a number of gun shots. Alice says (unofficial) that three boys were shot while trying to escape over the fence, one of whom is in the hospital. The administration won't take any moves to confirm or deny any of the stories so they continue to spread. This seems to be a short-sighted policy. There is no chance for the paper to bring such things out without being censored. They just won't allow us to take a definite policy on aims, except possibly Americanization. They are so afraid of radicalism. If it is being a radical to push American ideals and war effort among the Japanese without fear of stepping on toes, then we are radicals. The Japanese are really conservative and anything a little different is an indication of radicalism. They will have to get used to changes, because there will be many of them in the next few years. They will never go back to their old pre-war lives. If they cannot adjust themselves to changes, they are in for bitter disillusionment. I have hopes that they will, but the Americanization process will be slow. We can't expect anything else, I suppose, under the circumstances. Ever since Orientals have been in the U.S. they have had a difficult time. Denied citizenship and economic opportunities, it is not surprising that they have withdrawn and hung onto what they have brought with them. The cultural ties were stronger than the political ones. In a way it is a form of escapism.

.   .   .   .

Yesterday while we were playing our little card game, the police came in and arrested 88 men for violating the State Gambling law! This puts an end to our games for a while and is an "out" for me. I don't know where all of those single men get their money; they certainly have enough for those big card and dice games.

May 25, 1942   Monday

I'm probably a little uncertain of myself again. The past few weeks have given me a jolt no matter how much I try to rationalize to myself. Perhaps I have been too insistent on the Americanization angle, but that's the only solution I can see. A Nisei told me today that he wouldn't buy war bonds because he didn't know who would win the war. Such an attitude is inexcusable. The Japanese and Nisei are getting a raw deal but that does not mean that we should give up all of our ideals. Taro is going to write an editorial for Memorial Day and I pressed him on the point that it should be tied in with the present move to disfranchise the Nisei, but he didn't think that the administration would approve it. What about it—that's the trouble with the paper—we should have a policy and fight for it. K. says that it's no use to worry about citizenship, because it doesn't mean much any more. The so-called radical bunch seem to be the only ones greatly concerned with these matters.

.   .   .   .

The gals have a new fad of wearing jeans now and Alice, Emiko, and Bette were trying ours out. Alice has too broad hips to look streamlined in them and Emiko's stomach is too big. She looks funny. Bette has just the right figure for them, but Tom won't let her wear his new jeans. Mine are too big. Emiko started a fashion show by putting on our clothes, so Jack puts on Emi's shorts and brassiere and mimics their gestures before the mirror, while I did a Charlie Chan strut with her skirt. We laughed so much that I bet our neighbors think we are crazy.

Last night it rained all night and we are now back to slush alley. We sink up to our ankles every time we step out. They took up our boardwalk to gravel the street, but they never got around to it. So for the next few days we will have plenty of mud. Mrs. H. thinks that they pulled the boardwalk up on purpose, because they knew that it was going to rain and they wanted us to be inconvenienced!

.   .   .   .

The camp elections are coming off soon and there was a big row at a meeting to determine the qualifications of the candidates. The JACL are the largest single body in camp and they want to make sure that no radical element gets in. This, of course, is aimed at the Y.D.'s. They are still yelping, "We will cooperate," and they don't think that the Young Demos or any individuals should make an issue over civil rights at a time like this. This is an extremely shortsighted approach if ever there was one. My Negro and Jewish and Chinese friends are greatly concerned as they recognize what a dangerous precedent that they will be setting and they are already working or fighting it. The JACL will probably proclaim "we are loyal" and wave the flag and let it go at that.

May 26, 1942   Tuesday

The plane that crashed last night was an Army P-38. Y. says that there was rumor going around that the Issei clapped their hands in the Grandstand and said in Japanese, "It isn't anything just as long as it is an American plane." Another rumor (Tom) was that it was a Japanese Zero plane which caused it. The Zero plane was so small that it could go between the power lines, but the two P-38's that were pursuing it crashed. The newspapers did not publish the truth, because they did not want to admit that Japanese planes have come over. A third rumor (Emiko) was that it was Clark Gable who crashed, because he wanted to die the same way as his wife died.

.   .   .   .

Mom is also a little touchy and irritable these days. I guess we "ride" her a little too much on how badly she is bringing up the kids. Tom and Miyako yell at each other at the table and they are developing a selfish attitude which Jack and I are trying to break them of. Miyako is spoiled by Mom because she won't eat her fresh vegetable and Mom says it is all right even after we insist that she should. Tonight Miyako ate just rice and Mom got angry when we told her that she should not give in every time. Miyako has a quick temper and she goes into a sullen tantrum when her wishes are crossed. It's hard to break her of it, because Alice always interferes and says that we shouldn't do anything about it, because she will grow out of the habit. The number of arguments and bickerings has been increasing lately, but we all forget about them right away. Emiko gets mad at Bette, because she thinks that Bette tries to make Mom believe that Emiko is uncooperative in the housework, and this burns her up. Today Emiko stayed home from work and did it all by herself while Bette went to help mimeograph. Last Sunday none of the girls lifted a finger to clean the house. Jack and I did it this morning and Emiko this afternoon. Alice is beginning to get the idea that she is exempt except to get Pop's food and wash the dishes at night. Mom is now doing the laundry by herself. All of these petty arguments, I suppose, are an indication of the present inner tensions which we are all undergoing. I'm wondering about the future. Alice and Jack have their marriage[-plan] problems; Mom and Pop have not adjusted themselves to this situation; Emiko and Bette have problems about bringing boys in after certain hours and going to dances and coming home one at a time, etc. Mom and Pop have been very reasonable with them, but they see that Jack and I do as we please without any parental restrictions, and they also wish to be independent. But anything affecting one of us outside the family group brings instant unity.

May 27, 1942   Wednesday

Are we like the optimist who, while falling ten stories from a building, said at each story: "I'm all right so far"? If so, the thump will indeed be hard. L. thinks that this is the case and, therefore, no use in trying to stave off the inevitable. He was a former State Civil Service worker and has taken it pretty hard.

Jack told me this morning that he wrote the WCCA about Arnold and his attitudes and signed it with "M. D. S. Jordan," [29] and had D. take it out. By coincidence, a new police chief came in this afternoon to replace Arnold who is being sent to take over at Merced. Poor D. H. and Co.! W. T. will come back in as an internal chief and the police force will be completely reorganized. He even said something about getting horses for his force. The selection of the new internal force will be very carefully done.

Complaints are coming in that stuff is missing when delivered. They bring the packages around by truck now and since they have been opened for inspection, it is easy for the boys to lift a row of candy, etc., from the opened package. No letters

[29] The reference is to David Starr Jordan, president of Stanford University and a longtime worker for fair play for Japanese Americans.

have been opened yet. Tom says that they crossed "mail" off
from the petition which was circulating around.

.   .   .   .

Busy all morning sending out exchange copies of our camp
paper to the 15 other Assembly and Relocation Centers. A copy
goes to the Library of Congress, U. C. Library, and California
State Library. Mr. Greene provides a secretary to do the actual
work of sending it out. We are trying to get the third issue out
by Saturday morning so that we can have a special feature for
Memorial Day. Taro is really not aggressive enough. He should
push the paper a little more. Although there is a tight censorship and a lot of red tape, there are ways in which we can at
least have some sort of policy. I haven't talked to Greene about
social work for a couple of days, but I think I am continually
getting in his and Mr. Davis' hair with all my requests for the
paper. Wrote a little piece about the coming special elections
in S. F. and told the Nisei how to obtain the absentee ballot.
Then I asked Davis if they would provide an officer with a seal
for the ballot marking. Davis was not very cooperative, and he
said that they would do this if there were not too many Nisei
who came with the ballots to his office. It's very likely that a lot
of the Nisei will not even bother to vote. Even if they don't
think it means much they should keep in the habit. This is one
time that they should be on guard and fight for their civil
rights or else the disfranchisement movement will get stronger.
Mr. Davis scoffed at this and said that only a short notice in the
paper was necessary without any elaboration on the wider issues. Warren calls me "The Power behind the throne," because
I boss Taro around on what should be done for the good of the
paper. One of these days he might get sore, but he seems to
depend on me a lot right now and willingly follows any suggestions that we may make.

Dr. Thomas visited today, but I did not talk with her very
much as she was busy with Tom [Shibutani]. Am still very
much up in the air about the whole project.

Marge Spoelstra wrote from Pittsburgh and appears very much concerned about how I was getting along in the "concentration camp." She said that she heard Louis Adamic talk before 18,000 people and had a chance to talk to him. I don't know why I haven't written to Adamic. It must be the state of my mind. I just can't say anything definite. Marge says that he is working for a scholarship for me. This puts me in a funny position. I want to work in this evacuation and resettlement project because I think it is an important social experiment in which I may be able to help. But if a chance to go to school again comes up, I don't know what I would do. It would be an escape from reality and if I ever hope to get started, it has to be in this process. Although I am on several Federal Civil Service lists there is not much hope of getting a call. Making money seems to be a little futile. It won't give me any happiness. I decided a long time ago that my work, whatever it is, must have social meaning and I would never be happy in a dull routine position. Would going to school another year help me out much or should I go? What a difficult decision to make. I think I will do nothing now. In another couple of months I may be dying to get out of here. I doubt, however, that going to school another year will make me a better social worker.

.   .   .   .

Today I wasn't feeling so hot, as I have a cold, so I decided to take a rest on Wang's bed. Jimmy was typing away on a story and I fell sound asleep. Wang came in, growled a bit, lighted a cigarette and flicked the match in the wastebox, and walked out. I was only dimly aware of his presence.

All of a sudden I had a funny dreamlike sensation. I felt like I was in a terrific fever and my right leg kept getting hotter and hotter. I awoke with a start and was shocked like hell to see big flames shooting up to the ceiling. Like a rabbit I jumped out of bed and started yelling "fire" at the same time as Jimmy. I ran out in a daze to get the fire extinguisher but failed to see it when it was right in front of my eyes. Bob in the meanwhile had gone out into the Grandstand and told the men to get out as quickly as possible. I rushed back into the room and grabbed a blanket with Jimmy, and we smothered the flames. Jimmy burned his hand. I was still half asleep and feeling lousy so we just left the burnt mess, and I went back to sleep. Wang sure got a surprise when he saw the burnt stuff. He said that "this settles it. I'm going to quit smoking for sure now and I'll never throw matches in a basket again." It was a good thing that we were able to extinguish the flames as the whole Grandstands would have gone if it got a good start.

I started a rumor that an Issei tried to set the place afire in revenge for his incarceration in camp, and it probably will go around like wildfire. It's really surprising to see how the camp residents are willing to believe any kind of a rumor without verification. It must be due to the unsettled state of mind of the residents who are ready to believe almost everything.

.　.　.　.

Governor Olson is really in the political hot water.[30] The press seems out to get him. But Olson has made some dumb statements. The more I think about yesterday's remarks by the Governor, the less respect I have for the man. His demands that the military remove all Japanese are contradictory, because at the same time he urges that the Japanese be released for farm work under armed guard. This only whips up public fears and prejudices and is an about-face for Olson. The farmers, therefore, balk and are confirmed in their belief that these Japanese are really dangerous. If Olson is playing politics, he must be less intelligent than what I have credited him for. After all, we are not war prisoners or being punished for Pearl Harbor. The Army states that the move was made to protect vital defense zones and the Japanese also from possible violence. If the farmers continue to take the attitude that they would rather take a crop loss than have "Japs," the loss will be theirs, which is direct sabotaging of the war effort. And this sort of thing won't

30 The failure of liberal Democratic Governor Culbert Olson to stand up for Japanese Americans, and his occasional encouragement to the more vocal anti-Japanese, indicated once again to the politically conscious Nisei that they were essentially without important allies among western politicians.

encourage the Nisei to go out in the Voluntary Work Corps to help in the food for freedom program.

May 28, 1942   Thursday

Mitch was over tonight to discuss the possible points which he could include in a letter to the American Lawyers' Guild. They plan to make a study on the evacuation from a legal point of view. We were talking about the wage and employment setup, and I cited Alice and the T. sisters as examples. Mom got all excited, because she thought I was talking "bad" about Alice. I had to explain just what we were doing, but she still thinks that it is all right if families get extra favors and preference just so we are included. She certainly is funny about some things. She doesn't want to use the new sheets or bedspreads or towels and blankets but just keeps them packed away. Pop thinks that Alice is going around with too young boys and leading Emiko and Bette astray. He points out the girls on both sides of us who stay home, while the Kikuchi girls have to run off to every little dance and social. He said that he wouldn't mind so much if they went with nice boys. He fears that the younger ones will want to play so much that they will not want to study any more. But he never says much, because he gets in a big argument with Mom. And nowadays Mom resents Jack and I saying things to the girls. She feels it is her duty only she never does anything about it. Perhaps she feels as if she were being pushed aside and resents it which is natural enough. The children have definitely grown away from them. I wonder how it is like in some of the other families where the parents still hold the balance of power.

.   .   .   .

11:30—I was just writing a letter when Emiko came out and said that she was going to the lavatory as she had a stomach-ache. All of a sudden I hear a yell, and Emiko comes running in, white as anything. A man grabbed her by the arm as she was coming back, but Emi broke away. I put on my bathrobe, got the hammer and a flashlight, and went out to look around.

Some old lady going to the toilet probably thought I was a
fiend also. I looked around in the empty stables, but no sign.
One of the firemen came by, so I reported the matter. He said
that this was the second time that a case like this has been reported in this area. The girls are all talking about it now and
discussing what they would do if they were attacked. I never
saw Emiko so frightened in all my life. You can't tell what some
of these hard-up bastards will do around here. It's a good thing
I did not catch up with the guy or else he would have a dent in
his head. The sex problem in these camps is going to be quite
serious unless the young Nisei start to get married in numbers.
Every day I hear rumors about illicit relations but a lot of it has
no basis in fact.

May 29, 1942   Friday

A. says he talked to Dr. Takahashi of the [relocatee] Council
office today. Evidently they are still worried about the radicals
on the paper. He told A. that the YD's and the Writer's Group
were getting in as a clique. As a matter of fact, A. and Y. are
the only YD members and Taro from the Writer's Group. A.
explained how our staff has been open to all. Even Mr. Greene
stated that he approved the present staff and thought that we
should be put on the payroll, because we had worked right
along on a volunteer basis. Our full time staff, including the
part time workers, represents almost every group in camp. The
"conservatives" are a little cool to us, because they wanted Yas
Abiko of JACL as Editor. Kido [31] even wrote the administration
recommending this. With all the censorship now, it doesn't
make any difference who is editor as long as the community is
served. And if the JACL thinks strong Americanism is radicalism, they are the ones making a big mistake. But we have to
make every effort to work with them since their barking is fairly
large. They object principally to Bob Tsuda as the City Editor,
because they think he is a Communist. And I don't think some
of them are so favorably inclined towards me, because I once told

[31] Saburo Kido was an important national officer of the JACL.

them that the reason I would not join the JACL was because it was Fascistically controlled and the members were not given a democratic hearing. I still think this was one of the reasons why the JACL has made such a poor record in the public eye. But they can't be blamed for it. We just lack intelligent leadership and they just did not measure up.

I worked all day helping them mimeograph the 2800 copies off. And then we had to staple them and count them off for distribution. After this was all over we had to help distribute them to the house managers so that the camp could have them tomorrow at the latest. My feet just about kill me after all this. The cold has not gone away yet so I felt pretty weak for a while this afternoon.

Miss Todd of the U.S.E.S. [United States Employment Service] wrote and said that she had sent the copy of my survey to the Farm Security Agency for possible use in the Japanese Relocation plans. She has written a letter to recommend my further schooling at some University. Sometimes I wonder whether such things are actually helpful. They feel sorry for me and want to get me out of this mess and the only way they can do it is by getting me into a college again. But I just can't see this. If I can be of meaningful use in the relocation, I would much rather work. And it won't be so bad—not as they picture it anyway. My adjustment to the Japanese group is by no means complete, but I am coming along. At least I am not bored yet.

May 31, 1942   Sunday

I just can't seem to get my mind on this whole problem of the Japanese evacuation. I've lived and slept with this question for a whole month now. I can [not?] say that I am discouraged at the developments, but I am not too happy at my progress. I had hoped to be doing more. Working on a heavily censored camp paper is a long way from social work. And now I am even having a little doubt about the social work phase. Will I be any better off than I was in the Employment office? Not knowing Japanese puts one in a peculiar situation. Sometimes when I hear

Japanese being spoken I have an urge to shut the whole thing out as if I were in a nightmare experience. I don't hate the Japanese here, but their conventional ways get me sometimes. Perhaps they would be better off if they were not so law-abiding. They should really let themselves go occasionally, but you can't tell what is going on behind the Oriental mask.

June 1, 1942   Monday

Taro took the twelve names to Greene again, and he blew up when he found so many listed as editors. He said that only six would be on the payroll, one as a reporter. So A. will keep his job in the messhall, and one of the other fellows will do the same. B. H. has already quit his job, so that it was too late to put Warren in his place. We will pool our total salaries ($80) and divide it equally among the twelve of us. We don't know yet who the six on the payroll will be. Taro gave Greene my name along with the others and when he came to it he said, "Charles Kikuchi? Oh, the Social Worker! He's no newspaper man, is he?" Taro replied, "He's the best reporter that we have and he takes care of all the contact work." Taro said that Greene was reluctant even after that. . . . The fellows can't understand why Greene has singled me out, and they think that somebody in camp must have told him that I was a radical. They are more burnt up about the whole thing than I am. But I don't care too much any more; I feel that this is only a tempo-rary place, and I will get my chance later. That is why I have not asked for any letters of recommendation. Greene's personal dislike of the U. C. social workers would not make prospects too bright anyway, and he would be itching to get us on the first slip-up, seeing as how he feels. It's funny, because I seem to get along with him now. This morning I went in and insisted that we have some desks for the newspaper office, and he phoned the "OK" through right away. And he was sorry that the WCCA offices in S. F. would not allow us to send out the exchange pa-pers in the government envelopes. We told him that we would do it on our own, and he said that we should be careful "not

[to] get ourselves in a jam," whatever he meant by that. Taro and the rest of us are pretty disgusted with the whole setup. We were thinking of starting some sort of magazine, but we would have to work against too many handicaps so have given it up for the present. There are a number of Nisei in camp that have the ability to write—Jimmy, Toshi Mori, Warren, Lillian, Taro, Bob Tsuda, Toyemoto, Kawakami, K. Nishida, Alex Yorichi, etc.—and it would be interesting to accumulate their writings and thinkings for a magazine.

I have been dilly-dallying around for a month now, and I just can't feel satisfied with what I have done. I know I could have done a lot more under a better administration setup. I could think that the failure was personal, but this is the general opinion of most of the people interested in the camp welfare. The paper is serving a useful function, but that is not enough. I'm sure that I could be of far greater value. Sort of looking forward to the Relocation now. Haven't been here long enough to settle down, but I must keep busy at something in order not to get discontented. One interesting development is that I am getting to meet a lot of Caucasian American people yet, especially through Ann and Mitch. The visitors keep pouring in to see their Nisei friends.

.   .   .   .

The new police chief is much better. Interviewed him today for the paper. Jerry Easterbrooks is a great big 210 pounder with a very pleasing personality, and I got along well with him. He graduated from U. C. in 1935 and has worked for the past seven years in the Berkeley Police Force. He also played Varsity Football for the Bears for three years. He is only about 30, and looks quite young. He told me that he knows the Japanese well, and he has always found them to be honest, law-abiding, and peace-loving. There are 13 Caucasian patrolmen under him, all picked on the basis of their experience among the Japanese. Easterbrooks is directly responsible to the Army and not the Administration here. I discussed some of the problems which have arisen in camp, and he says that there have been 2 lar-

cenies, 1 burglary, 2 gambling raids, and one girl molested
(Emiko). Easterbrooks recognizes that sex will be the greatest
problem as the "Japanese are normal," and there are a lot of
young fellows around. He is not too rigid as far as poker playing
is concerned if it is a small game. What he wants to do is to
catch the professional gamblers in camp, because they will take
the innocent for all that they have. He is wise enough to see
that his job will not be an easy one and is working hard to get
the cooperation of the camp. Apparently he understands the
setup as he says that most Nisei are just like him, and he won't
allow his men to spy or put on a superior attitude while in
camp as this will be of great harm to his department.

The fire chief is of similar caliber. He has been on the San
Bruno fire force for the past 20 years and knows the Japanese in
this country well. He thinks highly of the Nisei, whom he is
teaching for the protection of the camp. He says that the fire
hazard is very great here because of the lack of equipment and
the prevalence of a strong wind that blows through here. There
are 11 regular full time Nisei in his department, and he is now
training 36 volunteers. Later on he plans to have more volunteers from each barrack. He thinks that the Japanese have a lot
of guts for taking this great mistake in such a smiling way. He
has dealt with many Japanese businesses and always found them
to treat him fairly. "But these things happen and you've got to
show them that you all have the real American spirit in you. I
know that you have from my personal experiences." It's too bad
we don't have more men like this in this camp.

June 2, 1942   Tuesday

Our newspaper office is getting to be a very popular place. A lot
of people were up today. It will be interesting to note what
they talk about. The big fuss today was over the coming elections. V. A. was worried about the candidates. He says the committee has made an age qualification of 25, plus citizenship.
H. T. thinks they should make an oath of anti-fascism as a part
of the qualifications. All residents over 21 will be able to vote.

This means that the Issei will be the biggest bloc, and they could shove in a Kibei. The average age of the Nisei is only 22 which means that a number will be ineligible to vote. The ratio of Nisei to Issei is about 65 to 35. But there will be many cliques and groups among the Nisei trying to get their man in. Bob Iki wants us to back him. The committee, composed of JACL leaders, hold secret meetings, and they haven't even announced the elections yet. They put a lower age limit on the candidates to keep some of the younger Nisei opposed to them out of the running. Henry Takahashi seems to be the most objectionable of the lot. He dominates the present council and bootlicks like hell for personal advancement. These God damn JACL's; that K. A. should be given a kick in the rump and thrown out. They are not even aware of the problem as a whole and yet they profess to be the leaders of the Nisei. Certain individuals like R. Carl Hirota are all right, but Takahashi, Tuni, and others are ignorant when it comes to the broader issues. They are the ones that have blocked the more liberal element at every possible turn. They were leaders in the old communities, and they want to keep controlling the power. The liberals are a threat to their assumed security, and so they use every trick possible to give the administration an unfavorable impression of the radicals. Like the newspaper deal. It's probably about the most censored thing in camp. This morning Greene went through the dummy with a fine tooth comb and made us eliminate Kotex from the drug store items carried, because it "was not in good taste." Then he makes the classic statement that there is absolutely no censorship around here! The poor guy must be getting sleepless nights now. He is waking up to the fact that there's a lot of discontent among the Japanese here. Wait until he reads Ann's piece in the A.C.L. paper. She really gave Besig the lowdown about the second-rate administrator and the problems faced here.[32] Greene will be able to trace her down, because he saw us with Besig the other day.

[32] The "ACL" (American Civil Liberties Union) and its northern California chairman, Ernst Besig, were leading bugaboos in California politics in the thirties and forties, and offered modest support for the Japanese Americans during relocation.

.   .   .   .

11:45—A tiny little field mouse just ran under Jack's bed, but I'm too lazy to get up and chase it. It's too cold to get up. Outside the wind is just howling. I can even see the glint in Mr. Mickey Mouse's eyes now behind Jack's tennis shoes. Why should I get up and make its little life miserable by evacuating it to the cold outside? We shall have to do something about the mice problem. There are plenty of mice around these stables. Oh oh! It just ran into the back room; Emiko would probably scream her head off if it got on her bed and tweaked her nose. It's no use going in there now and waking them up with a rumpus. They probably wouldn't be able to sleep tonight if I told them.

Felt pretty good today. Mari was here to see her folks and I got to talk to her. Tried to act nonchalant, but—. She was so busy trying to see all of her friends that I didn't get a chance to talk to her much. Anyway, I'm just a very impersonal thing to her. Now I have to start all over again trying not to let her bother my mind too much. She is now in the Berkeley office, and it is likely that she will continue right through as they will need her in the relocation work. She looks tired. Mari says that Stockton and Walerga are much worse off than we are. Ted, her brother, was full of gripes as usual, but that's his normal way. He doesn't mean any harm. Emiko, Bette, Alice, and Jack finally got their curiosity satisfied by meeting her. They seemed to like her. If they didn't I would have heard about it by now. When I think of her, I am conscious of all my shortcomings. Come now, Charles, don't be a suffering hero! Anyway—.

.   .   .   .

Kats told me that one of the Caucasians going around here was spying on the residents. The man came up to him and asked what he was reading (A.C.L. paper), but Kats refused to let him see. Kats saw him go snooping around the crowd at the sugar beet meeting, asking a lot of questions about the residents and he even asked Kats who the "radicals" were. This sort of witch baiting, whoever is responsible, is a dirty thing to do. It makes me mad as hell to think that they want to clamp down on the liberal group on the word of a few bootlicking Nisei around here just because they are so afraid that if any news of problems gets out, it will mean their scalps.

T. Y.'s aunt is going to Japan. She asked for permission to rejoin her husband in Manchuria. The U.S. will pay her voyage back and send her along with the exchange prisoners of war. What's to prevent the U.S. from doing this on a large scale after the war? As far as the aunt is concerned, it's good riddance. She was too old to ever become assimilated, and she will soon find out just how good America was to her when she comes face to face with the living conditions in Japan.

Saw an interesting Negro woman here today visiting some Japanese. She was formerly a Madame and ran a house of prostitution in S. F. on Buchanan Street. I used to see her in the dark doorways giving a *pssst* to the men walking by, but I was never tempted by her 75 cent offer! She didn't do much business among the Japanese, because it was too close to home. Her clients were mostly Filipinos, Negroes, and Caucasians. Jack says that she has a big car and owns an apartment in the Japanese section. In her spare time she solicits. Don't know whether her visit here was social or "on business." The Grandstand is a very public place, and she couldn't get on the grounds, so it must have been a social call. The Nisei boys never went to the "houses" in Japtown, but preferred to take their chances in the numerous places in Chinatown. I used to see many a pure Sunday school lad down there, so we must all be human.

Rumor going around that 700 babies would be born next month in this camp, so we had to run an item stating that the number of expectant pregnant mothers was only 70. Lillian still thinks 700 is not too high!

The mothers don't leave their laundry hanging out at night anymore, since one of the ladies had her whole laundry stolen the other evening. Mom, also, almost lost Pop's bed pan in the women's latrine. She had to yell at a lady as she was walking out with it. The woman got very embarrassed and said that she thought that it was hers.

Was surprised to hear that I'm supposed to be a speaker for

the Sunday Fellowship for High School and College Students
on the topic: "What Should the Nisei do to Help Democracy."
It's such a short notice and I haven't even been officially noti-
fied by the committee yet, so that it may be off.

.   .   .   .

As far as we are concerned, a lot of discretion has been allowed us in making our [research] reports [for the JERS]. They
can be handed in at any time. Strangely, the study doesn't excite
me too much. It should because it is a valuable and important
study. I'll have to go into it full-heartedly in order to be of any
value, yet I do have conflicts. I'm trained for Social Work and
I want to give it a trial. The idea of getting the facts as they
happen and don't worry about the future events is a sort of
negative approach to the whole problem of the Japanese. I want
to help more in helping their future adjustments and not record it after it is passed. This, of course, does have great documentary value, but I have long since given up looking for prestige and the hell with having my name connected with a
"Study." That is not the important point and if I go into this
thing, I'll have to make that clear. But then, later on, I may
continue with graduate school and I will be thankful for this
great opportunity. I should be thankful instead of having
doubts. It's not a matter of money. Jack wants me to go to the
sugar beets so I can make more money in a short time, but
there's no future in beet picking for me. It will be pretty hard
to keep this project quiet and from my family. Tom [Shibu-
tani], of course, is making too much of a fuss about absolute
secrecy as if we were doing a very dangerous work. Most people
don't pay much attention. Besides a lot of Niseis already know
that a study is being made and have already connected Tom up
with it. From now on, my diary will probably be more biased,
because I may let [Dorothy] Thomas have it, but I'll try to keep
it as I have—expressing my opinions freely.
  The only thing I won't do is discuss my intimate relationships with girls. But, this I haven't been doing anyway. I have
a victorian code about gentlemen should not talk and tell on
girls who give him favors. Anyway I always have doubts about

any person who tells of sex adventures freely and names names. That is poor taste, and not nice. Wang has a very moralistic attitude about sex and he thinks that I have no principles because I say that sex has nothing to do with ideals and the nobler things of life. He thought it was okay when I went over to Chinatown with Angelo and ran around with girls there "because they have no morals anyway," but it horrified him to think that I might be leading the young campus Nisei girls down some path to hell, especially "S." Now here, he is aware that when I go out on some newspaper "assignments" in the morning, or mid afternoon, it is to follow up with some interesting girl I met at a dance or some place in camp. Suffice to say, I have not been a monk in this camp as opportunities have been many. But I have not met anyone whom I feel serious about. I know the sex problem is here to stay in camp because one of the salesmen who comes in does a flourishing business in selling condoms, but nobody talks about this aspect of life here. It is swept under the racetrack. Because of lack of privacy, it goes on mostly during the day and not at night. Since I feel it is a private matter for me, I also feel that my time in "reporting" won't be on this subject except in a general way, as I am not about to inform on others who are having this kind of diversion in camp. It would ruin the girl's reputation especially, and I am not about to do that.[33]

June 3, 1942   Wednesday

Mrs. A. L. Wills, staff member of *Asia* magazine, and Mrs. Ellis were here all day to gather material for a forthcoming series of articles on the Japanese evacuation. Ann, Mitch, and I talked to them all day to present the liberal Nisei viewpoint. She wants to get the other side of the picture across to the public.

.   .   .   .

[33] The last paragraph was not included in the Kikuchi diary manuscript as delivered by him to the JERS during the war. It was later given to Dorothy Thomas by Kikuchi, who kept the paragraph as an "addendum" to the June 2 entry. It is the only portion of the diary so concealed by its author. (But see A Note on Editing *The Kikuchi Diary*.)

Jimmy Hirano also spoke his piece. He got very emotional about the whole affair and he said that they threatened to send him to a concentration camp where they put all the agitators. For a Nisei he is consistent in waving the flag of Americanism. Yas says he used to be very pro-Fascist and thought a Japanese victory was the only hope, so he questions Jimmy's motives a bit. I. H. is bumping his head against a stone wall. As long as we are here the Army is in charge and one can't buck them. He is only losing his usefulness among the group by being too untactful and not diplomatic enough. He says: "As long as I have breath left in my body I will fight for the welfare of my people in the barracks. I don't care if they take me away and split my family up even though my wife is having a baby next month. We've got to fight them. Look at the hospital setup. It tears my heart to see them put the babies in those wooden boxes on two-by-fours. And look at the dentist chairs. It's a camp seat supported by braces. We have the finest staff of doctors of any camp and yet they are stopped because they won't get the necessary supplies in." Jimmy got quite excited and every other sentence he'd put in a "see what I mean?" He said the police threatened the house managers with a curfew and zoning if they did not cooperate. He thought this made a farce out of the self-government clause. Mrs. Ellis had to quiet him down considerably and suggested that he save some of his energy and usefulness instead of getting all balled up over these problems which will be straightened out eventually.

.   .   .   .

During lunch it was announced that the rest of California would be evacuated and a curfew had been set for this area. A murmur of surprise went through the crowd and I could hear comments that they were out to get us, it was inevitable and planned all along; you couldn't trust the government to keep its promises; it was Governor Olson's fault; it was the Army; and so what? The prevailing attitude among the Nisei I spoke to during the day was that the pressure groups and the politicians were the cause of the whole thing and many of them felt a little resentment at this treatment. B. I. hopes that they take those bastard disloyal Italians and Germans next, and the hell with the Japs who are too old to be of any harm. One of the things that gets me down is that they invariably make their announcements in Japanese first and then in English if somebody like me is brave enough to yell "translation please" and feel out of place in making the request. Most of the Nisei can't understand them anyway; they never know what has been said when I asked them. Yet they don't protest at the use of Japanese too much. They feel that they can read about it in the paper or see a bulletin board whereas many of the Issei would not be able to do this. The habit of using a great deal of Japanese exclusively is a danger because it invites or encourages a withdrawal into a shell.

June 4, 1942   Thursday

This morning the third grade held their classes in the Buddhist Church up at the end of our barracks. Could hear them singing "God Bless America" at the top of their voices. It was interesting to hear one Issei say something about his little daughter was in there because she was an American while he was a Japanese. He said it with a smile and no trace of any bitter feelings. Most of the families around here are that way. They feel so sorry for the Nisei because we are in a tough situation. These married men keep more or less quiet on their feelings about the war in public whereas the single men are more outspoken. The married men are more stable because they have benefited more from America.

.   .   .   .

Talked to the U.S.E.S. man late this afternoon. He can't understand why he got only 13 volunteer workers to sign up for the sugar beet fields in Idaho. Told him that several factors could enter into the matter. Chiefly fear and uncertainty. The young fellows don't want to go off a thousand miles from their families at a time like this. Then the recent blasts in the newspapers against the "Japs" by public officials and the farmers are not conducive to their desire to get out among them. Some feared that scab wages would be paid. Those with farm experience did not wish to go because the season was getting late and the sugar beets were getting too high. Then not enough publicity was given. A printed pamphlet to be distributed with everything down in black and white would have helped. Finally, we do not have many agricultural workers in this camp. This small signup would show this fact. One fellow I talked to who signed up was a former salesman and buyer with a Japanese company. He feels that he can make a little money and he is getting tired of loafing around and wants to give it a trial. This will get him his "freedom." "But they will probably put a curfew on us and guard us, but I don't care as long as I am doing something instead of wearing out my pants here. What can I lose? I'm a prisoner here. Can't even get a beer."

Lawson is out as the Camp Manager and Davis will be in charge. He is a poor choice because everyone remarks that he is curt and sort of sneers down on the Japanese.

Sort of feel sorry for the soldiers. They are not supposed to talk to us, but they do. Most are nice kids. They can't get leaves and so have nothing to do. They work 5 hours and then have the rest of the time to themselves. One of the soldiers suggested that we get a volleyball team up and we can play each other over the fence, but the administration naturally would not think of such a thing. The corporal at the gate was made a sergeant and we congratulated him on his promotion. He says he is going overseas as soon as his foot gets a little better. Another one of the boys is from Boston and he thinks we are very American. He shoved a bologna sandwich into Alice's hands before she was even introduced. They must hear that we are starving over here. What a funny world. They feel sorry for us in our present situation and we feel sorry for them because things are so monotonous for them right now. But they have a cause to fight for and they are doing their part, but we are sort of left out on the war effort. On the draft questionnaires they want us to put "inmate of a public institution" in one space and "confined in an assembly center" in the other.

June 5, 1942   Friday

During the day several of the candidates came in to "create good will." I suppose they wanted a plug in the paper. In order to avoid this, Taro will give each of them limited publicity with a chance to insert a one line platform. Already many inner circle intrigues are going on. The JACL meets secretly and they will push some of their "big" leaders. If possible they will try to get all JACL men into the Council. The YD group is also active. They have met several times to get their candidate in and are systematically planning a campaign. They really are going about this politics in a serious manner. The JACL even are starting to "red bait" by spreading stories about the radicals who should be kept out because they will get all the Japanese into trouble. The Christian group is another powerful faction. If they get well organized they can swing the election their way. The leaders of this group are a little doubtful about the JACL plan of voluntary cooperation. F. H. was saying tonight that they should have fought evacuation more because it only serves to weaken our democratic institutions. He feels that military necessity should not have been so sweeping in character unless all citizens [born of enemy-alien parents, like the Nisei] were included. Otherwise, citizenship does not mean anything. He was a little resentful that the JACL did not test the constitutionality of the evacuation orders. Not questioning it is only an invitation for dictatorship which can disregard our other guaranteed rights once an inroad is made and left unchallenged.

T. K. then gave the other side although he is not a JACL member actively. He felt that we should see it more broadmindedly as a temporary sacrifice of our civil rights for the best welfare of national defense. As long as we are at war, he felt that the military forces should not be questioned. That is the test of loyalty. But we should be alert to the danger of the reactionary forces who may use the Army as a front to achieve their ends. In this case we should not cooperate but stand up for our rights before it is too late. On this point he disagrees with the JACL who still feel that pressure groups are not the primary reason although they may say they are. T. K. says that the Army still thinks the risk is too great from the military standpoint and pressure groups are only incidental.

.   .   .   .

Overheard Bette, Emiko, and Alice discuss breast development among Nisei girls. Bette is envious that Emiko is so fully developed while she has such a flat chest. Bette thinks she runs around too much and eats too much rice and starches. Alice says that Nisei girls do not have the right kind of glands. Emiko says all the girls are jealous of her breasts, but she thinks hers are too rounded and wished that she were pointed like Lana Turner's. Bette says that Alice never wears any bra and when she finally did buy one, it was a 15-cent kind. Then they started to talk about the dance tomorrow night. Bette already got a date, but Emiko does not want to go because she doesn't like program dances. Alice says she likes to go with boys like K. because he always sees that his partner gets around. From this subject they went to clothes, whether Alice should or should not wear jeans. In the meantime, Emiko sat on the bed and ate crackers. She is not taking her diet very seriously. Lately she has been complaining of pains in her side. Told her to go see the doctor because she may have appendicitis and she has to be careful because of the lack of facilities in this camp. Bette is worried about her pot belly but she looks like she has a cute figure, very boyish.

.   .   .   .

Wang (20 years old) pulled out today for Rupert, Idaho, to top sugar beets. They were only able to sign up 13 workers in this camp. Warren was only given two hours' notice and he had to pack his things and say his goodbyes in this time. The bus left at 6:30. We went up there and presented him with some candy and cookies as a going away gift. While the girls and Jack talked to him I interviewed all of the 13 in order to get a newspaper story. They had to open all of their bags for inspection so were busy and I had to go right into the bus with them to get the information. An FBI man is going with them and he wouldn't let me in until I told him that Mr. Greene had given me the "ok." Was I embarrassed when I turned around and found him right behind me! He didn't hear me, I guess, because he said nothing except "Reporter on the job?"

The farm labor shortage must really be serious since they are willing to pay the fare for those 13 up to Idaho which is over 1000 miles away. Warren had no contacts here and he definitely has broken away from his parents who wanted to send him to an eastern school. He said that he signed up because he would do "anything to get out of this camp." He also wants to make some money to go to school on. "We are going to have a good experience. V for Victory," he laughed. He was pretty excited about leaving and looked very forlorn when the bus pulled out. Warren has a brilliant mind and he can write well so that he should be able to find himself. I don't know what he will do about his girl problems.

June 6, 1942   Saturday   11:35 P. M.

Had my coffee over with Pat. Sure do miss the good coffee. Guess that's why I don't get up for breakfast. This easy life is getting me lazy, although I try to fool myself that I am doing something constructive on the paper. Only good thing about it is that I can get around to talk to people from the outside as well as residents. The rowdy bunch seems to have quieted down. About the most they do is to make a lot of noise. They don't go round in bunches and pick fights. Only heard of one thus far. They don't seem to get along well with the girls and they are generally ignored. A bunch was in the grandstands this morning. The majority of these young fellows don't have jobs here. They sit around telling dirty jokes and occasionally make wisecracks to the girls that go by. Sex is the one topic of interest and they go into all the details. The only mention of the war which I heard was: "That bastard Hitler should be castrated because he brought us here." Sometimes they go off to have a little game of poker for fun. They live in different areas of camp which may explain why they have sort of drifted apart. Most of them are former truck drivers, gardeners, and loafers who never did much work except in the summer. Not one of the group I saw this morning got beyond high school. They like to make remarks about the female breasts. "Look at that deflated set of cows." "I wonder if that wrinkled old lady had her tits all shriveled up." "If there is such a shortage of milk, why don't they milk that fat one?" Etc. Only one burglary has been committed: on the canteen. A radio was stolen from the hospital also. These boys gather around the prostitutes that come to see them. Harry, the internal policeman, says that they have their eyes on six of them. One blonde was asked to leave last Sunday, but it's hard to accuse them directly. Tony says there is a woman in camp who has established a good trade in her apartment, but he doesn't know where it is.

.   .   .   .

Talked to Ernie Iyama today about the politics in his precinct for the coming elections. The nucleus of the YD's are there and Ernie is going to run because he feels that he can swing a lot of votes among the Kibei and Issei. He plans to have his group leave his name in English and Japanese at each home he contacts in order to make sure that they vote. The YD's already have an organization and they are wasting no time. Most of the fellows on the press are of this group in mind, except perhaps Taro who has been connected with the JACL but he doesn't exactly see eye to eye with the "big shots" who dictate policies. Taro wrote most of the statements for the JACL to present to the Tolan Committee [34] when they were out here last February. Taro got his M.A. in English at U. of Utah and came out here to do newspaper work. Our press is going to be non-

[34] The House Select Committee Investigating National Defense Migration, chaired by Representative John H. Tolan of California, held hearings in Los Angeles, San Francisco, and Seattle dealing with relocation in early 1942.

partisan as a paper and we will try to serve the whole community on an equal basis. Ernie's precinct is important because Henry Takahashi is there. He is a reactionary JACLer and a red baiter. His only education and experience has been in optometry and he thinks that the fact that 10 of his brothers and sisters got through U. C. and a Doctor's degree in optometry make him a social leader. Carl Akiya, who used to follow the party line closely (he still gets *People's World*), wants somebody to represent the Issei and Kibei interests solely and this may cause a split in that area. All of the YD members who live in other areas have come into Ernie's to help him campaign. They feel that getting Henry out is the big issue and the battle will be interesting to watch. Toby Ogawa is running in our district. The YMCA group is strong in our precinct and they may push a candidate of their own since they split with JACL on the issue of evacuation. The Y group felt that it should have been fought to the end. The Secretary, Lincoln Kanai, has carried on to the end. He is now on the way east because he doesn't want to be in camp. Toby is a smart politician and he may be a good man because he can speak up when necessary. He announced the WRA requests for an occupational survey on the possibilities of industrializing this group. Toby made it sound like he and the house managers originated the idea, which is not true. Even the Tolan Reports recognized the fact that less than 30% of the Japanese in this state were in agriculture. But the serious farm labor shortage this summer will change these plans, I am afraid. No wonder Idaho was willing to take Warren and the other 12 in the sugar beets. The State employees are even going out into the fields in order to save the crop.

June 7, 1942   Sunday

Slept until 10:00 this morning and then read for another hour before getting up. Miyako went to the Catholic church with the I.'s and she was given candy and fruit vs. the "worldly temptation." Miyako has about the fullest daily schedule of any of us. She goes to school in the mornings and then takes dancing, art, and tonette classes in the afternoon. The rest of the day she is running around with Y. and F. Tom has established himself as the champion *Sumo* wrestler among the little boys.[35] They are much more interesting to watch than the regular tournament which they hold daily up at barracks 6. The events draw a big crowd, but it doesn't appeal to me much. Reminds me of the disciplined Japanese ways too much. They go through a formal ritual each time and the crowd has certain set phrases which they yell at the appropriate time. The boys wear only a canvas jock strap and they get into a ring about 8 feet wide. The idea is to throw the other fellow out on his back. The Issei turn out in large numbers for the events. In the infield the regular baseball league started today and a large crowd turned out. The police chief threw the first ball, the bugle corps played, and a speech was made to inaugurate the League play. The teams are divided into the American and National Leagues and each team is named after one of the big league teams. The strong wind is an extra hazard for the players.

.   .   .   .

Went to the College Fellowship tonight to hear the panel discussion on "What Should the Nisei Attitude as Christians Be towards the U.S. Government?" The messhall was jammed with college students from the Bay Area. As usual no questions were raised from the floor, except for the ones I asked. I felt silly and was disgusted at the same time. . . . None of the four [speakers] probed into the real reasons. They completely ignored the economic basis and stressed the opinion that Christianity would right all wrongs. I am afraid that this is not a very practical approach and I told them that they should fight for real democracy with the liberal elements, but they would not see it. Many of this group are pacifists and they don't feel that they can do anything in the direct war efforts, which I think is very harmful. If Americanization is the only answer for us, we must fight the vicious forces seeking to disfranchise and deport us. Bill

[35] *Sumo* is a traditional and highly ceremonial form of Japanese wrestling, still very popular in Japan.

Sasagawa, who testified on the Tolan Committee in Los Angeles, was the only other person to speak up. He pointed out that
the group was too complacent and that religion was not the
only answer. He said that the Negroes only get things because
they fought for their rights and we should do the same. He even
went as far as to tell them about the Negroes who came back
from the last war and returned to Chicago just in time to bear
the brunt of discrimination which became bitter due to the
fact that the Negroes had been brought in from the South during the war to handle defense jobs. After the war the Caucasians
made a determined effort to drive all Negroes out. The returning Negroes refused to turn in their guns, but used them instead to stand for their rights. Bill did not mean to say that we
should use guns, but that we should fight for what was ours and
we would if we really felt like Americans and believed in the
democratic principles. An outsider might have thought that
Bill was telling us to fight the government orders with physical
actions, but this is not what he meant. What a story this would
have made for the Joint Immigration Committee and the
American Legion to use as an argument for deportation! T. H.
told me after the meeting that he now feels that we should join
the liberals of this country and fight the thing out, and he hopes
that the government will follow its program of fair treatment
out. Emiko finally got interested because she came home and
started to read the Tolan Reports. M. Y. was so worked up that
she kept saying, "I hate the Japs." She thinks they (Nisei) are
getting too Japanesy in the concentration camp.

June 8, 1942   Monday   11:00 P. M.

Cast my absentee ballot today for the S. F. special elections.
Voted yes on both measures to increase the bond debt for no
special reason. The only reason I voted today was to protect my
voting privileges for the important elections which will come up
in the fall. The man elected at that time will shape the post war
policies for the world. A special deputy came in and notarized
our ballots. I counted about 630 Nisei voters in the room while

I was there. Lily T. said that she was voting just to show the American Legion that we were interested in our franchise even in times like these. Grace S. said that she was voting because this was one way of showing our loyalty and interests in America. Taro W. voted because this was one privilege which he would fight to retain because it was a symbol of his Americanism. James O. cast his ballot because the JACL told him to. He didn't think it was worth anything anymore. Nobu T. thought that voting was one of the few civil rights left to us. The general opinion was that the Nisei should take advantage of his voting privilege in view of the fact that there were forces that want to take this right away from us. None of them thought that the two issues on the question of county bonds was the important thing. And I doubt if the majority of eligible S. F. Nisei voters even went to the trouble to send for their absentee ballots.

Family difficulties again. Bette and Emiko just don't seem to get along with Alice and the rift is getting wider. Emiko and Alice had a nasty spat this afternoon and all of us tended to take Emiko's side. Alice was not completely to blame because Emiko is very touchy these days. We have been picking on Alice too much. She was very quiet this evening and she has the idea that we are all turning against her. This must have hurt her deeply because she went to bed and cried a little, according to Emiko. All of us will have to quit picking on her; she takes the brunt of the criticisms for some reason or other. And Jack bawled Mom out tonight because she was going to take a shower at 10:00 with a cold wind blowing outside and her with her cold. Miyako had been patiently waiting to go with Mom to the showers and when she found that she could not go, she became very disturbed. Jack started to tease her by saying we were going to send Mom back to Japan and what would Miyako do about it. Miyako took this very seriously and she kept saying, "I want to go with Mom." We said she was an American and would not get along in Japan because she was not a Jap, but Miyako said she didn't care because she was going with Mom. Finally Mom got mad and she came out and told us that she had no hopes of ever going to Japan and to stop teasing Miyako. Pop has long ago given up any idea of returning to Japan. Mom borrowed a Japanese magazine this morning and we ridiculed it as Jap propaganda, but she didn't mind. She just smiled and said, "Just a story book that I read. No can read American papers." Although she does not realize it fully, she is closer to America than Japan. The family has completely democratized her. We have much more freedom in our stable than in some of the other family units where the older generation still reign supreme. Mom is prepared for anything as long as she has her children about. All of the little children seem to make our rooms the general headquarters and Mom is good-natured about the noise and rarely rebukes them. And she is always giving them things to eat. It's no wonder our family never saved any money; Mom used to spend it all for food for the kids. Pop finally finished Tom's sailboat today, but Mom would not let him and Tom go down to Lake Tanforan to test it out because it was too windy. They were both disappointed. The boat is quite an artistic work of art. Pop never says anything about family affairs any more. He has left the policy making up to Mom and us older ones. Jack makes most of the important decisions as I still don't feel that it is up to me. I can't assume the privilege without taking the responsibility.

.   .   .   .

At present the government objectives are broad but indefinite. We must keep pushing for the widest policy, along with the progressive liberals, so that such anti-democratic moves like the NSGW disfranchisement and deportation program does not succeed. If we were certain, as a group, just what the Federal settlement policy would be, then the morale would take an upward swing and the Japanese [evacuee group] would be more positive in its actions. Yesterday Bendetsen of the Army [36] came out with a statement trying to justify the evacuation. Last week Olson roars about the "Jap" threats in California. Such statements are bound to instill fears, especially when the newspapers give such things wide publicity.

[36] On Colonel Bendetsen, see the Introduction.

But no federal policy can be complete unless it is made in terms of the worldwide issues of this war. Although we are a drop in the bucket as far as numbers are concerned, the social implications and significance are of fundamental importance to this country as well as to the rest of the democratic world. How can we fight Fascism if we allow its doctrines to become a part of government policies? The contradiction would be too obvious to ignore. Many of the American Chinese, Negroes, and Jews can see that a dangerous precedent can be set, which could easily include them later if this thing is not handled democratically. Already my Chinese, Negro, and Jewish friends have made remarks about the possibility. Perhaps we don't get enough of the other side of the picture, seeing that we are out here in California, in the hotbed of the greatest agitation. I can't blame the Nisei for being resentful when they read about "Jap soldier in U.S. uniform arrested!" I do so myself. One of the dangers of this is that many of the Nisei are getting more race conscious than even before because of this very thing—we are all lumped together as disloyal Japs. And I wonder how the Nisei soldier feels? This is one hell of a way to create national unity.

Furthermore, the growing Japanesy attitudes among some of the Nisei are unhealthy. It leaves me with an uneasy feeling. The more liberal Nisei have the same reaction; some are bitter in denouncing it; some feel helpless and wonder if the Nisei are really Americanized. There seems to be a definite split between these groups. The Kibei forms yet another separate group. The only time I see them in large numbers is at the *Sumo* matches. And the present administration actually is hampering Americanization. Greene told McQueen [37] today that the "Town Hall" writing incident would not happen again! This extreme shortsightedness makes our work very difficult. And we just cannot carry out a successful Americanization program without Caucasian leadership. We lack it among ourselves. A well-defined governmental policy would help the liberal cause greatly. One of the things about the Nisei liberals is that they

[37] McQueen, formerly the editor of a small San Francisco newspaper, acted as official censor of the assembly center press for the WCCA.

have more Caucasian contacts, judging from the visitors that come in. They have not been so closely tied down to the Japanese community in the past as the small-time businessmen who represent the JACL clique. Many of the liberals are now fearful of the program being allowed to continue under Army control. This is only supposed to be a temporary center; it may become a permanent one. This would hamper the WRA efforts enormously. The army is a military machine and not equipped to handle the social problems which have resulted from the evacuation, such as health, sex, personality adjustments, family problems, education, occupations, etc.

.   .   .   .

Relocation, thus, becomes very significant to the Japanese and the Nisei. After the war, the government will have to continue handling the problem wisely; the Japanese just can't be dumped out to shift for themselves. It's much better that they remain wards of the government until individual adjustments are made. But this may mean permanent segregation. Resettlement of small groups seems to be the most feasible program, but we would then have the problem of social isolation. In any event we have to be given a chance to contribute directly to this country. If the war lasts long enough the Nisei manpower can become very important in the war effort, given the right kind of training. The meeting of the WRA officials with the Advisory Council last Friday is a good sign.

We are not war prisoners, yet our constitutional rights have been taken from us, namely fundamental civil liberties. Viewed from this angle, it is no more than right that the government sees us through this mess. And a complete agricultural relocation is not the answer. Neither can it be on the basis of the former Jap towns which could not give economic opportunities for the college Nisei who usually ended up on Grant Avenue. That is out. Eisenhower [38] and the sociologists must have a head-

[38] Milton S. Eisenhower, Dwight's brother, would shortly resign as director of the WRA, to be replaced by Dillon S. Myer.

ache trying to get a long-range program with a wise social goal. As time goes on, the picture will become clearer.

June 9, 1942   Tuesday   11:30

Just got through having a long talk with Emiko, Bette, and Alice about the family problems. It's getting much more serious although not apparent on the surface. After two months of silence, Pop finally blew up and had a loud argument with Mom. Bette was so embarrassed that she had to send Pat home. Unless some adjustments are made, it is bound to have a bad effect on the young children. Already Tom and Miyako are getting much too sassy. It probably is our fault since we have practically taken all responsibilities away from Mom. She is fighting for her position although she does it in a quiet way. Pop bears the brunt of her suppressed feelings. This morning Mom told him to shut up and went out and slammed the door. Pop came to Jack and me to explain everything and we said that we would have to hear Mom's version also. To top things off, Jack and I bawled Tom out for wearing our woolen socks and making big holes in them. Tom said that Pop wore them and Pop in turn said it was Mom's fault for not mending the little holes. The argument got to be quite interesting for a while. I thought it was all over, but it started again this evening when Mom gave the kids some of the special cheese that Dr. Edwards brought for Pop. When he objected, she blew up and said he was too selfish. So Pop put on a suffering hero act and he got the big pot out and cooked about four pounds of asparagus and insisted that we should eat them. The fuse blew out and in the darkness Mom went off with the tub to take a shower. We didn't eat the asparagus so that Pop sulked and he just sat on Tom's bed and smoked until now. Mom got worried and came in and asked me to send him to bed because he might catch a cold. Now they won't talk to each other.

All of this indicates that all of us are a little uncertain about things and very touchy. Arguments result over little things. The next day they are forgotten, but they should not have started in the first place. Pop feels he is getting neglected by the family and sort of pushed aside. He has become very gentle and rarely loses his temper these days. Bette and Emiko say that they like to have long talks with him nowadays because he has such a sense of humor. Emiko rarely talks seriously with Mom because she has sort of grown away. Pop rarely talks much with Alice because he thinks Mom is spoiling her and turning her mind against him. Miyako is about the only one that is really close to both of them and it hurts her deeply when they argue. She doesn't know what it is all about. It's all a complicated mess. We have decided to avoid arguments as much as possible after this and see if that will help the situation any.

June 10, 1942   Wednesday

Our censor came around today. He objected to a statement made by a couple of people I had interviewed: "Don't mind if he runs around a little"— he said this was bad for morale. And the sugar beet statement: "It's better for us to work hard than to stay here and be idle." He didn't like the idea that people were idle here and so cut that out. We just couldn't say anything. I was so damned mad. We are nothing but a kept press.

The daily count will go into effect shortly under order from General De Witt. The house managers are responsible for counting us in the morning and at night. It's practically a curfew. Don't see the necessity for it here, but there must be a reason.

.   .   .   .

The third town hall meeting was held tonight and it was the most successful one to date. About 1000 residents jammed the social hall to listen to Mr. Ferguson, the Regional Attorney from the WRA, explain the policies of his department in the relocation program. Prepared questions and questions from the floor were also answered. There was a lively interest in asking questions, mostly about physical needs and policies. Henry Tani was the chairman. Ferguson: "I'm glad to see a typical American institution here in the Town Hall meeting. You should keep it up as it is the best method of Americanism. As far as I am concerned, your loyalty has been demonstrated on many occasions since I came out here. I don't know too much about the Japanese, but I am learning fast through contacts with you people." In general he discussed the organizational and functional machinery of the WRA and admitted it was a plan without any precedent. Therefore, it would be necessary for the WRA to feel its way along, although certain basic policies have already been drawn up. It was refreshing to hear a man of his caliber speak and be frank to the audience. He told what he could and did not paint a rosy picture of the relocation area. Its relationship to the Army and WCCA was defined.

.   .   .   .

No information was given as to when we would move although he thought that it would be before fall at the latest. The audience reaction was very good. The chief questions asked were about physical provisions. Only a few inquiries were made on the broad policies of the WRA. A surprised gasp went through the audience when somebody asked whether there would be free speech, press, and assemblage there, something which was denied to us here. Mr. Ferguson said that military necessity would determine this although his outlook was very promising since the relocation camps would be inland. In all, 28 questions were asked and he answered most of them very frankly —e.g. questions on Issei activities, work corps, wage scales, types of jobs available, the franchise, church groups going together, etc.

June 11, 1942   Thursday

Mom wants to enroll in the English classes but Pop won't hear of it. He doesn't want her to get ahead of him and he thinks that she is just doing it for social purposes, which is undoubtedly true. Mom is gradually taking things into her own hands.

The Catholic groups are petitioning to be sent all together to Tule Lake [Relocation Center in California] because they don't like the heat. Since the I.'s are getting very friendly with us and the relations are very good, Mom took Mrs. I.'s suggestion and signed the petition, even though we are not Catholics. Pop got excited and thought this would mean a splitting up of the family but we explained that we were doing it for him because he had to have a cool climate for his health. This made him feel so much better that he was very cheerful today. We still have to work on him for the English classes for Mom. We told her to go ahead anyway, but she doesn't want to do it if it is going to create resentment on Pop's side. This evacuation is making a new life for Mom. For 28 years she has been restricted at home in Vallejo, raising children and doing the housework. Her social contacts have been extremely limited, and this has been hard for her because she is more the extrovert type of personality. Now she finds herself here with a lot of Japanese, and it has given her a great deal of pleasure to make all of these new social contacts. Pop on the other hand rarely leaves the house and he still retains his contempt for the majority of the Japanese residents. This attitude is intensified when he sees that Mom is gradually pulling away from him. He naturally lays the blame upon these people. The only ones that he likes are the I.'s next door. They are so agreeable that we get along with them famously. Bette and Patsy are real chummy these days. Bette borrows her checked shirt to wear with her jeans—all of the H. S. age girls dress this way—and they go into lengthy huddles to see what to wear each day. We go to the messhall with them and stand in line together. Since our family takes a whole table, we sit as a unit but frequently we join them as individuals. Miyako and Yuri are inseparable. They do everything together. Not a day goes by that some sort of food is [not] exchanged back and forth. English is the chief mode of conversation. Mom and Pop do not speak Japanese with our friends unless addressed in this language. This morning the kids and Mrs. I. and Mom all went together to the Flag Day ceremonies held at the new center flagpole.

.   .   .   .

The Issei are getting very steamed up over this election business. They are holding group meetings to endorse certain candidates who they think will give them a fair deal. Yuki said that an ugly rumor was going around about Bob I. and Ernie. Her father is helping Professor Obata campaign for them and he wanted to know if it were true that these fellows were formerly acting as stool pigeons for the FBI and if this were true the Issei would withdraw their support. Yuki did not know how to handle this dirty situation so Bob Tsuda and I told her to have them go before the Issei group and set things straight without repeating the rumors. Henry Takahashi is taking this election very seriously and his particular precinct will have the most interesting battle. In our precinct, Jimmy Horano is Toby Ogawa's campaign manager, but he says they will not do their heavy campaigning until the night before the elections. A camp-wide parade will be held at this time to stir up the community interest. The Issei are already steamed up about the whole thing. It is unfortunate that they were never given citizenship; they would have made damn good citizens, not that they weren't, in spite of discrimination. The fault in not being more easily assimilated into the American life on the part of the Issei is not one sided. Given an equal opportunity vs. other immigration groups, they would have taken a vital interest in things American. Even if this particular election will not mean too much, it is good for the Issei and a subtle step towards Americanization. The Japanese have to go more than half way in this present situation.

.   .   .   .

Just got talking with E[miko]. She couldn't sleep so she came out here and we started to talk on things in general. We talked about everything including sex. E. says that the Nisei girls still think it is a sin to discuss such things frankly and she has learned most of her things from her Caucasian friends. She went around with Caucasian and Chinese girls in H. S. chiefly since there were no Japanese in Vallejo. Because she lived in the slum district she learned a lot about what was going on in the red light district and discussed these things quite frankly, even at home. But after coming among the Japanese, she finds that these are unmentionable subjects and feels that the Japanese are too narrow-minded and suspicious. E. thinks that the sex problem will increase in camp and believes that the only solution is for the young people to get married. Already she notices that the boys are getting more vulgar. They whistle in a suggestive manner at the girls and some of them are peeping toms.

We got talking about the war and E. says that she really feels that she is an American and wants the U.S. to win the war. "Sometimes I feel inferior to a white person, but most of the time I feel equal or superior. I don't know why I feel superior to a Filipino, but I guess it's because there were so many single ones in Vallejo who chased the prostitutes." She sometimes feels superior to the Japanese here because they can't speak English so well. She is not ashamed of her Japanese ancestry even if she does feel that she is an American. She says that she has way more arguments here in camp but she doesn't know why. Mom nags her a lot but E. feels that she can dismiss it lightly now because Mom can't do much about it. E. also has her personal problems, chiefly the matter of excess weight, but she just eats anyway because "I get hungry." She is a little envious of Bette, who has such a cute figure. E. wonders if it will interfere with getting boyfriends. She doesn't seem to have any trouble as they are always popular at the dances. E. doesn't know what will happen to the Nisei in the future. She thinks that we will get along in our rightful places after we win the war, but she is not so sure that we will go back to Vallejo. She is particularly worried about further schooling right now and hopes that she may be able to continue in some way or else get married. She is glad that our parents are not Japanesy like some of the Issei around here.

June 13, 1942 Saturday 11:15

The political campaigns for the camp elections are going full blast ahead now. Mitch and the YD bunch are having a big rally over in their precinct tomorrow and they have planned a bunch of questions to fire at Takahashi in case he starts to redbait. The YD's are well organized and have a good chance of getting Ernie in. In our precinct, the Isseis got together again to endorse one candidate tonight, but did not come to any decision. Posters are plastered all over the place. Somebody even got the bright idea of putting posters in the toilet bowls. Y. K. has the most signs up. They state that he is the only Nisei patent attorney in the U.S. This will win him many votes because the Japanese look up to a person with a little position.[39] Toby is also doing a little campaigning on the side and giving the glad hand to everyone. The Berkeley group seems to be pretty well behind him. The S. F. "Y" bunch is backing Tod Fujita solidly. Tod is a nice fellow, but he doesn't have the aggressiveness of the other two. I have an idea that Toby will win. Really not much choice among the three as they are similar as far as ideas are concerned. Toby would be the best choice.

Pop has finally broken down and he has decided that he will go and learn to speak English in the class with Mom. He is afraid that he will make many mistakes and be ashamed for showing his lack of education. But "Oh light, I go. Learn the ABC. Maybe one month, I learn pretty good. No use Japanese school no more." Jack said that he should study it hard because the Issei may be given a chance for citizenship after the war and if they show that they are being Americanized enough.

"Oh no, first generation, never give him citizenship. Maybe government he take way Nisei citizenship too, no?" We said that he should learn English regardless because the young kids are growing up and soon they will not be able to talk to them in Japanese. All of the kids that come here speak English. Pop accepts this. "Humph, what the hell. Me 67 years old. Too old

[39] On June 15 Kikuchi wrote in a personal letter: "Mr. K. is blowing his own horn. He is the most objectionable of them, although he may have the stuff. But the people don't like his conceit; he goes around telling everyone that he is the only [Nisei] patent attorney in America and what great initiative he has in starting the First Aid classes, etc. I guess I distrust him because he plays up to both the Issei and Nisei with contradictory statements in order to win their votes. He probably is not up to anything except to gain personal prestige. (I don't like his Jap looks.)"

to start school, but me smart and learn fast like Miyako in the head."

Our messhall looked very pretty tonight with all those fresh flowers on the table. Some Caucasian florist nurseryman gave them to the residents and they divided them among all the mess-halls and the hospital.

June 14, 1942   Sunday

T. M. heard a rumor that we were going to Arkansas in three weeks. Mrs. I. has a premonition that we will all go to Tule Lake together. At least it is a good topic for conversation. Similar to the anxiety of the pre-evacuation days when everyone was all packed up and waiting for the word to go. A lot of people would rather stay here permanently as they are more or less settled down. For some reason everyone would rather be sent to Tule Lake if we have to go. They dread to think that we will be sent all the way to Arkansas or Arizona. The majority of the Japanese here still think in terms of returning to the Bay Area as soon as the war is over.

This afternoon we went up to the grandstands to look at the visitors. There were not so many people today. The Negroes are coming down here in increasing numbers. Peter Ray, a well known dancer who used to perform with Duke Ellington's band, came to see Mornii and the other jive boys, and he drew a great crowd by his dancing exhibition. He is now at the Town Club. The jitterbug craze is still strong with the young kids and for them nothing else exists. Most of them are from S. F. Last night at the dance they were all dressed up in their draped pants and bright shirts. These boys are really extrovert and many of them speak the special jitterbug language with the facial expressions which they copy from the Negroes. They are not too popular with the majority of the Nisei girls who are more conservative.

A few Chinese were also here visiting their friends. The only way I could tell the difference was that they were wearing Chinese buttons. Some of the Forbidden City and Chinese Sky-room showgirls were also down to see Grace S.   Walt Gordon,

Jr., the well known Negro football player at Cal, was also here today visiting Bobby O. and Joan N. Melvin Stewart introduced me to him. Melvin is also a Negro. He is now working in the Post Office, but plans to go into social work. He graduated from State with me and then worked as a redcap with the Santa Fe railroad for a couple of years before getting his present Civil Service job. When he saw all the Negroes around he said, "You know who are your real friends now. A lot of us are behind any movements that will fight this thing because we have had to face a lot ourselves and so are opposed to anything so un-American. The trouble with the Negroes is that we have been so involved in our problems that we didn't see the danger of this war hysteria against the Japanese soon enough. It's so impersonal with us, but when we actually see you people in camp, we go out mad as anything and want to do something about this great injustice because we know you Nisei are just as loyal as we are. The color of the skin is no indication of loyalty—we can testify to that."

Jose and Machado were also here. They also finished S. F. State with me and were doing graduate work at U. C. last year when I used to see them occasionally around the campus. They are Filipinos and have been told to report for army service this coming Thursday. Both of them expect to return to the Philippines and help reconstruct their country after the war.

Alice and Jack have cultivated Sergeant Boyd Horton to such a point that he gives our visitors special privileges. The alert is now off so that the soldiers can get leaves and Boyd is going to look up Angelo and Delores in S.F. He expects to be sent overseas at any moment. He has a heart and does not turn his men in if they talk to the Nisei through the fence. The Army evidently wants no inter-group friendships formed for fear that the soldiers will also see that we are not treacherous spies but average Americans. In spite of that the Nisei are getting to know a lot of the soldiers. The latest Army rule is that the guards at the gate can't even speak to us except on business.

The *Sumo* exhibitions continue to draw about 2-3000 people each Sunday. They had a tremendous audience today watching the exhibits which are now stripped of all their ceremonial Japanese traditions. The stronger Nisei boys are taking up the sport which is not so easy to learn as there are many tricks to it. I don't like the thing; it's too much a reminder of the Japanese conservatism that clings to the old ways and customs.

Got up late this morning and so went to take a shower clad only in my bathrobe and slippers. Had to push through a crowd of Buddhists going into the church. They all looked at me so shocked at my lack of dignity. Tonight I went to their dance with a bunch and had to face some of those I saw this morning, but they did not say anything.[40] Met the cutest girl from San Mateo, but have already forgotten her name. About 400 Nisei were present. The Buddhists are a more conservative group of Nisei. Not many outstanding leaders among them except Ted Hirota. Many of them don't even know how to dance so that they announced a special dancing class for their members. A lot of Kibeis are in the group, and even the Nisei Buddhists speak more Japanese than other Nisei groups. Bette and Emiko and Patsy went to a High School Social of their stablemates club and they also had a good time.

June 16, 1942   Tuesday   11:45

Had a very busy day running around to get election information for the newspaper. As if there is nothing else of concern in the world! It's funny how isolation can cut one off from the realities of the great outside. We seem to get so wound up in our little camp affairs. In a sense this may be a little bad; but on the other hand a positive interest by the residents towards camp life is a healthy sign. It indicates that they are not contented in a wholly passive role. This energy can be guided into useful channels if we could develop the right sort of leadership among the Nisei.

Dr. Thomas was here today to discuss the University study on the evacuation. Felt sort of silly not having a well outlined

[40] Kikuchi's June 15 letter added that "only one girl mentioned it so that I had to inform her that I really was a Buddhist priest and that the green robe was my ceremonial gown."

report ready to present, but she was understanding and told us that we should not make a task of the work. I felt that this was the right approach since we could not be wholly objective and our personal feelings would creep into what we wrote. However, I gave her part of my diary to read over and will know by next week if my approach is all right with her. I just can't approach it in an academic manner like Tom [Shibutani]; it would be too biased and artificial unless I had a good background in technique and procedures. Perhaps I should do it on a voluntary basis and then I would not feel duty bound to get out a definite report each week.

Election started early this morning and interest was rather high. Precinct #2 was the one I covered for the paper because this seemed to be the most bitterly contested. Talked with several of the YD's and got the lowdown on how the campaign developed. When the elections were first announced, the chief move was to get Dr. Takahashi out by any means. A lot of the dislike was on a personal basis. But among the Issei there was an undercurrent of opposition due to the fact that they felt the JACL had failed them during the evacuation. I was greatly surprised to hear this remark because I had believed that the more progressive Nisei were the only ones to take this viewpoint. But the reasons are not the same. The Issei look at it more in terms of personal discomfort rather than from a wider viewpoint.

The strongest opposition sprang from the Berkeley Methodist Episcopal church group. "They hated his guts" because they resented his bragging subtly about the "Berkeley Takahashis" and how important they were. This church group distrusted his motives and had no confidence in anything he did. Takahashi used to be fairly prominent in this church, but dropped out because of conflicts in policy. The M. E. group, therefore, held a little secret meeting and invited a few of the Issei who were opposed to Takahashi in. They decided to put up Yuasa, who was a prominent architect, liberal, and a member of the church group. One of the reasons for this resentment was that Takahashi put on too much of a pose as a "savior of the Japanese" and that he didn't get anything done. They didn't stop to consider the fact that he had to work with an inefficient administration. A few of the liberals in the precinct also came to the meeting because they wanted him out since they did not think he had an "advanced idea or policy" as a member of the JACL hierarchy. They also resented the fact that he expected to keep his former prestige and position instead of starting from scratch as everyone had to do. One of the ways he used to advance himself was to "redbait," which the administration apparently approved.

However, the other YD members thought that an even more progressive person should run. Ann and Mitch did not think they should put up one of their own members because he would immediately be tagged. However, they went ahead and put up Ernie, since he could appeal to both the Kibei and Issei element. A meeting was held with the Yuasa group and Yuasa agreed to withdraw and support Ernie. So the YD's immediately organized a campaign committee. C. A., a former communist, took over the task of winning the Kibei vote. H. I., a former Party member and writer for *Doho*, [41] took over the Issei vote campaign. Mr. U., an Issei who had obtained citizenship through his war service, was made chairman for Ernie's campaign. U. is an American Legionnaire and had taken a very active leadership in the Japanese post in San Francisco.[42] He had attended many of the state conventions and has had 12 years of voting experience. Prof. Obata and the other liberals were also drawn into the committee. The artists took part by drawing posters and the whole precinct was canvassed from house to house by all the backers.

In the meanwhile, Y. insisted that Yuasa should run because he did not like the YD's. Since his petition was not filled, a huge "write-in" campaign was started and the church groups swung back on the bandwagon. The chief argument was that a few of Yuasa's backers thought that Ernie was a communist,

[41] *Doho* was a far-left-leaning Japanese daily in Los Angeles.
[42] Naturalization was briefly possible for otherwise ineligible persons who had served in the American armed forces during World War I. Very few Issei had the requisite service, of course, but these were enough for segregated American Legion posts to be established in both San Francisco and Los Angeles.

which was not true. Mitch particularly did not like this because he thought that a smearing campaign by both opponents
would greatly reduce Takahashi's chances. At the polls today,
Mitch and Y. almost had a run-in. Mitch and C. were disturbed
that there were no voting instructions posted in the booths for
the Issei so that they had some made up and tacked on the
walls. They also insisted that minor technicalities be clarified
in order to be fair to all candidates. Y. came in and was mad as
hell because he thought that M. and C. were campaigning right
in the polling place, and strong words followed. The result was
that Mitch was asked to leave in order to protect his candidates
from an accusation of "dirty politics." All day long, the YD's
and Issei-Kibei supporters were out urging people to vote.

At 9:30 we heard the news that Ernie had won by an over-
whelming vote and that Yuasa, the write-in candidate, was
second, while Takahashi came in a poor third. Mitch, Ann, and
I rushed over to the Center to congratulate him and from there
we proceeded to the laundry for a "victory party." About 35
people were there, including some Kibei and Issei. It was surprising to find them backing an anti-Fascist liberal, but they did
it because they felt that the camp needed strong leadership in
order to work for the welfare of the whole community. Then
these were the more liberal ones, while the rest of the Issei
voters selected Ernie chiefly through the efficiency of the campaign organization and in protest against Takahashi, plus the
fact that they felt that Ernie was the best candidate. They arrived at this conclusion chiefly by holding meetings and discussing the respective candidates and their platforms.

June 17, 1942   Wednesday

Censorship note: Ran a statement for the paper about how the
Nisei could get the complete Tolan Reports and where to send
for it. McQueen sent it back censored completely and gave no
reason. We were all pretty burnt up, but what can you do except protest? Taro suggests that we all quit and get into education. The paper is not worth that much trouble. It is now

checked and double checked. Mitch and I thought that perhaps we could get some organization to donate $20.00 for postcards and have the ACLU print the notice and distribute them by mail. Then we could find out whether they are absolutely against the Tolan Reports circulating widely. We could probably get one placed in the library, but not run a notice for all the camp.

The administration makes the mimeographing of the paper hard because of the lack of cooperation. Yet they take about 200 copies to send out. We were not able to get the complete election results. Ogawa got 492 votes, Fujita 126, and Katayama 85. In our precinct, 725 cast votes out of a total of 779 eligibles which is over 90% and the highest % of any of the precincts. Ernie won in #2. In #3 and #4 there was a difference of 1 vote and of 2 votes in the results. In the Infield, Ichisaka, a JACL man from Washington township, won. The progressives, thus, got 3 men in. One person is supposed to be a sort of reactionary Kibei. I. does not belong to the inner JACL clique of S. F. All of the farm groups in the infield voted for him. Because of the close votes, Davis would make no official statement for us. He sealed the ballot boxes up and will wait for demands for a recount before issuing a statement. This means that we will not get a lot of statistics in for this week's issue. I went to the two losing candidates and both Tosh Suzuki and Dave Tatsuno said that they were perfectly satisfied with the results and would not contest it. But Davis was "too busy" to let us get at the returns today. On top of this, the sentry at the gate is balking at keeping our copy for McQueen to pick up because he claims that he is too busy. Besides, I don't like the idea of putting out a paper all "sweetocated" as if everything is running smoothly.

.   .   .   .

In the infield there is an interesting garden. It is laid out beautifully and has some fragrant flowers already blooming. Around it is a sort of bamboo-like fence and right in the middle on a post is one of those Japanese lanterns. The whole thing looks like old Japan. Some people just can't divorce themselves from Japan and cling to the old traditions and ways. The garden is an outward indication of this sentiment for Japan. The odds are that the builder of the garden is pro-Japan, although he may have built it for cultural reasons.

.   .   .   .

Tom carried the blackboard to school for Jack [who was teaching social science] but classes were dismissed because the Jr. Hi is moving to the grandstand with the Hi School and adult education. Physical facilities are sad and the teachers are not so good. They sit in the messhall tables for a class and these classes are strung side by side right down the length of the grandstand. The teachers have to yell to get attention and compete with their neighboring teachers. On top of that the classes have to be chiefly lecture due to the lack of textbooks. The Hi School students are much more noisy than the others and already Toyo is having difficulty in controlling them. She is so tiny and timid that she should stick to writing sentimental poetry.

.   .   .   .

Another argument tonight over the dances. Jack picked on Alice and insisted that she either go to Kenji's birthday party or go alone to the Rec. Hall Dance. Emiko and Bette got mad at us, but decided not to go at all when Pop said he did not like them to go to dances so often. He backed down. Alice was very burnt up because we said she chased young boys and was too social minded for her age. Alice resents the fact that we called her friends "rowdy." Emiko and Bette went into their room and started to cry because we said that they were too selfish and did not stop to consider the fact that their going to dances continually caused friction between Mom and Pop. Finally Pop and we gave in and all three went to the dance. So we went to "Rowdy" Kenji's party and had a very good time.

It was Kenji's birthday and the messhall 18 clique composed

of S. F. Nisei chiefly managed to get steaks from the commissary
for the occasion. About 40 were present and they were given all
sorts of trick gifts. They were able to help themselves to everything. We just gluttoned ourselves on steaks, fried potatoes,
cake, fruit, jams, lemonade, ice cream, and coffee. They were
not too noisy, in fact very orderly. No off-color jokes were told
and girls [were] treated with a great deal of consideration and
respect. What girls can do to men! We danced after the boys
washed all the dishes. After-dinner speeches also were made
while the dishes were being washed. I told them about the time
Kenji almost got himself and me stabbed by a Filipino while
cutting celery in the San Joaquin Valley two years ago.

June 18, 1942   Impressions of Tanforan Hi School

The High School teachers met for an hour and a half today to
discuss clothes. The problem was: what to wear to classrooms.
Some of the girls come in slacks, some of the boys in jeans and
without ties. Others come dressed very formally in suits and
dresses. From a disciplinary point of view, the teachers were undecided as to what they could do. After great discussion, they
decided to leave the matter up to the individual teachers and let
them decide what was the most comfortable wear. Most of them
still come garbed very informally.

The school is a vast hubbub of voices—some low, some high
pitched. The Jr. Hi and the Hi School hold classes in the morning. The men's dormitory in the grandstand is full of mess
tables occupied by chattering students. Above this din, the
teachers try to compete and they have to speak very loudly in
order to get themselves heard. Blackboards have been made
from painted plywood. A painted sign "Tanforan High School"
sticks up from the mutuel windows and a girl stands behind it
giving out information instead of selling mutuel racing tickets.
The unerased race results high in the air lend a further racing
touch.

The teachers appear to be doing fairly well considering their
lack of training and experience, plus the handicaps. The stu-

dents generally do not mix—the boys and girls prefer their own group. Many of those in the back look bored and idly chew gum and are not very attentive. A few try to catch the attention of their friends in an adjoining class. The more studious ones sit in front wide awake and attentive. Jimmy S. teaching chemistry to his class but it looks like it went over their heads from all the puzzled gazes; Toyo looking very timid and small; she had a hard time controlling the noisy ones; Jack exploded the myth about the moon being made of green cheese, but his moon on the board did not look so round; Marie asking her class about how their standards of living have been affected by the diet here; she has everything under control; Ann the most popular teacher, she has the largest class so she stands on the table to make herself heard. Most of the boys wear boots and jeans—and they leave their woollen caps on. The topics assigned are fairly practical. They are on some phase of life at Tanforan.

June 19, 1942   Friday   11:05

The sailboats of the Issei are getting bigger and better. One old man even has a motor in his. They take a radio down to the lake and play it while sailing the boats all day long. The wind makes them go fast as hell and it looks rather picturesque. The recreation department is planning to hold a regatta in the near future. K.'s father has a three-masted schooner which he is going to enter. The Issei haven't anything else to do and I see them around all day long painstakingly carving out these boats.

We had beans for lunch today and the pile dumped in the garbage can was evidence enough that they were not appreciated. Tonight, they served us one small fish and rice. This has been the worst meal for quite a while. Prices must be going up on everything on the outside but we are not much aware of it here. Charles Pine told me today that haircuts are now 75 cents. The only way I feel it is in the cigarettes which no longer have tinfoil. The "South S. F. Industrial" sign is no more. It has been stripped for the tin on it. The large hill looks bare without it since it has been quite conspicuous coming up the peninsula for many years. We are only beginning to feel the shortage of every-thing.

Yesterday another statement was made against the "Japs" in the U.S. Day by day these native fascists are getting louder and louder. So far, few liberal groups have rallied together to stop them. Dr. Willis H. Miller of the California State Planning Board addressed the American Association for the Advance-ment of Science in Salt Lake: "There must be no negotiated peace in this war, nor no armistice. This is a total war. The Axis nations must be crushed and divided into little units. The U.S. must maintain a military force capable of enforcing world policies. At home all citizens of Japanese ancestry must be ex-pelled from the U.S. No longer need we regard our country as an asylum for all who wish to enter. After all, who wants to live in an asylum?" I would hate to entrust the future of this country to those fascist forces. The hysteria has gotten them so much that they reason emotionally.

Pop and Mom went to English classes for the first time today. Pop is the oldest one to sign up (67) among the 250 in the class. He feels pretty proud because he did not make any errors while Mom made one. Classes are two afternoons a week and it is good that he is taking a new interest up. Mom will also benefit from the social contacts. They now want regular notebooks to take along.

.   .   .   .

This afternoon I went up to Hi Korematsu's room to discuss his brother's case.[43] Ann, Mitch, Nori I., Vic A., Marie K., Ernie I., and Ernie T. and a couple of Issei world war veterans were also there. Fred Korematsu wanted to get the group's opinion on whether he should plead guilty to [evasion of] evacuation orders. He is here on $1000 bail furnished by the ACLU and has until Monday to make up his mind. According to paper reports he had his face lifted, but he looked quite Jap-

[43] The Korematsu case (*Korematsu* v. *United States,* 323 U.S. 214 [1944]) ul-timately went to the Supreme Court, where with three dissenters the Court de-cided that the evacuation orders did not violate the Constitution.

anese to me. The only thing was that he had an operation on the slits of his eyes. Fred was working as a welder for one of the shipyards. He has a clean record, and Besig wanted him for a test case to determine the constitutionality of evacuation. Besig has wanted somebody all the time, but so far nobody had come forward. There is another case up in Seattle but Besig thinks that this one is better.

Fred, as far as he himself was concerned, is perfectly willing to fight the case as he feels that it may determine a principle. However, he was a little uncertain as to what repercussions it would have on the group if it got wide publicity and he wanted to sound out opinion. Vic who is legalistically minded said that the case should not be fought because it would only make the pressure groups redouble their efforts and they would put through a constitutional amendment to this effect. He thought the decision would be obvious enough and it would be silly to think that they would free us now. However, I pointed out that this would not necessarily be the outcome as it was the principle that was being tried and the case would drag on for years. Ann suggested that a more logical outcome would be that they would set up "hearing boards" to determine our loyalty and that we did not necessarily have to leave camp.

Mitch thought that evacuation was an established fact and that our prime efforts should be in the direction of the future and make this program a success, which would at the same time prove our loyalty. However, he thought that it should be fought, but was not sure that this was the proper time.

Nori opposed it on another basis. She agreed that this case may serve as a rallying point for all liberals, but at the same time, she was a little doubtful about the labor unions. The war is their prime objective and she was doubtful that they would let anything split their ranks at this time. In this way, the Japanese here would be left holding the bag.

Ernie T. believed that all Nisei would be hurt by a test case at this time. I could not see it. Neither could Ann, Marie, Ernie I., Nori, and Mitch. We were undecided on other points. Hi K. believes his brother should fight it and he had only until Monday to make up his mind. We decided to meet in the Dental Clinic after dinner with Dr. Carl Hirota's group to discuss it further.

After the roll call, about 10 of us met and we went through another discussion. Some of the JACL's were present and after about two hours, we agreed that the discussion could not be ours since Fred would be the only one to suffer in case he lost. But we told him that we would all back him as most of us by this time believed that the pressure groups would go ahead with their program regardless of whether we kept quiet or put up a fight. Since evacuation, we believed, the liberal groups had come more to the fore and this would be the time to test the principle since we did not think evacuation was purely a military necessity, but partly on a racial basis. The fact that Italians and Germans are not going to be evacuated now or they will be able to appear before hearing boards would lend support to this argument.

Fred has the "guts" to fight the thing. I don't believe that the group would suffer by it. In fact, we have everything to gain. We are not prisoners of war and our civil rights have been taken away without due process of law. Fred has not made his mind up yet, but he is thankful that many Nisei believe as he does in regard to this situation. It was a well rounded group representing the "radicals," progressives, JACL reactionary and church elements. We believed that unity would be helped in the war effort.

Afterwards the groups started to talk about the feeling of the Issei and I was disturbed to hear their opinion that the Issei still believed strongly —hoped—for a Japan victory, and influenced the Nisei accordingly. Ann even went as far as to say that she would question the loyalty of most Nisei.[44] I objected to this, saying that she was being too harsh and impatient, but the others generally agreed with her. The question, therefore, arose as to what could we do to combat this force. I insisted that the

---

44 One presumes that "Issei" was intended. Whether this suggestive error was made by Kikuchi, or by the JERS typist who transcribed the no longer extant original, cannot be determined.

Issei were mostly sympathetic and felt sorry for the Nisei position and they said that I should get around and listen to them more. Ann said that my father and mother were not typical of most Japanese families. Art K. said an Issei grabbed him the other day and told him to wise up as the only hope was a Japan victory and that the Nisei were only fooling themselves by calling themselves Americans. He said that the Nisei were a bunch of damn fools. Others cited similar experiences. We all thought that education was the chief way to maintain the morale and ways and means of developing an adequate program were discussed. Later Ernie I. showed us a letter which the CIO had sent to District Attorney Hoyt denouncing his stand on disfranchisement of the Nisei.

Since it was only around 8:30 when the meeting broke up, Ann, Mitch, and Eleanor came over with some symphony and rhumba records. Earl and Mamie and Patsy were at home when we arrived so that it was quite a crowd by the time our family was included. We played *Porgy and Bess, Rhapsody in Blue, Joe Hill, Red Army Songs,* Rhumbas, etc., until about 11:00 p.m. Pop was quite contented because the gals could be under his watchful eyes. Jack gave Eleanor her "Russian grammar lesson," which provided a good laugh.

June 20, 1942   Saturday

Pop and Mom are going at their English classes very enthusiastically. They practiced writing all afternoon today. Pop feels proud of the fact that he is the oldest student in the camp. He told us tonight in broken English that he has not attempted to read and write for over 50 years. His stepmother hated him as a child and was jealous that his father planned a full education for him. The family was well off and Pop was sent to the best school in the province. His stepmother mistreated him and nagged him so much that he finally chopped up all of his books and slates in her presence and told her that he would stop his education if that made her any happier. Pop was 13 at the time. Shortly afterwards he ran away from home to go to sea.

Later he joined the U.S. Navy and during this time he learned to speak a little English and "went through 5 grades of English studies by myself." His hatred of his stepmother was always associated with learning and he says that every time he would try to educate himself he became full of mixed feelings against her memory and the buzz was so loud in his head that he could not apply himself fully. His brothers inherited all the property and there is only one brother alive now. Pop never wants to see Japan again as he has no connections there. The last time he was there was 30 years ago when he went to get married. At that time he built a $3000 shrine in memory of his father who was the mayor of the town at the time Pop ran away. He was received in awe by the townspeople who last knew him as a "black sheep." The family had all returned to Tokyo in the meantime. It seems that his father was a political exile; he supported the overthrow of the Shogunate rule and the restoration of the emperor.[45] Pop says a lot of his nephews are now army or navy officers in the war. What strange things fate can do. Instead of being in some old Jap home tonight, we were having a typical American argument in the stables. We tried to thrash this whole matter of the increasing number of petty arguments out and find the reasons for them. Alice just can't or won't realize that they are due to the unsettled minds of the people who fear for the future. That is why Mom nags so much one day and then is so kind the next. She will do anything to retain her place in the family and won't be pushed aside. Even at meals she has her methods. Since she doesn't do the cooking, she attempts to maintain her position by carrying all the plates home and by dividing the desserts or watching our Miyako and Tom unnecessarily. Lots of fellows tell me that they have more petty arguments too, but the thin walls help to keep them in a low voice. One girl says that her mother gets her under the blankets to bawl her out. They are so conscious of what the neighbors may say or think.

.   .   .   .

[45] The Shogunate (rule by feudal lords) was overthrown and the emperor restored to power in 1868. Kikuchi's father was born in 1875, on the island where his exiled father had continued to live.

Most of the rumors these days concern the time and place for the next move. Everyone feels that it will be before fall and a great deal of speculation goes on as to the exact date. Two weeks ago the rumors were chiefly about food and crime. The way that rumors spread like wildfire also indicates the lack of news for the Issei. Most of them can't read the *Totalizer* so they don't know what is going on. From now on, it will be almost impossible to put bulletins out in Japanese. No reading matter in Japanese at all is available for them. Without authentic news, they seize every piece of gossip as gospel truth and are too eager to believe it. Most of the Issei don't know what is going on around here and many don't want to move again now that they are settled down here for the duration. They have a lot of free time to go around and pass the gossip on. The stories get bigger and better as they are tossed around from [one] barrack to another. Stayed up until 2:30 a.m. talking with Alice, Jack, Bette, and Emiko. Emiko was the last to fall asleep on me. Funny sight of the day was Emiko at 2:30 at the foot of Tom's bed. She fit into it so well!

June 21, 1942   Sunday

Lots of visitors as usual. Many of them probably came out of curiosity to look at us and the camp. Makes one feel like being either in a zoo or a prison. The person who owns the property across the highway in front of the main gate has opened up a very profitable enterprise. He has a 15 cent parking lot!

.   .   .   .

Heard that Eisenhower has resigned from the WRA due to clash of authority and too great hampering of his policies. He was too good a man to lose.

Pop was studying his English again and Mom did hers in the other room. The competition is getting keen and they eat up the praise that we lavish on their achievements. Patsy came in to compliment Pop and he said with such a pleased grin on his face, "Oh scram! I study now." Mom was struggling over spelling words. She writes "las wick" for last week. Mom says she learned to write a little English 30 years ago just before she was married.

Miyako's comment: "Veddy veddy good, Pops."

Tom: "Two studious Japanese students doing their home-work!"

Emiko: "Gee that's good. What dya know about that, hey?"

Bette: "Pretty good, bub. You can do my English lesson for me next."

They then redouble their efforts. Pop will stick to it now that he has started as he is very persevering about things that he starts. The teachers need a little handwriting lesson also. They write out the assignment very illegibly and the Issei have a hard time following it.

Tom and the bunch are starting to think about learning Russian and want me to join the class as they feel that this language may become very important after the war. Ann wants to import someone to teach us once a week. It might be fun at that. I don't have the inhibitions against Russian that I do against the Japanese language.

June 22, 1942   Monday

Last night Mrs. I. was disturbed and scared because she told us over the wall that somebody was tapping the window pane as she came from the latrine. Immediately Alice and Emiko "re-membered" that they heard it also. Then a couple more women spoke from the other rooms and said the same thing had hap-pened to them, insisting that it was not the wind. So Jack and I went out with a flashlight to investigate. While we were on the other side Pop heard a man come running by. We found the door open in the art room and went in to investigate, but didn't find anything. I think that the imagination of the women is working overtime and they are too willing to interpret strange sounds as a "man" waiting to pounce on them. Anyway, talked it over with Toby, and as a councilman, he was able to get the administration to finally install about four lights in our block.

Yas Abiko came into the office to talk about ways to combat the NSGW. He wants Taro and some of us to get some actual data on the number of Nisei holding dual citizenship. This material will be provided to the Rev. Somers so that he will have something to go by. The NSGW are basing their drive of taking away dual citizenship on the basis that only 12½% of the Nisei have dropped their Jap citizenship. The JACL claims 75%. The latter figure would be nearer the truth since those born since 1924 would not have it,[46] and the bulk of the Nisei have been born since then. There is no way of checking the exact figures. The house managers and barracks captains will assist in roughly determining the number of dual citizens in this camp in order that Taro may have some reliable statistics. The NSGW want to disfranchise the Nisei because they believe that we always vote as a group along solid nationalistic (pro-Japan) lines. The group is not large enough to carry that much influence anyway, except perhaps in the Hawaiian Islands. If the people of this camp are an accurate cross-section, there is not much danger of the Nisei voting in a solid group on anything. There are too many individual differences present. The dual citizenship argument is a bit silly. There are thousands of other immigrants [sic] that hold dual citizenship, but they are not denounced as dangerous citizens. Most of them, including the Nisei, simply ignore the claims of the other nation. Why should the Nisei even recognize the asserted rights of Japan? The American concept of citizenship is what we go by. It is a bit amusing to see how some of the clever writers tie up dual citizenship with the family system and draw something insidious out of that. Even among many of the Nisei who hold dual

46 The matter of "dual citizenship" was at some times of seemingly great importance to active oppressors of the Japanese Americans, although in fact the purely formal question of the official relationship to Japan of persons born and raised in the United States was no more sensible than the (conflicting) argument used by the same people that "blood is thicker than water." In any case, to alleviate this source of pressure upon the Japanese Americans, certain of their organizations successfully requested that the Japanese government change their procedures so that after 1924 an Issei couple had to make a special effort to register their offspring if they wanted them to be citizens of Japan as well as of the nation of their birth. Procedures for formally renouncing Japanese citizenship were also available.

citizenship and who believed a little in Japan had these Japanese ideals shattered by the Pearl Harbor incident. And from now on, American loyalties and ideals will be stressed in the relocation camps. The NSGW and similar groups only hinder the process.

This morning the medical students had quite a "beef" with Davis, according to reports by an eyewitness. Dr. U. told Davis off and he said he would resign if he did not get better cooperation from the administration. The Med. students also want more time to study for their medical examinations. T. K.: "That Davis is a cold son of a bitch."

The Army photographers disrupted our day by taking a moving picture of our pressroom in action. These official documentary films will probably be used to show the "bigwigs" how well off we are and they will also be kept for the record of the "greatest mass migration in American history." We can't write about it in the *Totalizer,* the sergeant says. Anyway we were excited about being in the movies. They put the huge klieg lights in and it made us sweat like hell. I had on Jack's Hawaiian shirt and typed out a letter while they took some shots. The director made us go through the motions of being busy. Bob Tsuda kept his back to the camera except when he turned around and asked for a cigarette. Yuki and Emiko posed under our office American flag to lend inspiration to the scene. Lillian was too bashful. Jimmy, Taro, and I played "starring" roles with them. We told Mom that they are going to put the films in time capsules for man to dig up 10,000 years from now. Emiko also got in another picture in the grandstands. They were going to take pictures of Tanforan schools in action, but did not get the equipment set up in time and there were no students around.

June 23, 1942   Tuesday

Kenny certainly can pour out the copy, but Warren and I always doubted his sincerity. He was too interested in justifying his own personality conflicts. Although he has great potentiality as a writer, his defense mechanism was irritating to me, perhaps because I myself may have experienced the same. To me, it appeared that he was compensating for frustrating situations by plunging away like a "bull in a china shop" leading, as he sincerely believed, an "intellectual" cause—the fight against racial discrimination. He is still on the same track—very subjective and emotional. To him, the activities he lists such as the "Y" were a personal matter. He used it as a place where his emotional problems could be worked out, although he always denied this vehemently. He used to derive great pleasure out of his "sacrifices" for Nisei welfare. But to me, it looked like it was only himself he was interested in saving. He felt that he had to serve because he was hostage to a sense of guilt and unworthiness. He did it to reassure his own sense of insecurity, his states of anxiety. He was perpetually afraid for his own future. He constantly expressed his "dumbness" to us so that we could reassure him. He constantly sought out the pseudo-intellectuals among the Nisei. Last summer he believed that communism was the only answer to the "hollow mockery of democracy" and he used to take me to the rooms of the fellow travelers who amused me with their almost religious fanaticism. They lived in a world by themselves. Now he wants to go to Howard University to plunge into the Negro problem. I told him that he was doing this because he was afraid to face reality. He still is naive and never has been able to cut away from his mother's apron strings, a mother who "rules him like a tyrant." Evacuation won't be hard for him; he'll enjoy it because it gives him another cause. K. is a very maladjusted young man, like all Nisei who have more than average brains. His immaturity is his salvation.

.   .   .   .

No visitors were allowed in today because of Army orders to search all barracks for contraband. Rushed home to hide all the knives and tools. Went to Chief Easterbrooks to ask for a clarification of the order and he said that the search was necessitated by the fact that the luggage was not gone through at the time of our arrival. He had a whole pile of saws, hatchets, knives, and

Japanese literature in his office. He said that the tools were not collected because of the stealing of lumber here (10,000 square feet), but because they were "potentially dangerous weapons." Who in the hell would we attack anyway—the Japs surrounding us? The poor Issei have nothing left to read, except their bibles and religious books. They even collected anti-fascist literature translated into Japanese. Their interior police were not very consistent or thorough in their search. In the first few barracks they even went under the mattress and searched thoroughly, but by the time they got to ours they mainly knocked and asked if there were any contraband articles in the stables. Only the more timid gave up articles. The others figured that nothing could happen to them anyway since they were already prisoners. All Jap signs taken down. Hurrah!

.   .   .   .

Tom teaches Pop how to pronounce English words every night. He is getting very good at writing; he practices about 6 hours a day. His tenacity is surprising. He says he is doing it for my benefit so that he can explain his thoughts better to me.

.   .   .   .

June and no weddings yet! What about that 3 to 1 ratio of women to men now? The Nisei just aren't ready to take the plunge, the future being so uncertain.

.   .   .   .

Lately I've been getting that restless feeling again. I feel so useless at times. And I resent the term "white bastards" which I hear many of the Nisei using. And E. T. refers to the Jewish people as the "Kikes" who gypped hell out of the Japanese in the evacuation. Won't minority groups ever learn not to hate another minority group because of their seeking some scape-goat? This sort of thing can only lead to further hatreds and the Japanese here are in a swell position to get it right in the neck unless all of the minority American groups learn that their problems are common and should be worked out together for the future good of this country.

Roll call is a farce. They don't even check up; merely call in and ask if everyone is present.

June 24, 1942   Wednesday

Awoke to the blaring of the radio and almost got up to breakfast for the second time since I have been here, but didn't quite make it. It looked too cold and windy outside. The June Bay Area fog keeps the temperature down; nothing like the hot country. This time last year, I had just returned from Canada and was on my way to Reno with Jack in my little jalopy. We thought we would be in the army this year, little did we realize how our lives would be changed by evacuation. It was unthinkable, although Issei internment was a possibility. I wonder where that former Japanese captain who picked pears with us [is] now. We used to have such arguments. He was a member of the Black Dragon Society so probably is in Montana cooling his heels now.[47]

The radio announcer very dramatically told us about the 6 Japs arrested in Santa Anita for holding secret meetings and speaking in Japanese. The Army has definitely clamped down on Japanese even here. All of the Japanese signs were torn down today by the interior police.

In the paper today there was an interesting letter to the editor. The man ranted and raved that the Nisei should be disfranchised because they could never assimilate by intermarriage "because the Japs will always have those short arms." He stated that the Nisei have high birth rates and would soon outnumber and outvote the Caucasians unless they were all disfranchised and deported. Just can't understand the utter stupidity of some people. They would make good Fascist stooges.

.   .   .   .

[47] Many known Issei members of several ceremonial Japanese nationalistic and militaristic organizations, like the Black Dragon Society, were picked up by the FBI immediately after Pearl Harbor and were interned under suspicion for varying periods.

After the auditions we went over to the laundry for Horno's farewell party. He is leaving tomorrow for Tule Lake to work with Shibs. All of the communists and the progressives were around. Jack thinks they are queers. At least the aims are one. A Caucasian internal police came in and we shot the baloney for a while. He is an Italian-American, but he did not even know about the Tenney committee [48] and its *exposé* of the native Fascists in North Beach [an Italian section] in San Francisco. Nori got quite excited and mad at the idea that they were allowed to run around loose while loyal Americans like her were locked in by barbed wire fences—facing in—because of the yellow faces. A petition was signed for FDR asking for an opening of a second front. Bill Hata is the only reactionary on the paper staff and he refused to sign it this morning. He thinks that these matters do not concern us and that we should confine our energies to gathering material for the church groups, "who are the only friends the Nisei have"! All the time spent on world problems is time wasted, according to him. Bill got an honorable discharge from the U.S. Army just after the war broke out. He doesn't think much of the "radicals."

•   •   •   •

All of the [Town Hall] speakers dodged the main issue, except Vic. The Issei are not all loyal, that is foolish. All of the people I have spoken to state that the Issei still feel for Japan. Cannot blame them in a way but the future must be left in Nissei hands, sink or swim. Pre-evacuation days did not show Americanization of the Issei. They clung to their old traditions, had language schools, and even praised Japan. We can't wait until they become Americanized, if ever. We have to work right now. The Army is wise in forbidding Japanese in public meetings; this only encourages them to be more Japanesy. I feel sorry for the Issei fighting for their former positions, but they are too pro-Japan to be trusted with our future. The break with the past must be clean.

48 State Senator Jack Tenney for some years ran the spectacular California "Little Dies" committee, investigating "un-American" activities on the right and (especially) on the left.

June 25, 1942   Thursday

One of the 6 Japanese arrested at Santa Anita was the [assembly center] mayor! What a black eye for the Nisei, even if he were innocent! We can't afford these things and the safest way is to keep the Issei out of office. The morale at Anita is very low and dropping fast. They can't get enough workers to sign up to make camouflage nets. Probably this is primarily due to the low wage scale, rather than any proof of disloyalty. Morale is also dropping here with the recent contraband search, the ban of Japanese language, the row at the hospital, the maintenance crew still not being provided with shoes. Some of them are wearing gunny sacks around the holes in the shoes. But at the same time, people are too willing to accept the worst and do not realize that we have the best food of any camp, best roads, only camp to have cotton mattresses instead of all straw ticks, and the shoe and clothing requisitions have gone in.

June 26, 1942   Friday

Dr. Thomas wrote Fred and he says that she is sending us $15 for June and $20.83 for July. I feel like a heel taking it. Perhaps will be able to make some arrangement with her to let her keep the thing in a lump sum. I certainly don't want it here. It will only give me reason to put my prestige on a higher level. That is one of the chief things I notice about the others; they get a sense of self importance because they feel in a little better position than the other people in camp. I certainly can't accept money for doing nothing. There is no method or plan to my approach. I can't type the stuff up because of lack of privacy, too much noise with 9 of us here, and I wouldn't be able to concentrate. My correspondence is really getting neglected. My reading is done in snatches—sort of morbid to hunt up articles on the evacuation. Most of the articles say about the same thing. Trying to get the rest of the family to read more than magazines and funny books is hard. Jack is keeping up with current

events since he is now a teacher. He has an eye on Mitzi and
Lil now. Such a fickle guy; Dolores hasn't been down for about
a week and he is getting restless. Bette has her days full with
her young crowd. She does more reading than any of the others
and now she plans to read some current novels if I can get hold
of any. Today I was talking with her about the future and she
says that she would never go to Japan even if Pop and Mom
were deported because she just doesn't like the Japs and
couldn't get along with them. She feels that they are too conventional. Today she yelled, "Hey you Jap" at one of her
friends and the older Japanese were shocked and stared at her.
She said that she felt much closer to the family, but has more
quarrels than at home. She can't understand why Mom gets
cranky more than before. She thinks that she benefits a lot from
the family discussion. In Vallejo Emiko and she were the oldest
and they told Tom and Miyako what to do; but here she finds
that she has to contend with us. Alice sometimes takes advantage of it. Bette said that she resented it at first, but now feels
glad that we are here because we don't know what is going to
happen next. She believes that we will go back into normal life
after the war.

Alice is getting much easier to get along with since our talk
last week. More than anyone, she resented the fact that she is
not the head of the family any more, but has to be satisfied with
making decisions in a family council. She has a bad habit of
shaking her finger at Pop and telling him what to do instead of
respecting his feelings more. Pop came in this noon and asked
if shaking the finger was bad. We told him that it didn't mean
anything so he was satisfied. He accepts anything that Jack and
I say because "you have college education."

.   .   .   .

One indication of the tightening up by the Army is the sudden resignation of Police Chief Easterbrooks at 3:00 p.m. this
afternoon. John Yoshino, the press representative, said that one
of the interior police told him that Easterbrooks quit because
the Army thought he was being too lenient, and wanted him to

clamp down. He refused to do this on the basis that it was not necessary and that he was having little trouble with the residents, and that they cooperated. He was scheduled to speak at the joint Christian-Buddhist Mass Meeting tonight on our "moral responsibility." He used to give me all the crime news for the camp and appeared to have more of an interest in the people than the other officials.

.   .   .   .

One of the other rumors floating around is that two dead bodies were found at Santa Anita today. B. H. says K. N. told him. So I went out and started talking with her in the grandstands. She stresses Americanism and acts it in most respects; yet she has a few peculiar Japanesy ideas. For instance, she told me that she would not think of marrying any Nisei here in camp, because she respected her mother's wish on this matter. "You know, the Japanese have some set ideas about heritage and while here in Tanforan there is no way of checking up on a Nisei's background. How can I tell if he comes from a good family line?" K. referred to the Japanese custom of going back into the family records and investigating thoroughly for the past two or three hundred years. Certain clans are taboo and social ostracism will result in Japan if married into. The *Eta* group are the lowest on the social scale and even in America they are shunned.[49] One *Eta* family in Berkeley offered $5000 and a home to any Nisei that would marry the daughter, but no takers. The daughter was pretty sad, Mitch says.

I told K. N. that this practice should not be continued in America, especially here in camp where all must prove themselves on their merits. K. insisted that she would not oppose her mother on this point. I asked her if she would agree to an arranged marriage if her mother fixed it up, but she did not think so. K. is a Buddhist and somewhat conservative in her opinions. She has done two years of graduate work in history at U. C. and

[49] Generally living in segregated villages in Japan, the Eta often hoped to and in many cases did shed their outcast status in America. The care taken by Issei in their children's marital choices was great by American standards, and often resented by their children.

is now teaching in the High School. She is about 25 years old (guess) and not unattractive. She thought that Emiko would make a greater hit at the talent show "if she could only sing in Japanese." She believes in America, yet is a little confused and not willing to make a complete break. "How do we know what our future will be?"

June 27, 1942   Saturday

Today was one of those real hot days. We all sweltered in the heat. Saw the first shorts on girls, aside from the baseball field. The light, pale S. F. Nisei are certainly getting dark in this open air life. Soon it will be difficult to distinguish them from their country cousins. The girls are going in for sun baths and dark tans. They wear dark glasses to shade their eyes and go out in the grass in the infield to sun themselves. I don't know whether I prefer this heat to the wind. It seems so confined here. We just can't jump into a car and go swimming out at the beach or go into a nice air cooled theater. About all the people can do is go sit in the grandstands and watch the heat waves in the distance. They must really suffer in some of the other centers like Fresno and Merced. The infield barracks get very hot.

June 29, 1942   Monday

Heard over the radio this morning that 100 of the former restricted areas around power plants, etc., have now been reopened to the Germans and Italians under orders from De Witt. Implying that the danger of sabotage is now gone with the Japanese evacuated. The liberals around camp are disgusted as hell. They said that this action proves that evacuation was only on a racial basis, and De Witt's order is rank as hell. And just yesterday five German spies set ashore from a submarine on the Florida coast were caught along with some American-born agents who are being rounded up by the FBI. It doesn't make much sense. I believe the assembly centers should all be closed up and the government should give us a hearing right away and if found "loyal" be helped back into private life where we can be of some use instead of a financial burden on the government.[50]

.   .   .   .

The 50 constitutional delegates met in the House Managers' meeting tonight and it was well conducted. Guy Ueyama was chosen chairman and he conducted it according to parliamentary rules. The best organized group were the politically-minded liberals from Ernie's precinct. . . . The struggle for power was again evident. The liberals had skeleton outlines all planned from which they made suggestions. Katayama was there blowing his own horn as usual. The Issei are strong for an assembly to act as the legislative body and want to give it most of the power. This doesn't give much for the councilmen to do. Tod Fujita spoke in defense of the house managers who have been doing much of the administrative tasks in nature. Roberts' rules of order were followed so that the group could not get too far off the track. The Issei in back rows never said a word during the meeting, letting Ikeda be their champion. All of the Nisei spoke in English except Katayama who spoke of us as "Japanese" and the Caucasians as "Americans." The nerve of the guy; he should be in a camp for having such reactionary views, according to Jack. Three representatives from the administration and the internal police came in to see that nothing subversive was said.

June 30, 1942   Tuesday

Had a very busy day rounding up news for the paper so that we can get out on time. But Marguerite dealt us a harsh blow when she said that Davis has sent a rush order for 5000 cards to be mimeographed for the records on which scrip tickets will be issued. Free scrip books are a sort of standing joke among the Nisei; and the Issei just don't believe such a thing is possible.

---

[50] Selective rather than indiscriminate evacuation was the most that liberals could hope for before the relocation was set in motion. Afterward, theoretically quick release of those administratively determined to be loyal formed the basis of WRA policy, and in 1944 was the basis of the decision in *Ex parte Endo* (see Introduction).

Mom and Pop believe I am kidding when I say that each individual will be given an amount up to $2.50 per month, including children, by the government for purchases of necessities. And the idea of getting free shoes and clothing is beyond them. Mom said that one Issei woman told her that we would never get anything free from the U.S., but that Japan is paying for our protection.

Emiko does most of the art work for us now besides working in the mimeograph department. She has a knack of making those little drawings quickly. At H. S. she did all of the cartoons in the annual and was the art editor of the H. S. paper. She is also good at other things along artistic lines, but she is not much interested in a career. She would rather get married and settle down to a home life. She wants to get married at 19 and says that if she gets a chance then she will not hesitate since she might as well get all the happiness that she could. Evacuation makes no difference since love is of prime consideration with her. Last night I made a $5 bet with her that she would not be married at 23. This leaves her almost 6 years to go. She has a trail of boys interested in her now but she is too busy with her work. Recently she decided to get her own group so that she doesn't go around so much with Alice and Bette's friends, but the three of them still stick together a lot. Bette has expanded the most. She has a whole host of H. S. friends and is considered to be one of the most popular along with Pat and Tsuki. But Tsuki was sort of left out on the yell leading. They didn't encourage her to come and practice with them. Tsuki was formerly a yell leader at San Mateo H. S.   Professional jealousy.

At the Rally this morning, Bette and Pat did quite well in leading yells. Pat also gave a baton twirling exhibition. She looked a little awkward in the yells but was full of the old pep. Bette was a little more stiff. She looked more graceful however. She said that she was scared stiff to get in front of those 700 H. S. kids. The rivalry between the 30-odd H. S. is noticeable. The S. F. ones go around with a strut, and they are more outspoken and intelligent as a group. All of the talent in the Rallies thus far has come from the Bay Area Nisei. They are beginning to form little cliques. All of them think that their particular high school was the hardest. Bette is rapidly adjusting herself fully to this existence, although she still longs for the outside. Some of her Chinese friends came to see her last week and she gets many letters from her Caucasian high school friends.

Miyako is completely happy. She enjoys it very much out here in the country. She only writes occasionally to her friends since she is only 10 years old. She and Yuri do everything together. They even try to look and dress the same. They try to take the same classes and they like and dislike the same people. The only trouble we have with her is her temper, but she hasn't had a tantrum in over a week. In Vallejo she used to lock herself up in the closet when she got mad, but we haven't gotten around to building one for her here yet. Miyako is the leader of her group since she is stronger in body and mind and she decides what the other girls should do. She in turn does a lot of things imitating Bette and Pat.

Alice is more or less settled down in her secretary job. She still takes it seriously. She is going to work July 4th because "all government officials and offices will not have any more holidays for the duration." Angelo comes down to see her every Sunday and they shock the Issei by necking in public. She doesn't say anything about her plans to us. Jack had mentioned several times that she could go out to get married if she wanted to, but she apparently can't make up her mind. She and Angelo have talked it over quite a bit in their weekly huddles.

July 1, 1942   Wednesday   1:45

Two months here and I'm not feeling so rebellious this week. Time certainly can go by fast. The days hardly seem long enough to do everything I want to. Got to thinking today that all of the things we have been striving for can hardly be blamed since we are living in a Democracy—and a Democracy is not supposed to have everything all planned out in a concentration camp. That's why they call it a *center*. If things were cut and dried, life would be unbearable. But the full day's activity makes things rather interesting—even if only on an insignificant paper. But I suppose it does serve a certain purpose in the morale-building. For myself it is a good opening to get around and see what others are doing and talking to all sorts of interesting people, with all sorts of attitudes. Perhaps I feel good because I ate so well today.

.   .   .   .

My news note on Kochiyama got in the *Berkeley Gazette* via the *Totalizer*. First time we have hit the daily metropolitan press. Taro and I went to see Greene and argued him into letting us increase up to 10 pages. No doubt that we rank among the best among center papers. Administration thinks highly of it; no wonder, we paint a bright picture of things inadvertently. As long as I get my plugs on Americanism in, it suits me. Had to run around like hell to get news to fill the extra page. I slop the stuff in and let Jimmy rewrite and polish it up if necessary. I hate to stay cooped up there writing when I can be out and around. Bill covers sport and recreation, Jim and I education, Ben odds and ends, and administrative news has been piling up on me. Swiped some occupational survey figures, copied them, and returned the original. Gunder will throw a fit since he doesn't want to release anything until after completion, but we can't wait that long and I'm unscrupulous anyway.[51] Have got fair contacts with most of the administration and Taro makes me do most of the dirty work, but it inflates my ego to hear them say that they have to depend on me for the news.

.   .   .   .

Outside I can hear the swish of the cars as they go by down the highway. The barbed wire fence way below us reminds us that we are on the inside. On the other side of the highway there is a huge glass hothouse where they raise chrysanthemums and dahlias. The tiny men working hard way in the distance look like ants, but they are free men. The armed soldier, some lonely boy from the middle west, paces back and forth up by the main

51 Gunder, Kikuchi remembers, was "some sort of a guard for WCCA."

gate. In the sentry boxes, the soldiers look bored. They probably are more bored than the residents here.

Eight men came back from North Dakota to rejoin their families yesterday and their collective families greeted them with buckets of tears. Everyone was trying to tell each other how bad it was in a concentration camp—in North Dakota and at Tanforan. Lorraine's father was one of them. He was some sort of a merchant who did a lot of traveling around the country and in the deep south. As one of the "big shots" in the Japanese Association,[52] he was picked up when war broke out and shipped to N. D. Lorraine did not think that she would see him again as he was so old, so was greatly overjoyed when he got back.

In checking up on the number of visitors at the gate, I was burned up by a notice I saw on the wall. The police chief has ordered that all Negro visitors be checked closely and their slips be kept in a separate file. Evidently they think that there is a great danger of the Japanese stirring up the Negroes. (They call it race hatred.) Another list is kept separately for people that they want watched for one reason or another. People as they drive by look at us as if we were some sort of caged monstrosity. Over 7000 visitors have been here since May 14th and they include many professors from U. C., Stanford, Mills, S. F. State, and other Bay Area colleges. Many church and Y people also come down. The peak of the visitor rush has probably been reached and there has been a drop in the number in the past few days. A new system is being set up. Visitors are to be given blue badges when they come in and a previous application has to be made before they are allowed to come in through the gates.

Mom and Pop went up to interview for the barber shop, but Greene told Pop that he was a little too old. Pop protested that age did not make any difference because he was a "first class" barber. Greene told Mom that she could work if she wanted to on the girls' hair, but she did not want to do it alone. Besides, she felt that she had too much to do at home. We told Pop that

[52] The Japanese Association, extraordinarily influential during the period of Issei immigration but less so after 1924, was at its peak a voluntary association which directly or indirectly could coordinate the interracial efforts of a large majority of the Issei generation.

he could concentrate on his English lessons now. For the past few days he has not taken out his razors to sharpen them. We bring a few fellows home for haircuts occasionally just to keep him in practice. He took it surprisingly well; perhaps he is not saying what he must really feel. Being cast aside is not easy to take. It is fortunate that he has another interest to keep him occupied now.

Draft registration for the 18–20 years olds took place during the past few days, and 271 signed up from here. I asked the member of the Burlingame [California] draft board just what our status would be but he would not commit himself. He said that a ruling would have to be made by the federal government on the matter. Right now most of the Nisei have been placed in 4-C: aliens ineligible to citizenship.

July 2, 1942   Thursday

Another censorship note: McQueen put "seeming" in front of "injustice" in the editorial Taro wrote for the 4th. We tried to get Taro to run it with quotes around the word, but he thinks that this will only make our work more difficult as they will check us more closely if we did a thing like that. Perhaps he is right. Sometimes we react as a child who has had his candy taken away. On the other hand, certain principles are involved.

.   .   .   .

   Jack: "God damn you, turn the music off."
   Emiko: "God damn you too." Jack: "Go to hell." Emiko: "Go to hell too." Jack: "You son of a bitch" (laughing). Emiko: "You son of a bitch too" (mad). Bette: "Oh how vulgar this concentration camp is making you."
   Talent show just ended and the boy scouts are blasting away on their instruments in the grandstand playing patriotic music for the residents. What a racket.

.   .   .   .

Wang's opinion of me from the far-off sugar beet fields: "One thing everyone notices about you, Chas., is not any of your correctable faults; it is your intolerance. In a word, you are a damn Nazi. Yes, you are intolerant. Let the Japs use Japanese and be Japanesy if they want to be. Hell, they haven't but a few years on this paradise we call hell anyway. Hell, and it is a hell of a paradise, too. That uses up my quota of hells for the duration. You should read *What Makes Sammy Run?* (he was a Jew who hated Jews).

"What is an agitator? An agitator is a man, usually unpaid, who has given his life to the Cause, who tries hard but vainly to spread the gospel. The Cause may be one of a number of different Causes, big and small, ranging from the Communistic Cause to the Cause of Jehovah's Witnesses. Or it may be the Democratic Cause. Prime example: Charles Kikuchi. He will be persecuted by the administration and the people to whom he is showing the Light. The prophet, not Wang, has spoken."

Wang often likes to hear himself talk. Now that he is out of my clutches, he can philosophize, dear boy! He is trying to make me feel heroic, or he is pulling my leg.

July 3, 1942   Friday

The Council members are working very hard. They are still busy on the setup of the self-government system and so have not devoted too much of their time to other problems although they are taking more and more of the former activities of the house managers. Each councilman has his advisors and they help them with many of their problems. . . . A more important group are the communists. N. I. and group. They are intelligent. They have direct contacts with the Party, the CIO, and the Party Press. They are Ernie's Kitchen Cabinet. This group is important because they receive ideas from the outside. I know most of the group but haven't joined many of the discussions yet. Mitch is opposed to them on one point. He feels that evacuation is not a completely closed book as N. advocates.

N. says our efforts should now be placed on physical improvements. It looks as if they are following the party line of nothing to hurt the war effort in any possible way. Therefore, they are against Korematsu fighting his case and have approached him a couple of times in order to influence his decision. Jack says a party member is always distinguished by his "queer" looks. They do look different at that. There is something intense about them verging upon the fanatic. N. is about the most intelligent of the group. Then C. A. and another Kibei. The other three or four are mere satellites—E. fits in somewhere. A lot of the welfare of the Japanese could rest with the group with their outside contacts and they are quick to speak up here in camp through their speakers. But, they do not do much in physical activity, they do the thinking. And they support the liberal forces here whose ultimate goals are not entirely the same.

July 4, 1942   Saturday   Independence Day   11:00

I was talking to Mr. Besig, Fred Korematsu, Mitch, and C. H. when I saw Mr. Gunder rush up to the administration office. "Oh! Oh!" says I, "he is going to raise verbal thunder, that Gunder!" And then Nobby rushes down and tells us that Davis ordered that all copies of the *Totalizer* had to be collected at once. Taro was called up by Davis and given hell, but he wouldn't tell him what was wrong with the paper. I surmised that it was the employment story since I had obtained the figures by devious methods. And the Constitution story was a little doubtful. We had distributed the paper without getting the double check. The staff was lined up and told to see the house managers and get all the papers back in an hour. I spotted Mitzi going home for lunch so I temporarily lost interest in the proceedings and walked her home. The rest of them rushed around excitedly getting the copies back. The whole camp got in an uproar and they hastily read the paper to find out what was wrong. The house managers did not know what it was so they collected them very seriously. It will probably be the only time that the *Totalizer* got such a careful reading (Gonzales thinks it is the greatest morale builder in camp). Everyone was mystified. I met a few people on the way back from lunch and they asked me the reason so I told them that the army and Davis were cracking down because of one of the articles and from there the rumors began to grow. Some thought it was the lend-lease articles about goods intended for China ending up here. We finally found out from Davis that he objected to a part of the Constitution story and the scrip book item, which had to be changed. He said that he had marked it out, but we told him that there was no initial on the copy so we ran it as it was. Greene came up and he was very sympathetic. He even helped us unstaple. In order to stop rumors we decided to get the copy out as soon as possible and so spent most of the afternoon unstapling 2400 copies. About 300 copies were not turned in.

From now on the paper has to be triple checked. I saw Toby and asked him to bring up the matter of freedom of the press, within limits, and he will do so Monday. Davis allowed the occupational story to go through, but Gunder is still in an uproar about the whole thing. The two pages have to be run over tomorrow, on our decision. We haven't much to make an issue out of it and this was not the time to quit. The three articles in question were mine but Taro had to take the verbal lashing for it. Told Pop I was going to jail for the crime and they got excited for a while.

July 5, 1942   Sunday   12:00

Bob Iki and Fumi dropped over briefly this evening. He said that the "liberals" were trying to decide whether to blacklist the "Kremlin" bunch or not. He felt that they were getting the liberals tagged also. But since the liberals were in such a minority, it was his idea that we should not pull apart from them. He says N. I. is the brains of the group. I asked him why he did not get along with Mitch and he said that he was too immature at times and dogmatic. He even thought that Mitch would not get elected in the new assembly because he was over aggressive. We want to get as many liberals in as possible because we will be able to influence the Council. Since only Nisei will be able to run, Bob thought that Jack and I should try for the Assembly. The important thing was for the liberals to get known and into things because the future leadership will have to come from the young Nisei now reaching mental maturity. By the time the Council and Assembly get organized we will be on the way out.

July 6, 1942   Monday

These superstitious and gullible Japanese! Or it could be called the Blue Ghost of Hollywood Bowl. A Japanese couple living out by Bob Iki started the whole thing. Bob says she is a high grade moron. Yuki says he is her friend! Anyhow, last Friday this man was playing mah jongg with a neighbor when he thought he felt a fly on his leg. He reached down to brush it off casually and was chilled to feel something slimy and cold. This turned to terror when he saw a snake wrapped around his leg. He managed to kill the garter snake, but by the time the story had gone around it had been transformed into a rattle-snake!

That night the F.'s went to bed but he felt uneasy because the Japanese have some sort of superstition about killing snakes. While lying in bed they looked up at the ceiling and were terri-fied to see a faint blue eerie glow. They thought that it was some sort of a spirit so they ran to a neighbor and slept with them. It didn't take long for the story to get around and by breakfast time the crowd began to gather. All sorts of rumors spread around. They were retold in the messhalls, toilets, and wash-rooms. Some said that it was a ghost of a jockey who had been murdered. Others believed that it was the spirit of a departing horse. Some said that it took the shape of a monster and waved its hands around. After roll call, the mob increased to about 1000 people and the internal police force had to disperse them. The occupants of the stall moved out for certain that night when they saw it again over the board which had been placed over the spot by Bob Iki, who thought that it was a phosphorant glow showing through the wood. The police came and locked the room up, but some of the more curious broke the door open to get a view. Bob Iki went in and sure enough there was the blue glow. After all the stories about it being like the blue light seen near cemeteries in Japan, etc., he felt very uneasy. But they looked around for the cause until they finally located a tiny crack in the far wall near a beam. The moonlight from outside came through this crack and traveled behind this beam, emerging as the mysterious blue glow! So they boarded it up. Marie said that ten people have already moved out of the Bowl, and all sorts of stories are spread about its cause. Chief Davis had to go to the house managers' meeting this morning to clear up the whole thing. I never knew that the Issei were so superstitious. They must be extraordinarily limited in intelligence. All day long I heard different versions of the "ghost." It was the chief topic of conversation up in the school and Jack's class swears that it actually was a ghost. Sam says one of the Buddhist priests was so upset that he couldn't pray. Bob says many of the Issei still think it was some sort of a spirit. And here I have been telling everyone about the high intellectual level of this center. They are now calling the Hollywood Bowl by the name of Ghosttown!

Pop has another "suffering hero" mood tonight. Mrs. I. phoned from the office and asked the doctor to come see Mom. Dr. Fujita came over and she said that Mom had a pulled muscle and for us to get some alcohol for Mom to rub it with. Pop got all excited because his older children did not call the doctor and had to let our next door neighbor do it. He felt that this was a personal reflection upon the family. And Alice got in an argument with him over it so that he refuses to speak to Mom because Mom took Alice's part and called him dumb. To retaliate he tells Bette that Mom doesn't take care of him any more. He sat in the other room and practiced writing until after 11:00. Alice just can't realize that the incident itself is not the important point. Pop resents the fact that he feels he is being left out. So when Mrs. I. called the doctor, Pop assumed wrongly that Mom had consulted her without saying anything to him about it. He uses the "older children" argument as a front to cover his real feelings on the matter.

.   .   .   .

Taro and I talked to Greene for 45 minutes today and he is not such a bad guy. He has the right attitude towards the Japanese even though many of his ideas are a bit distorted. Greene feels that the Issei are a millstone around our necks. He feels that it is up to the Nisei now and blames much of the lack of assimilation on the Japanese alone. "You are Americans, but you have not entirely worked into our melting pot, but preferred to stay in your isolated communities. Things are not so bad here and you can contribute to the war effort by not causing too much trouble. You can handle your educational and recreational system completely. And you Nisei have a large task ahead of you to keep the young ones Americanized and not fall under the first-generation influence. The Issei are hopeless." Some of his illogic brought faint glimmers of smiles to Taro's face. But Greene is better than some. He was sympathetic about the whole paper mess and was a little griped at Davis. The whole thing probably goes back to the WPA politics.[53] Greene should have been made center manager (God forbid) or assistant, but both Davis and Estes got placed ahead of him. Greene says the welfare division has been started but all they will do is to take applications for clothes. "No case work is involved because it is not based upon need. Later I plan to put the division in with the barbers, beauty operators, and shoemakers down in mess-hall 19"! (This is his idea of social work—a clerical stooge.)

McQueen came up while we were talking to Greene and censored some of my stuff on "Your Opinion." He marked out fight fascism "from within as well as out" and Jimmy says that he is more anti-Communist than [anti-] fascist and considers

[53] The Works Progress Administration, where Kikuchi believed many of the WCCA employees had had their last bureaucratic positions, was known, especially among anti–New Dealers, for the inefficiency associated with makework projects.

Communism as the greater danger. It's not any use in bucking the army and I may as well take Taro's advice and become less excited about the whole thing.

July 7, 1942   Tuesday   12:00

Pop is still irritated. It seems that he feels that Mrs. I. butted into his affairs when she called the doctor for Mom. He says that he raised eight children and he knows when to call a doctor without having anyone else do it for him. The thing that set him off was the fact that she did it without consulting him. "What the hell! Me still boss." Pop thinks that Mrs. I. considers him a helpless old man not able to handle his family problems. We explained that Mrs. I. was a nice woman interested in the welfare of her friends and was only thinking of Mom's best interest. In such a community as this where there are such few doctors we cannot afford to take any chances. Pop realized this but the sore point was that Mrs. I. did not consult him first. He said he did not tell her off but was very polite for which we breathed a sigh of relief. "In Vallejo I would kick her out of my house; here live close and can't do." We stressed the point that this should be a democratic community where everyone should be interested in the welfare of his neighbors. Pop conceded, but was still mad. He was shaking with emotion for a while but cooled off. He feels that he is being neglected and compensates by a persecution complex at times. Basically it is a deep feeling of inferiority, covered by a seeming superiority complex. He never has gotten on with the Japanese and thinks that they are all cheats. Then again, it may be his strong feeling of individuality which makes him a non-conformist. Now that he is getting old, he uses every possible means to be prevented from being shoved aside. We understand that and have been trying to help him make the adjustment. He even wanted to go out and cut hair in the new barber shop, but after talking of all the possibilities he decided that it probably was not worth it. If he and Mom worked, then the children would get neglected. His argument was that he and Mom would make $24 a month. He even had it figured out to $288 a year. He said that we could save this money for after the war since he lost everything during the evacuation. We only got about $100 for the whole business (after 38 years of work). It is no doubt that Mom and Pop have been through a terrible mental strain. They came to S. F. without Bette and Tom who stayed on with Mariko taking care of them. (Mariko had lost her job as a necktie designer in L. A.) Miyako came to S. F. with them and they worried a great deal about economic problems, the kids in Vallejo, and what would happen next. Perhaps it wasn't the wisest thing to let Bette and Tom stay on in school, but they were so set on finishing their term and staying with their school friends. I put Miyako in the Raphael Weil School and she found friends right away. Now Pop is worried about how we will make a living after the war. He doesn't think that he will be allowed to take out a license in Vallejo again, but I keep re-assuring him that he will have no trouble. We told him that money was unimportant here; it was more important for him to make friends and learn English so that I could talk with him better about the family problems. Mom probably has varicose veins and has been laid up for the past 5 days. We told Pop that it was necessary for all of us to be in harmony and stick to-gether because we all had to share common problems. There-fore he should take care of Mom and not be mad and not speak to her. We told him in a democracy all people were equal and should be treated so, especially neighbors.

July 8, 1942   12:00

The chief topic of conversation these days is our next move. People are getting uneasy about it. A rush is being made to spend all the scrip books at the canteen because they won't be any good in the relocation centers. The residents all believe that they can't stand the hot weather. Most want to go to Tule Lake but this is not very likely. The majority, I suppose, just want to stay here in the hopes that the war will end quickly and they can all return to their former homes. But things just won't turn out that way.

.   .   .   .

Talked to Toby, Ernie, and the Council today and they gave me a lot of confidential crap on why they could not let us have their minutes. Ernie and Toby are the only two that are of any use; the other three are nice puppets. They tried to tell me that their minutes will be closed and that they would give me a "news release" for the paper after getting Davis to "ok" it. Then we take it and rewrite to suit space. Then we send it back to Davis for the second ok. From there it is to go to McQueen for the army "ok." Then we put it in the dummy and take it to Greene for final "ok." They certainly do trust us! The council-men tried to whitewash the administration and I told them that their duty was to represent the people who elected them, not to be glorified office boys for Davis. Ernie got the point. What is the use of having a sham form of self government? The Constitutional Committee was supposed to meet tonight and change the Constitution in compliance with the army regulations. Frank Y. wanted to make changes in it without even consulting the Committee, but Ernie told him that this could not be done. We are going to push the Council on this "closed minutes" deal. How else can we tell what they have been doing? They are not too hard to handle if one boosts their ego a little. Taro told me to take a day off because I got too much news for them. Strange how I get so involved in getting that paper out. At least it is one way of keeping morale up although very superficial at that. Taro and Greene will have a fit when they find out that I requested the Council to ask Davis to allow us to print the Constitution as an extra!

The paper is one way in which we can show the Americanization of the Nisei. For example: The *Berkeley Gazette* carried the Kochiyama item on his inheritance that I wrote up and it was sent to Mrs. Roosevelt who printed it in her July 5 "My

Day" column with the remark: "This should remind us that among the group are really good loyal Americans and we must build up their loyalty and not tear it down."

Tule Lake letters were censored for one day but Dr. Thomas says that it has been stopped and the man who initiated it is in hot water. What the hell do these lame brains think we are— prisoners of war?

Bessie says that Greene held up some Tolan Committee Reports in the post office and she had to go and insist that they deliver them. Tampering with the mail is a federal offense. Mitch is getting an extra set to put in the library.

Heard a new sidelight on the cause of evacuation by Morton Grodzins of the U. C. evacuation study. He says that as much as he hates to believe it, the accumulating evidence is beginning to indicate that it was not so much the pressure groups that forced the evacuation order, but the reverses in the southwest Pacific. Every time a strategic area was lost, there was a surge of public feeling against the "Japs" at home.[54] However, the Tolan Reports would show that it was the pressure groups that spurred this fever on and organized the movement and helped to mold the feeling along these lines.

Camp politics are not the only thing going on around here. Bette has a bunch of boys who are managing her campaign for vice-president of the student body. They have made over 200 little cards to pass out to the innocent students in the morning. A lot of posters have been made. One has a horse on it with the words: "Keep them riding, with Bette Kikuchi!" She is running against the girl who gave such a good talk on democracy at the H. S. rally the other day.

.   .   .   .

Dr. Thomas came down this morning to place a difficult proposition before us. She wants us to decide within a few days whether we would be willing to go to the Gila River [Arizona]

[54] But compare the emphasis in Grodzins's, *Americans Betrayed* (Chicago, 1949).

area on the U. C. study. She can only guarantee us wages for
a total of 6 months, with the possibility that the Columbia
Foundation will come through with some money. But money is
the least important consideration. She wanted us to talk it over
with our respective families and make a decision by Friday.
However, I stopped over to shoot the bull with Marii, Ernie T.,
Ann, and Mitch about the education possibilities in the relocation areas and did not come directly home from Town Hall. It
was 12:00 by the time I got in and I have been mulling over it
until now. And a god damned flea is distracting me. Maybe, if the
wind keeps howling outside, I can do some thinking on it. Left
a note on the light switch for them to wake me up early so that
we can discuss it in the morning. It's a tough nut to crack.
Strangely, I felt nothing when she told me. As far as I am concerned, it doesn't make too much difference where I go, but
there are nine of us and we all have individual problems to consider. Pop has diabetes and high blood pressure so that he cannot stand the heat; Alice is thinking of going to Chicago to
work, and if Angelo can get into the signal corps they may get
married; Jack wants to get out and go to school or marry
Dolores; Mom dreads the idea of moving all over again. And
so it goes. It's chiefly a psychological matter; I try to feel and
appear calm on the surface, but inside I am disturbed. There is
no doubt that adjustments will be difficult to make and if I
happen to get into a Japanesy group, I will become terribly unhappy. That is why I want to develop our family solidarity. It's
taken evacuation to finally bring about this to such a strong degree, in spite of bickerings and arguments. It's something I have
missed especially during the time I was in the orphanage (10
years) and then on my own through college and post-graduate
work at U. C. It never completely satisfied me. This isn't
escapism, but in times of great uncertainty, group loyalties become more intense for some unknown reason. Hell, maybe I
am afraid to face the future and not so confident and certain
like I try to pass off. Sometimes I feel almost frustrated, with
jangled nerves. Other times I get mad as hell and feel that I

am bumping my head on a stone wall. Then the sun comes out and I feel nothing or life may look like a clear vision. I keep saying to myself that I must view everything intellectually and rationally, but sometimes I feel sentiments compounded of blind feelings and irrationality. Here all of my life I have identified my every act with America but when the war broke out I suddenly find that I won't be allowed to become an integral part of the whole in these times of national danger. I find I am put aside and viewed suspiciously. My set of values gets twisted; I don't know what I think. Yes, an American certainly is a queer thing. I know what I want, I think, yet it looks beyond my reach at times, but I won't accept defeat. Americanism is my only solution and I may even get fanatic about it if thwarted. To retain my loyalty to my country, I must also retain family loyalty or what else have I to build upon? So I can't be selfish and individualistic to such a strong degree. I must view it from either angle and abide by the majority decision. If I am to be in a camp for the duration, I may as well have the stabilizing influence of the family. If I go my own way again at this time, it will be the end as far as the family is concerned and they may feel that I ran out on them in a time of crisis. If they were holding me back, it would be another matter; but actually they are shoving me forward. The family setting gives this whole thing a more normal balance. When I feel the need to break away, I will go, but I don't feel it is necessary or wise right now when there is no need for it. The single men alone in camp here are not stabilized to such a degree as those with good family relationships. I suppose I could go out to school, but that is escape into an Ivory Tower and I am too curious to miss all this. Actually, it is exciting and there are opportunities. Something fine will come out of this, I am hoping. If we degenerate, we are lost. Gods, Chas, quit trying to dramatize and get back on the beam!

Anyway Thomas consulted the WRA and it seems that three possibilities are open for us:

1. We can stay on and take the chance of being cut off from the U. C. study (not important in making the decision) because

we probably will be relocated out of this area. Tanforan will most likely be split up anyway. Personally, I would rather travel a distance. At least I can get to see a little more of America and it's more adventurous and pioneer-like. Debit: We don't know where we will go.

2. We could go to Gila River at the request of Dr. Thomas. The climate is hot for two or three months of the year but good for the rest of the time. We will get there right in the midst of the hot spell (good ole S. F. fog, how I will miss it!). The physical setup will be the best and Dr. Thomas assures us of a good administration. This place will be the check study and we will be allowed to work along independently in our study. Some of this group may go there, but not likely. This means that new contacts will have to be made again which takes time. Debit: Pop can't stand extreme heat.

3. Finally, it may be possible for her to get us to Tule Lake, but this center will definitely not be going there. There is a good administration, but not so good physical facilities as in Gila. Extreme cold down to 27° below. Debit: The people there are more Japanesy and [I] would find it harder to break in. The main study is located there and we will have to be under supervised direction. This is too restricting. This place is as isolated as Gila if not more. We have to work in the center also so that choice openings may all be taken. But, it is in California and family may think it is most desirable for this reason.

Parker Dam (Poston) is improbable for the Tanforan group. Colorado or Arkansas possible if this center goes last. Gila sounds the best, but other four members of study object from what they said this afternoon.

Thomas wants decision (favorable) by Friday. Now to work on the family and present the case to them. It has to be the group decision that will be final.

Attended a most boring Town Hall meeting tonight. The idea is good, but the speakers were lousy. I'll probably be much worse next Wednesday. Midori S. is supposed to take the negative side with me on the question of remaining single in camp. I really don't believe in this side, but am doing it as a duty.

July 9, 1942   Thursday

We had our family discussion on whether we should go to Tule Lake, Gila River, or remain here. I told them that personally I did not care and it would be up to the majority. Pop did the most worrying and he is taking it most seriously. He is still up thinking about the matter. Jack doesn't care; he thinks the heat will be too much for Pop at Gila, and questioned whether asbestos walls would be provided. Alice is in favor of going to Gila because of practical reasons. Pop wants to be near a big city where he can get special foods, he doesn't want it too hot or too cold due to his old age, diabetes, and high blood pressure. I had to draw a diagram for him to explain how low 27° below zero was. He doesn't feel that he has any say in the matter as the government will make the final decision. He would rather stay in Tanforan where the climate suits him but realizes that this will not be possible. If he leaves, he has an idea that Tanforan may become a permanent camp. We told him that this was definitely out. He looks very bewildered. The reaction is similar to the days when evacuation orders were awaited with so much anxiety. However, he has decided that he will go where the family wants to go. I explained that we may not go at all since Earl was the only other one in the U. C. study group that favored leaving. Fred H. wants to stay here because he knows a couple of girls and wants to get married. Doris wants to go to Tule Lake. Ben wants to stay here because he wants to go out to school. Earl wants to go to Gila because this will be his chance to escape his mother.

In any event, Mom is not fit for any traveling at this time. She has been in bed with a bum leg for a week. Since she has come here, she has been ill off and on constantly. Emiko and Bette want to go to Gila, Tom wants to go to Arkansas, and Miyako wants to go back to Vallejo with her other friends at school. Breaks are hard to make. Heat seems to be the primary consideration. Colorado, Arkansas, or Utah seems to be the choice of the family from the climatic point of view. I wonder where we will end up? The vote was Gila 4, Tanforan 2, Tule Lake 1. We took a secret ballot.

July 10, 1942   Friday   1:50

Mr. Davis must be getting tired of reading all our copy. He takes his time and I have to spur him on via his secretary. After we got our main material back, a little at a time, we sent up some old stuff that we will not use in the hope that he will get tired of reading our stuff so many times for objectionable items. I asked Ernie I. to tell Davis that the present method of censorship is an added handicap and a better arrangement would have to be made. The council doesn't get as much attention as we do. We are not carrying anything in the paper about their activities this week because they were so secretive about their minutes. Toby brought some news releases from the council, but I had all of them already—from reading Ernie's minutes while I was in the council's chamber this morning. Ernie doesn't think much of the other councilmen because they are too willing to kowtow to the administration. They work hard, but it seems to me that Davis is shoving a lot of the routine work on them such as setting up the organization of the laundry shop and clothing distribution.

The council met this morning, but I only got in on the tail end. The Issei were allowed to serve on the Constitutional Committee since the idea was to get the final ratification on the Constitution. The age qualification for running for assemblyman was raised to 23. Mitch, Marie, Jack, and 4 other Nisei objected, but the Issei voted them down. Ernie got Davis' approval for us to run the Constitution off as an extra next week so I went down and requisitioned 120 more reams of paper through Greene. He doesn't know that I put in another order through Mr. Merz of the Supply Department. At least we won't run into the difficulty of running short on paper again for a while. Greene has washed his hands of the paper now so that we won't have to contend with his objections any more, we hope. We want to get the Constitution out so that residents can keep it as a souvenir! From the way the council is being ignored, it doesn't look as if the Assembly will mean anything. At least expressions of feeling will be heard through them.

Last night I appeared on the talent show as one of the participants in the quiz program and I missed the 32 cent question by saying that a woman's heart beats slower than a man's. The *Totalizer* staff had a notice on the door this morning saying that I had disgraced their fair name and was fired! I certainly had to take a ribbing from them. Some man from the health department came in and he told us that the milk companies that sent in the pint bottles of milk here have threatened to stop sending milk unless the residents refrain from urinating in the bottles! It makes the sterilization more costly. I was surprised that the Japanese would do such a thing. But I suppose it is such a long way to the latrines for some of them and so they grab the nearest container handy. Many families have chamber pots for this purpose, especially if one member is aged, crippled, or ill. It is such a great convenience. It gets windy and cold at night. Since there are no individual toilets in these stables, various systems have been devised. But urinating in the milk bottles is a pretty bad thing.[55]

.   .   .   .

When Pop thinks about the heat there [at Gila River], he worries all over again. He asked me if it was like the Panama Canal, full of mosquitoes and snakes. He was at Panama for a short time during the time the canal was being dug and he said that all of his friends died from the fever. He came back to the U.S. as soon as he could get a berth on a boat. Panama was one of the ports where he got his prejudiced unfavorable opinions about white women. That was one of the reasons why he would never let Mom out of the house in Vallejo when he first

[55] Kikuchi was later (July 22) to report that "the source of the urine in milk bottles . . . [was] traced to the Protestant church where the elementary children receive free milk daily. . . . The parents will have to pay for the damages."

got married. In other words, he never did associate with a good group of Americans in his early days here, except perhaps for his contacts in the U.S. Navy. He has his honorable discharge framed and hung on the wall in the stable. I told him that the government was planning wisely in these relocation centers and the sanitary conditions would be well taken care of. I hope nobody will start to tell him about rattlesnakes now! His final words before I left for the office after lunch were: "Me old now but start over with family. You 'hana' [young sprout] and John take care of Emiko and Bette and Miyako and Thomas now. I no say nothing." But I could see that he was worried yet. Mom is taking it more calmly. Bette: "Gee whiz, I wanna be the vice president." Jack: "Well, let's pack up and go. We can make friends easily enough. All of our present friends are new here and it doesn't make much difference where we go as long as we stick together." Emiko: "Gee, I feel funny about it, just like leaving S. F. for here. Heck, we won't get our free clothes either." Mom: "I no vote. Papa fight if I say yes so go with my children." Miyako: "Is Yuri going to be with us?" Me: "No, I don't think so." M.: "Oh gee!" Tom: "I want to go to Arkansas and see the Arkansas travelers. I don't want to be a desert rat, but I'll go to help build good shelves for you."

I didn't get in until almost two and Pop was lying at the foot of Tom's bed, wrapped in his overcoat and smoking that pipe, which he has been using for the last 25 years. I could see that he wanted to talk so I sat down for a few moments. He wondered again if the government intended to send us to the desert so that we would all die off, seeing that the Japanese could not stand heat. So I had to go through the whole thing again. He was so easily convinced that I became suspicious and wondered what he really wanted to talk about. He hesitated for a while and finally said that he wanted to talk to me alone at the latrine after the roll call tomorrow evening. It seems that he had another argument with Alice. I said it was late and that I would talk about it tomorrow so he went to bed.

Jack woke up for a few moments and he said that Pop wanted to turn full authority over to me and Jack, but Alice objected and treated him like a child and he got very angry because he thought that Mom put her up to it. He thinks Bette and Emiko are getting bad because they go out so much and want us to control them more. Jack said some of his arguments were very illogical. Pop probably is getting confused with all sorts of psychotic fears. He never says anything to Emiko and Bette any more, but expects us to take care of the situation. We have more or less been ignoring it because they are normal and can't help it if they make friends. Things are so unsettled that they have been finding release in all of these social activities. And the school here is not conducive to studying. Further, it is summer vacation now.

July 11, 1942   Saturday

The whole family problem was aired tonight. I met Pop for a conference out by the *Sumo* ring. At first I was going to discuss it lightly, but it dawned on me that he had been brooding on the thing for quite a while. He is trying desperately not to be rejected and this has been one of the main causes of friction with Mom. He told me all sorts of stories about how unfaithful she was and that she wanted him to die so that she could be free again. He is 17 years older than Mom and so feels that she is ashamed of him. He has built up all sorts of imaginative stories in his mind, and this was one chance in which I had an opportunity to practice social case work. He felt resentful against Alice because she stood up for Mom, and last night's argument was almost the exploding point. He said that he waited up for me last night to tell me that he was going to hit Alice. He was grateful for all that she had done in the past, but he could not stand being talked down to. "God damn. I mad. She think me dumb, no head. Me have very best head. Haruka [Alice] no listen. She too sassy. What you think, I go hit her now?" It was all I could do to persuade him to talk himself out of this resentful anger. It has been accumulating for quite a while and had reached the breaking point. He spoke with such hatred of his relationships with Mom and it made him see red when Alice would not consider his side at all. He said Mom was cold to him and wanted him to die; that she thought being a barber was low class so that he should not do it here; that she was too proud to walk with him in public because he looked like an old man; and that he really loved her after marriage but she did not care for him, making him crazy with jealousy and resulting in his trying to get a response by being mean. He said that at one time when Mom went to S. F. for a divorce he almost killed the four children and planned to commit suicide. That was one of the reasons why he never lived among the Japanese—because he feared that the men would try to steal his wife. I let him release his pent-up feelings and then tried to get him to advance some solution. He wants me to handle the problem of Bette and Emiko and their running around with boys. For Mom and Alice he would not budge an inch. He even wanted to go to another camp or else be left behind. Finally he accepted a decision that the best thing to do would be to talk it over with all the older children and Mom. He absolutely refused to do this, but thought we could get some measure of family solidarity if I could talk to Alice. He did not think that it would be any good because Alice was too sassy.

After the festival, 11:00, I talked with Alice and explained the whole setup. Emiko and Bette listened in and I told them that they would also have to consider Pop's feelings more and talk with him occasionally so that he would not feel completely left out of everything. I told Alice that an aged person undergoes a difficult period of adjustment just previous to retirement and is not willing to be shelved.

In the meantime Jack talked to Pop trying to indicate the necessity for family unity in order not to affect the personality development of Miyako and Tom. So we got Pop and Alice together. They sat on my bed and Pop explained his feelings and why he did not want to be treated as a baby. Alice cried and they talked for about an hour getting all straightened out. I tried to explain the situation as best I could to Emiko and Bette and I think that they have some sort of understanding now. We felt that this was the most opportune time to get him together with Mom. We had to play on his ego and explain why he must give Mom another chance for the sake of the whole family unity. Pop thought that this was no use. He wanted to be left behind, but we told him that he was needed to do the important thinking for our family, which would fall apart or split without him. Even though it was 1:00 a.m., we insisted that Mom be awakened and the matter discussed with her. We thought it would be better if Jack and I did the intermediary work and the girls just listen. Pop finally consented to talk it over so we all went in Mom's room. Jack explained everything to Mom. We said that the fault was on both sides and that from today on they should decide to make a new start. Mom caught on at once and she said that it would make her glad to have the air cleared up and that she would pay more attention to Pop. Pop did not think it could work although he would be very happy if they had better relationships. We said that this would be up to him. Pop thought maybe they should split up and divorce, but we assured him that it took more courage to face and work out his problems. Gradually he began to get less stubborn and more open to reason. We laid the whole thing up to him. With the placing of everything upon him, he assumed more importance in our eyes, so that he began to reason a little again. It wasn't an easy job and we had to talk like "Dutch uncles."

Around 2:00 a.m. he finally said he would also try to be friends with Mom and it looks like new adjustments will be made by both him and Mom. I suppose all of this time was really worth the end result. Only hope that it lasts more than a few days.

July 13, 1942   Monday

I got to the office real early this morning (8:15) so that Taro would have the Constitution to work on. But Jimmy had gone home with the keys yesterday and as usual he overslept. We finally had to send Nobby after him with a club. I fooled around with my "Your Opinion" column and then talked to Alice S.

for a while. She is a member of the "Party." She is starting a movement to help the war effort by getting the residents to buy one or more packs of cigarettes with the scrip books, and then re-selling them through the committee at social affairs, to be paid for in cash. This money would be sent to buy medical supplies for the boys overseas. We thought that this was a very good idea so we gave or promised to give one or more packs. Mitch came in and he thought that we should start a move to donate 10% of our scrip books back to the army as our part in the war. Then he suggested that we should find out whether we could buy war stamps with them. At this time, this is not possible. I know that many people would be interested and willing to buy stamps if this were possible. We recognized that all of this is part of the flag-waving stuff, yet sincere. And since we are expected to be more loyal than President Roosevelt, it is these things that indicate evidence to the public that we are American. The Pomona center recently collected about $200 in their USO drive. Here, the house managers sponsored a rubber drive and a few people gave their worn out shoes. The rubber matting going up the stairs into the social hall has also been torn out.

.   .   .   .

Henry T., H. S. principal, came in and he sort of kidded Ernie along because he thought that his teachers were giving the students so much. "After two months can you actually say that you have taught them anything new? All we are doing is reviewing what they have had before. You can't expect much more from us. We have a long way to go and we need plenty of outside help. Let the State pay for good facilities and salaries for competent teachers and we will learn in time."

Wandering around in the classrooms by our office I think Henry is right. The front row pay a lot of attention; children in back fool around and try to attract the attention of the pupils in the next classroom. And I overhear many remarks that they are not learning anything. They don't have confidence in their teachers; it's a psychological thing. How can the Nisei be expected to discuss social subjects when they have had limited contacts with such things. Most of the teachers have just come out of school and they use such an academic approach. In fact they already consider themselves as members of the teaching profession. The other day while the scrip books were being distributed, one of the teachers came down and wanted to get her book quick. She was directed to the workers' line. "But I'm not a worker, I'm an educated person!" was her remark. This indicates in a way that they are placing themselves in a high class by themselves. Ann says that this sort of thing is increasing very rapidly. They want to be known as the "faculty" and put down any attempts at familiarity as if their dignity is at stake. Johnny I. of the Jr. Hi is more practical. He realizes that his teachers are not 100% competent and he says so. Jack says that they have near-riots in some of the elementary classes. This was not in Ernie's report. He wants to shove the Nisei teachers ahead too fast and they are nowheres ready yet. It may be that he is also shoving Mr. Ernie T. ahead at the same time. He has good ideas but he should keep the "I did this and I told the WRA to do that" stuff out of it. Otherwise, he will only harm himself.

July 14, 1942   Tuesday

The whole family is beginning to get into the excitement state of packing, but nobody wants to start. Emiko bought a couple of cardboard boxes from the supply room, but we need strong wooden boxes to crate our accumulated belongings together. Jack and Bette even want to take "our" linoleum with us, but I thought that we would perhaps be overburdening ourselves. There is a chance that we may be able to find some there. The Gila project is still uncompleted and people won't be moving in until the 25th. We decided to take the dressers, but the table might be a little too awkward to handle. Ann wants one of our barrel chairs.

Our home certainly has changed since the day we first entered here. We have a table and some chairs in there. Apt. #5 is

Apt. 5		Apt. 4	
		Door	Window
Front room		CK Front room	J
	T		
	M		E
Back room	X	Back room ·	X
Mom Pop		B A ·	
X X		X X	

Pop and Mom's and Miyako and Tom's side. Tom sleeps in the front room which is also used as a kitchen. On the sides we have the shelves and closets. Tom has some books, a radio, and odds and ends around his bed. Our toothbrushes, towels, and dirty laundry occupy the other corner. Pop, Mom, and Miyako sleep in the back room. There are two home-made closets for their clothes, plus a lot of our trunks and boxes. Pop keeps his little toilet chamber in the front corner since it is difficult for him to walk all the way to the latrine at the far end of the building. Five of us stay in apt. 4. Jack and I occupy the front room with our army cots. The "Tanforan" club bureau is at the foot of my bed by the side door. The bar desk is in the other corner. In the middle of the room we have the table Jack made. Home-made chairs and benches are scattered around. Miyako usually accumulates a lot of her junk on our dresser. At the head of Jack's bed, we have piled some more trunks.

On my side I have a shelf for my books, magazines, and radio and a lower shelf for the lamp, art objects, and diplomas. My pot-bellied "Buddha" stands guard over my head. The walls are decorated with college banners and painted scarfs. Jack has a shelf for his books on the wall over his head. Most of the books and magazines are stacked on the desk built at the foot of Jack's bed. Yesterday, Alice finally got around to putting the curtains up.

We have taken the stable door down and a curtain has been placed between our rooms. Emiko, Bette, and Alice sleep in the back, two of the beds are put together. On the wall there are a lot of maps to brighten things up a bit. The two closets are jammed full of our clothes and Emiko takes up most of the space. Jack and I only have 1/3 of one closet and she needs 2/3. We put our good clothes away in our trunks. Jack's bureau with the large mirror is at the foot of Emiko's bed. The phonograph is between her and the other two on top of the linen box. Shelves have been put up for odds and ends. Emiko has her framed H. S. diploma hanging on the wall. Some more trunks fill up the remaining space.

My room is used as the social room, study room, and barber shop. Pop usually lies around on Tom's bed. He never bothers us although we make it a point to introduce him to all our friends that come over. Today he was feeling more sociable so he did a sort of jitterbug dance with Miyako in front of Bette's friends.

.   .   .   .

Alex came in this morning and wanted a big write-up on the Bon Odori festival which the Buddhist group is putting on.[56] It is a folk dance and has some connection with the Buddhist religion. We got into a very heated argument when Taro and I said that this was worthy of burial in the most insignificant page. Alex contended that we needed these Japanese sort of things. I told him that he was not being very realistic. Although I had nothing against the better part of the Japanese culture, I did not consider this an opportune time to stress Japanese culture. I told him that the Buddhists should stress Americanism more since the group has been looked upon so suspiciously. Alex contended that the festival was necessary for camp morale. This is a lot of hooey; it is only an evidence for the Caucasian

56 The Bon Odori festival honors the spirits of the dead.

public to believe that we cling to Japan and don't want to Americanize, unfair as that may be. Alex admitted that the Buddhist group were more conservative but he could not see the harm in encouraging Bon Odori now. I thought a camp-wide folk dancing festival, without religious lines, would have been a better plan. In this respect, Alex is a little conservative. But otherwise he is fairly liberal. He used to go fishing in Alaska with the CIO union men; was active in the YD's and wrote a column for the *Nichi Bei*.[57] His father owned a little restaurant in Oakland.

.   .   .   .

Marie, Ann, Mitch, Jimmy, Jack, and myself got into a long discussion about how much democracy meant to us as individuals. Mitch says that he would even go in the army and die for it, in spite of the fact that he knew he would be kept down. Marie said that although democracy was not perfect, it was the only system that offered any hope for a future, if we could fulfill its destinies. Jack was a little more skeptical. He even suggested that we [could] be in such grave danger that we would then realize that we were losing something. Where this point was he could not say. I said that this was what happened in France and they lost all. Jimmy suggested that the colored races of the world had reason to feel despair and mistrust the white man because of the past experiences. The treatment of minority groups even in this country is contradictory to democracy. Jack thought this was the reason why so many minority groups did not feel for democracy, because they have never had it. He said that before we could do anything, race prejudice had to be eliminated, and he did not see how this was possible. Marie said this feeling of hopelessness was one of the reasons why many Nisei were rejecting patriotism. But this was a negative approach. A lot of things would be cleared up if the Caucasian Americans showed their good faith by letting the bars of immigration down and by giving the Negro a democratic chance. Asia would never trust the U.S. unless we showed good faith at home first. Ann thought

[57] A San Francisco Japanese daily.

that it was worth the fight to make democracy right and eliminate the patronizing attitude of the white man. Whether America could shake off the stupid mistakes of prejudices was something that none of us could make a definite answer upon. We did not know whether economic greed would still be the dominant end of these nations at war. We hoped and believed that the world would be changed for the better, under a democratic system. Jack thought that this was not being practical enough, but the rest of us could not agree to that. Jack ate almost a whole box of crackers during the conversation.

July 16, 1942   Thursday   12:10

I was down at the gate talking to Mr. Rodney today to get some data on visitors. He did not have the exact figures so that I had to go through the whole list and count them. He says that a lot of people come there to look at the menagerie, but he won't let them in. I happened to glance at the wall and I saw three names on the wall. These people were not to be admitted under any circumstances. One of the names was Helen Gahagan.[58] I asked him if this was the singer and movie actress (wife of Melvyn Douglas) but he shut up like a clam so I did not press the point. There is another man in the office who sticks a long needle through all of the packages (for smuggled weapons and contraband). The inspector is very dumb. He stands there and argues with the visitor without explaining why he takes the packages and does not return them. It really is for the visitors' convenience since they are delivered directly to the residents by truck, but the inspector gives the impression that it is all [confiscated as] contraband.

---

58 Helen Gahagan Douglas was a noted California liberal who served in the House of Representatives from 1945 to 1951. She was defeated in a bitter senatorial contest by Richard M. Nixon in 1950. The political left in Hollywood was among the best known targets for rightists in the late 1940s and early 1950s, and Mrs. Douglas's defeat was an occurrence of national import.

July 18, 1942   Saturday   12:35

Bette cleaned up the house, but she appeared a little cool so I
did not say much to her, although she tried not to show it she
was greatly disappointed about not getting to go to the dance.
This afternoon they all went out to take a sunbath on the infield. After dinner they came over in the hopes that there would
be a last moment relenting. Jack said that he did not care if she
went and he asked her if she still wanted to go. Although she
had been saying all day that she did not care she answered with
a hurt "sure I do!" This is the one time that she did want to go
because of her new-found crush. It made me feel like an old
meanie for taking Pop's side so I went and asked him if he
would mind. He said that he did not want Bette to be going to
dances because of her age. I almost was going to say for her to
go, but Alice said that perhaps it would be better not to let her
have her way by pouting because she would do it every time.
Pop says he wants Jack and me to take all the responsibility—
at the same time he emphasizes that Bette is too young. Jack
says he doesn't care; which places the responsibility on me and I
don't want it because her feelings are unconsciously vent on me.
God, I would hate to be a parent. And to top things off Jack
goes to the dance. He put on a show about how excited he was
to take a 25-year old girl to the dance. I was going to take Marie,
but I felt guilty about going myself while they stayed home. I
did not say "no" to them, only "Well I don't know, you had
better ask Pop." Pop knows he will weaken so he wants us to say
it for him. Emiko took it surprisingly well. She didn't even blow
up or say anything. A lot of the young kids started to drop in.
I had intended to do a little writing, but it was too noisy so I
got dressed and went over to Marie's. I don't know why I feel so
funny and think about the situation. Perhaps I am a little disappointed in Bette because I expected much more of her. I have
always wanted her to go on to college, but I can see that relocation camps are going to make her lose interest. Here she has so
many social functions to compete with that she is losing interest

entirely in schooling. Although she would be the last to admit it. The environmental circumstances just make it that way. Bette has a great intelligence and she would regret it later if she did not do something with it starting now. The amount of her present reading is limited to funny books and movie magazines, a great comedown from the sort of books she read before evacuation. An overemphasis on dancing is not going to make her a well-rounded person in the long run.

·   ·   ·   ·

I was sitting in the toilet today when an old Issei came in. He took some tissue paper and scrubbed and scrubbed the seat for about three minutes. Then he carefully laid some more paper on it. This done, he then took down his pants and sat on the toilet next to the one he had cleaned! What an absent-minded person. I looked funny at him and he suddenly discovered his error and blushed like anything. With a silly grin, he said, "What a dumbbell I am, né?"

July 19, 1942   Sunday   11:30

I went around asking the question: "What do you think will be the greatest problem facing the world in postwar America?" The surprising part was that so many had given it no thought (19), and about half were college students. They just didn't want to think about it. Some thought that it was hopeless. Most of the people I asked had something to offer and the general opinion was that there was hope and that the Nisei would meet the test. One person thought that the psychological problem was the largest and that all the rest would stem from it. The majority were of the opinion that getting a job was the basic problem. One believed that the Nisei should go back to their old Japanese towns and pick up from there, while the rest favored a scattering of the group. Several feared that the isolation of the resettlement camps would make the adjustment back into the normal life a most difficult task. Acceptance into the American society was another big worry. They felt that the Nisei never had been completely accepted and it would be that much more difficult if we were taken away from the mainstream of life for several years. Two believed that cooperatives were the only answer to the problem and advocated that they go to the Middle West and join the Caucasian cooperatives.

.   .   .   .

So many rumors are going around about when Tanforan will be cleared that I decided to start one of my own. I told a couple of fellows that I had confidential information that 1000 of the ablest and youngest Nisei were going to be drafted by the army and sent to Alaska to build a road as a defense measure against Jap raids. By early evening I heard the rumor again, only this time the story had grown to a road made from Mexico to Alaska and all the Japs in the U.S. were going to be put to work making it.

July 21, 1942   Tuesday   12:30

It seems that my week will be very full. Sunday night: party; Monday: folk dancing; tonight: precinct meeting for nomination of Congressmen; Wednesday: Town Hall; Thursday: lecture; Friday: invited to party held by the file clerk girls or work on paper; Saturday: dance; Sunday: invited to party. And yet the social activities are meaningless—they seem so unreal. But it is so difficult to read. Somehow, it seems that nothing matters any more except the war and the future. I know I am disturbed. On top of that I resent this unreal environment and the people who look like they accept it. I also know that adjustments would be more difficult on the outside. I'm trying to escape reality at the same time I face it. It doesn't make sense. Sometimes I get such an awful empty feeling; my nerves are so jangled. Waves of resentment come over me at the funniest times. Outwardly, I try to pass off as adjusted to this setup, but things happen or I read something which brings almost a violent reaction. The psychologists would call it frustration, I suppose. The only stabilizing thing in this whole mess is the family. I am afraid that I would go to pieces except for them, in spite of arguments. Other people I have talked to say much the same thing. It may be due to an unconscious feeling of loss so we clutch on to what we do have. Fear of the future?

Yet I don't honestly say that I am unhappy here; but here is only a short time. We still have a long future. My self-confidence has taken a jolt. I'm not really doing what I had hoped to do. And the Japanese language looms up as an inescapable obstacle. Will it always be my Waterloo? Every time some Issei addresses me with the lingo, I feel like a damn foreigner. It should be the other way round, but that is intolerance. Friends from the outside say that I will be of great use to the Nisei, but I sometimes doubt that. The thing I want to do—Americanization of the group—is not going fast enough. I get so impatient. Then I have to catch myself or else assume a smug feeling of superiority over those "Japs." But pointing the finger of scorn is not the answer. I think I can see the road clear ahead of me; then doubts about the Caucasian-American good faith enters. In short, I am a very confused young man.

Events of the past few days may have something to do with that. They sent a car down for Mom today.[59] Bette was home to go up with the car. Goro S. and Rick M. came up to the door, but they had no stretcher. Mom insisted that she could walk to the car. The ride to the hospital was bumpy. Mom did not say anything about the severe pain in the region of her stomach. She tried to walk to the medical room, but collapsed.

Bette waited around outside for the news. She thought it was a routine checkup. Drs. Fujita and Togasaki came out. "Your mother had better not travel," they said, "she is weak from the loss of blood and her blood pressure is extremely low. It is caused by fibroids of the uterus." "What's that?" asked Bette. They then told her that Mom had tumors. Just the thing we had feared. Mom has to go to the San Mateo hospital for a further check, but there is not much doubt. We can only hope that it is not serious. Going to Gila is out until Mom gets better.

[59] Mrs. Kikuchi had been suffering for some days from severe menopausal hemorrhaging.

Dr. says that she may have another hemorrhage if she travels now.

Pop was hit pretty hard. He kept saying that the doctors were wrong. It was just an ordinary sickness indicating a change of life, he kept saying, trying to make his wishes come true. He didn't eat dinner tonight. He sat around on the edge of the bed. He looked so forlorn that Bette went in and put her arms around his neck. Mom even tried to comfort him. Bette told him that he should not worry so much because he would get gray hairs (the only hair he has left is white). Pop asked me what about Gila. I said that I would contact Thomas tomorrow. This will also put her in a fix, but she is human and will understand.

.   .   .   .

Emiko has sort of a persecution complex. She takes things so personally as if people want to pick on her. She fails to realize that much of it is her fault. The point tonight was that she shouldn't have danced and made noise just after hearing of Mom's condition. I talked to her until 12 o'clock and we got clear on a lot of things. Emiko says she can't help getting mad. A lot of it is cover-up for her feelings being hurt, especially references to her plumpness. She is also worried about the boy situation. She feels that she is not meeting enough of them because she works all day. She tries to picture herself as a "sad" case: one weak eye, bad teeth, bites her nails, twitches her feet, hands feel sticky, nervous, etc. I think she was just feeling sorry for herself. She is very attractive and has an unusual personality. As she is only 17 she fails to realize that this is a problem common to most Nisei girls. There are few fellows in her age level and many of them are in the army. And times are abnormal now so that social functions are no longer of the greatest importance. We are not living in a normal environment. The administration may also clamp down on social activities because there are so many of them going on. Orders for a ten o'clock curfew have been received but the new [internal police] chief, White, is not going to enforce it unless necessary. Emiko has adolescent worries that she will not be asked to dances anymore if she turns a boy down, as the story will get around that she can't go out. I can see that she has some valid points and I certainly would not like to clamp down on her. She gets around a lot and much of her role of martyr is exaggerated.

Bette and I had a long talk earlier in the evening and we called a truce to our feud—on her part chiefly. I was not aware that she was feeling badly. I explained that environmental conditions had a lot to do with her lack of interest in studies and current pursuits of boys but that she had nothing to worry about. Bette wants to go on to college. Emiko wants to stay in camp and take care of Mom and Pop in case Alice leaves. Emiko doesn't want a career, only to be happily married. I agreed with that, but I said that she should be doing something positive in the intervening period in order not to become stagnant. Emiko calls the diet kitchen workers the Dies committee because they snoop around so much. She went to sleep in a good mood.

.   .   .   .

I notice that a certain Miss Endo is going to bring suit against being moved to WRA centers against her will.[60] What the hell good will that do, is the comment I heard from about 10 people. They say that even if she wins they are not going to release the 80,000 Japanese anyway.

July 24, 1942   Friday   1:00 a.m.

Miyako and Kozuko had a fight with Setsuko today. She says that Setsu speaks Japanese all of the time and they can't understand her. So they asked her to please speak English. Setsuko wouldn't so they wouldn't play with her. Setsuko got angry and went home crying to her mother because she has been left out of the group. Miyako says that she is not going to play with her until she uses English like all the other children.

Emiko, Alice, and Miyako went out for a walk this evening.

---

[60] By the time the Supreme Court ruled on *Endo* in 1944, the relocation program was being phased out, a situation, however, that may have been speeded by the impending Court decision.

They went way down to the far end of camp—near the fence where the highway goes by. They were watching the cars go by when a very "high class car" drove by. A "high toned" lady was sitting in back with a chauffeur in front. Emiko said that she suddenly stuck her head out of the window and with a look of hatred stuck her tongue out at them. It was so funny that it made them laugh. Then they got mad so they thumbed their noses at the fast departing limousine! Miyako asked me tonight why the white people did not like the Japanese. I told her that Japan was upholding certain principles that were opposed to those which we have. I said that this camp was a little sample of what the Japanese in Japan live under, only much worse, and that the world had to eliminate these doctrines that restricted the freedom of man. Miyako said that she was an American but did not know why the white Americans disliked us. It doesn't bother her too much now. She went out to play before I could finish my explanation.

July 25, 1942   Saturday   12:10 p.m.

We are getting adjusted to only one phase of this one wider problem. Many think that the camp affairs in our "Utopia" are the whole problem. For example the boys in the Rec Department are working towards putting in a recreational program based upon the more normal conditions which they knew on the outside. They believe that everything will be hunky dory when this objective is reached. So they are working hard to get sent to relocation centers as one body in order to reach this goal. It is a mistake to aim the whole recreational program towards such a limited purpose. It is important, but it should be relegated to its proper proportions. Bob has the opinion that recreation is more important than education. The boys of the Rec Department are doing a great service in community organization, but they just have not grown up yet. Fellows like Kim O., Tod H., and the H.'s have the idea that the way to solve the problem is to keep the people from even thinking about the issues involved. The whole bunch of them (about 40) are mak-

ing a career out of recreation. I think that the more capable ones
are making a mistake. In the WRA centers, the stress is not going to be on recreation. A pioneer community organization
must be well rounded so that all phases of the problem will be
considered.

In a way the overstressed recreation program is proving to be
a handicap to the advancement of the Educational Department.
The kids all kick about the school because the Rec Department
holds more pleasure out for them. Thus, few of the students
have anything constructive to offer. They'd rather be occupied
with the socials. Bette is a good example.

.   .   .   .

Right now Bette thinks social life is the most important. She
would rather cut classes to go to the Rec Hall. She expects to be
led by the nose for her education, and protests when some of the
responsibility is put on her shoulders, like writing constructive
compositions. If this keeps up she will so limit herself that it
will restrict her chances for growth. She won't be prepared to
meet the changing social situations that are now developing.
Like many of the others, she will become essentially a conform-
ist and when she discovers that the established system is changed,
she will be utterly lost.

Without being a "sad" girl, Bette is capable of getting a firm
understanding of these new situations in order to further round
out her personality. Ann thinks that she has great prospects of
being one of the more well balanced leaders for the pupils of her
age if she would get over the puppy love stage and discipline
herself a bit before she falls into the rut and becomes a con-
formist to everything without ever questioning. Like many of
the other Nisei she will develop negative attitudes based on the
emotional experience of evacuation instead of on a broader intellectual basis. The time to start for her is now. I have been
encouraging her to read *Time* magazine as a starter, but without success. If assimilation is the only answer for the Nisei, it
must be via an educational process. It is not too early for her to
develop a sense of social responsibility and democratic group

consciousness. To do this she needs some sort of guidance and I don't know whether I can be of much use until she gets some idea of why this is important for her.

Today, Key gave her an expensive locket with her initials on it. This phase will pass over, but what should an older brother do to help her get a better perspective on things? I certainly can't butt in, but Mom and Pop cannot do much in the way of guidance. Under ordinary conditions, this would be unimportant. But when Pop finds out (as he is bound to sooner or later) there will be hell to pay. He doesn't understand such things as puppy love. Alice is no help; Jack is not interested. But family conflict between Issei and Nisei in such a confined place as this is not a pleasant thing. I may as well wait until the storm breaks.

Ann is very disturbed about the young Nisei. She doesn't know how to combat this growing feeling of "don't give a damn" among the younger Nisei. She does what she can in her class and also by having some come over to her stables to "expose them to magazines, books, and good music" in the hopes that this will be a counteracting influence against pessimism. She sees Bette more in school than I and she says that she is beginning to reflect some of the limited attitudes of her group. I can see some of the answers for the young Nisei as a whole, but when it comes right home to my sister, I don't know what to do. In the meantime, she is drifting along in an unhealthy mental adolescent stream.

Emiko is growing out of the adolescent phase and lately I have noticed that some of her thinking is along more mature channels. She worries about what is going to happen and what about Pop and Mom. Lately she has been thinking of getting some training as a dental hygienist so that she will have something to start out on. Her idea is that she is going to enter the mainstream of American life again. Life in a real Japanese group permanently never enters her mind. One of the reasons why she likes to work up in the supply room is that she "gets to see white faces occasionally" which is a reminder that the "Japanese world here is only temporary." Sometimes I think she worries too much about the future. Like most of us, there is no clear-cut answer yet, to everything. Emiko is so much more Americanized than most Nisei girls that it becomes unusual. Everything she does is western. She has an extrovert personality and gets along easily with almost everyone, but is quick to resent a "Japanesy Jap." Tonight she said that she got to thinking about the woman that stuck her tongue out as she passed in a car and the possibility occurred to her that a more fanatic person may even go as far as to throw a bomb sometime. It disturbs her to think that the Nisei are considered as "Japs" by the majority of the population and she wondered if we will ever become accepted on an equal basis. I was unaware that she ever gave such things more than a passing thought since we never talk about it much in the family group in a direct way.

July 27, 1942   Monday   11:15 p.m.

Looking through the reports of the Council, I found out that the K. case has been closed. He is a very big Nisei, about 21 years old, who was working as an ambulance driver. A speed limit of 15 miles per hour had been established for the safety of the residents. About two weeks ago, K. was sent out on an emergency call so he speeded up. One of the Caucasian police was sitting on the bench and he signaled for him to stop but K. kept going to get the patient. Upon his return words followed and K. told the police that he was neglecting his duty by sitting around on his ass, etc. K. then said that the administration was corrupt and that a lot of graft was going on. Davis got burnt up at this and said that K. would be taken care of and shipped out immediately. K.'s mother was seriously ill and so friends sent around a petition asking for a fair hearing. Davis refused and he was brought before the Council and after much work the thing was ironed out. K. will not be allowed to drive any more cars here, but he is not blacklisted as far as other jobs were concerned.

T. S., the electrician foreman, is also in hot water. The crew dislike him so much that they don't ride to work with him. It was charged that he lets a girl ride in the cab with him which is against the regulations. It was recommended that he be transferred to another department. Davis states that no case history of each worker is sent to the WRA to blacklist them.

.   .   .   .

One of the fellows sent a letter to the Red Cross yesterday to complain about the unhealthy stables. He pointed out that ventilation was very poor, especially in the back rooms, and that due to the open spaces at the top, lots of dirt came in and settled on things. This is most certainly true for us. Everything gets dusty so quickly. Bette is continually dusting the shelves off. When she sweeps, it gets just as dirty on the floor again in about a half hour. They have put rough gravel out on our walk, but it has sunk into the soft earth and the wind that blows through here does the rest.

.   .   .   .

At least they are planning to sell contraceptives to some of these married people. The plan is to sell them over the counter in the canteen by some minister who is in charge. They feel that this is the way they can control the moral problems! The hospital has been deluged by requests for contraceptives so they are going to wash their hands of the whole thing. What is needed around here is a birth control clinic to give the young couples guidance. It would be silly for them to have children now, considering the environment and lack of facilities.

The doctors here just haven't got any of the equipment which they were promised. They are understaffed and working under serious handicaps. The more serious cases are being sent out to the outside hospitals. At present there are 30 of these cases. Only the doctors can go out to visit them and carry the messages from relatives. The doctors naturally are not pleased with this arrangement because it cuts into their limited time. They have requested the administration to allow close relatives to go out themselves to visit the cases.

It looks like the curfew will go into effect now. A father is very disturbed because his 13-year old daughter is pregnant.

He wanted something done about it so he went to the church group. These people got very excited about the moral problem of the young and so they asked Chief White to put in a curfew. I don't see how suppression of this sort will solve the problem. It's not as superficial as that. Many of the Nisei are taking the attitude that they may as well have as much fun as they can now. It so happened that the army had issued instructions to put a 10:00 curfew into effect, with all lights out at 10:30. This is certainly going to interfere with the reading by many of the residents. White did not put it into effect because he felt that this restriction was not necessary for this camp. But since the people (Issei) have asked for it, the ruling may be put into effect. . . . The Nisei reaction is that the ruling is silly and cannot be enforced and why should the older Nisei be penalized. They don't like the idea. The Issei are for it because there is nothing for them to do in the evenings anyway.

The Japanese phonograph records were confiscated today and already 2000 have been brought into the police department. The innocent ones will be returned but Japanese military music will be stored away and returned after the war. The chief has to play and listen to all of these records. I feel sorry for him because Japanese music is hard on the ears; it sounds out of tune. All of the other contraband things are being returned, except Japanese literature, dynamite, and the sharp-pointed saws. All other tools were given back today.

Ernie is going to investigate the complaint from #83. They claim that the Caucasian patrolman walked in six times without knocking on the suspicion that gambling was going on. Ernie has also arranged that drunken soldiers will be kept out of the camp. A drunken sergeant bothered the people down around #16.

July 29, 1942   Wednesday   11:25

Jack was baiting Pop and Mom about the war today. It all started when he was making out Red Cross messages to Mom's relatives in Tokyo. He made a remark that they may have been wiped out by the bombing of Tokyo. Pop said that this was a lie and that Tokyo was not bombed.[61] From there they went into the war situation and Jack said that more Jap and German soldiers were killed in battle than American and Russian ones. Pop said that both sides were sending out a lot of propaganda. He believed that Japan was fighting for the equality of races. I was left to argue with him and it distressed me very much to see how restricted in thinking many of the Issei have made themselves. Pop recognizes the fact that the war was brutal and he said that it was hard for the Nisei because they did not understand things so well and that much of their book learning did not give them the true facts. He gave the typical Issei argument that we did not have much chance in a democracy. I pressed the point and showed how much better off we were here and why we could never go any place else. He granted this point, but said that I should not get caught up in the war hysteria and hate all Japanese. Mixed with this sound logic were many limited views about how honorable the Japanese soldiers were and that he did not like to see them fight America because they were only protecting themselves. He blamed it on both governments and not the people although he resented the idea that the white people wished to "stamp on the necks of the yellow man." I said that the Japs were more notorious for this, citing the cases of Manchuria and Korea. Pop said he did not wish to have arguments splitting the family up and that we should wait and see after the war who was right. He doubted the promises of the Allies to give more equality to all races. He based this conclusion on the results of the last war, plus the treatment of the Japanese and the Negroes in the U.S. We just don't think from the same basis, and if I admit the defects of democracy, it gives him a winning point. Pop and Mom would rather have us put wars out of our minds, but this very camp makes us aware that a war is going on now. I am afraid I was a bit irritated.

.   .   .   .

[61] A B-25 raid on Tokyo by Colonel James Doolittle's small detachment had been staged in April, 1942, with morale and not direct military benefit in view.

What the Issei should do is to realize how they are benefiting by democracy right now, even in this camp to a limited extent. Since they are not well acquainted with the wider issues, they tend to formulate their opinions from limited personal experiences or from rumors. At the same time they forget that it was a minority group that treated the Issei so harshly and that this treatment was not based on democratic practices. But there would be more possibilities if they realized that this was not a race war but a war of principles arising from world economic problems. Pop believes in democratic practices, only he mistakes the fallacies of democracy as the real thing and therefore would not label these beliefs as such. The way we bait them naturally puts them on an extreme defensive as any references to the bad qualities of a Japanese soldier are taken on a personal basis as a reflection on their own characters.

Pop holds the capitalistic idea. He is prejudiced against the Russians because they are "bullsheeveesky." He says that if a man makes a million dollars, the government takes 90% away and gives it to a lazy person. I asked him what was wrong with that, pointing out how he had to charge 35 cents for haircuts when he was a better barber than the Caucasian that charged 65 cents. He said "no," a man should get what he could. This led to a discussion of prejudices. Pop thinks Hitler is a sourfish and distrusts the Germans; Koreans are not the same as Japanese. A Jew is a cheating kike, a Filipino goes around raping women, and the Japanese in the U.S. are cutthroats (only when I am not arguing with him). Pop is a mixture of past fears and frustrations.

.   .   .   .

It's a funny thing that the Nisei will give great talks about democracy. Although we may not have much chance at self-government here, the right to vote is important. We should be laying the basis for self-government in the relocation areas right here. Much will depend upon the Nisei and the present apathy is not a good start even though the elected persons are comparative greenhorns. We have to develop leadership gradually and not expect it to turn up suddenly. At least they can gather a little experience in the procedures of self-government here, although the practice of it will probably be denied by our WRA administrators.[62]

July 30, 1942   Thursday

The radio announced this morning that General De Witt had ordered the clearance of all assembly centers (including Tanforan) to relocation centers by August 7th. Everyone got greatly excited and the news spread around camp like wildfire. I saw a couple of kids getting boxes to pack. Taro wanted to check on the story so I went up to see Davis. I couldn't get by the secretary so I sent the message in. He said that there was absolutely no basis to the story and that he had received no news of it. So I guess that we will be here for a little while. The favorite pastime is speculating where to go next. There is a mass dread of going to Arizona and the people are willing to believe the worst about it. Letters written by people who have been sent there paint a black picture of the place. The place seems to be unbearable. It won't be long now before we are all moved and there is an increasing tension among the people. The attached letter [63] was received by one of the Issei. K., a Councilman, got a hold of it and made a translation. He showed it to me yesterday and at that time planned to carbon copy a lot of them and pass them out. Today about 15 Nisei showed me the letter and hundreds in camp already know about it. I heard about 8 different oral versions and each was exaggerated a little more.

[62] The JERS text reads "WPA administrators," in which case Kikuchi would be talking not about future relocation centers but about present difficulties at Tanforan.

[63] The letter, from Poston (Arizona) Relocation Center and dated July 20, stressed climate and exhorted that "this HELL on earth is absolutely not a fit place for human beings, especially for the aged and for the very young who have no resistance. . . . I do not know where you are to be sent, but I urgently advise you to ask to be sent to Tule Lake or some other area of temperate climate. I know that anyone from the [San Francisco] Bay region would simply die of the heat if he were sent to Arizona."

July 31, 1942   Friday   12:30

Three months in a concentration camp! Life goes smoothly on. I should be more dissatisfied and rebellious, but much against my will I'm forced to admit that I'm getting adjusted to this restricted life and falling into a smooth and regular rut. There still is something within me that makes me feel uneasy but these momentary lapses are getting more infrequent, or else I am feeling better tonight than usual. The idea of doing social work is fast fading from my mind as far as this place is concerned. And the language difficulty has to be recognized. If I can't establish rapport with the residents via language, there is not much use of me doing it. There is one social worker now—a former YMCA secretary—and her prime function is making up order forms for the people who need clothing. All of the other social problems are handled, many badly, by the police, house managers, council, administration, churches, school, and rec department. It is usually an incidental factor. The house managers think they solved a social problem by recommending that a man be sent to another camp because he beat up his wife recently. They did not see that the conflict was more basic than that, a case that needed intensive handling by a very experienced worker. If I did social work now, I would be in a similar position as the schoolteachers here, with the added advantage of one year of training. But I would have to have a sympathetic and experienced department to back me up and give me practical guidance, impossible under Greene.

.   .   .   .

The paper has come along to its peak. We have to fight for every inch and never have received much cooperation from the administration. We take the censorship in stride, feeling that there is not much use in trying to buck Davis and McQueen with their Fascist ideas. The work has fallen into a routine and some of the old zip is gone. I wanted to get it up to 12 pages, but Taro and the others absolutely refuse to expend more energy under the present setup. And I hardly blame them. We have sort of developed a policy of subtle Americanization and avoid loud protestations of loyalty, of waving the flag. We minimize things Japanese. I notice that the other center papers play up such things as *Bon Odori* and *Sumo*. We did not even mention the repatriation business.[64] The *Totalizer* gives much space to all educational activities and minimizes sports, which is usually given double and triple the space in other center papers. We are the only one to have regular features and the paper is planned out in magazine style, the chief credit going to Bob and Taro. Standards of writing are kept up by them, plus Jimmy and Lillian. I get the stories in and they all take turns giving it a thorough going over. I don't mind since it makes our paper more polished. Bill H. is much worse than I am. He uses typical H. S. style. With our limitation on space we thought that it would be better not to develop a straight news style. My "Your Opinion" column is getting on to a higher level, but then I run into difficulties because there is always the uncertainty of censorship on a controversial subject. McQueen only tentatively "oked" it for this week in regard to wages. Davis let it go through when I added that the question applied to WRA centers.

Bob and the rest of us are informally discussing what type of paper is best for WRA centers. We would like to see something that could circulate to all centers with something more solid to it than what we have been doing up to now. I don't see much future in a center newspaper so will try to get into something more along the line of my interests and ability, if any.[65]

.   .   .   .

Messhalls are well organized now and food has improved 100%. From the excess starchy foods we got the first month, the diet has become very well balanced. We get lots of vegetables

[64] The possibility of repatriation to Japan became a subject of very great appeal, to whites who hated the Japanese, to many of the oppressed Issei, and, ultimately, to some Nisei.

[65] Before relocating to Chicago, Kikuchi worked at the Gila River Relocation Center as one of the directors of the Social Service Department.

and everyone has probably gained pounds. There is less confusion and meals are served in an orderly manner. Manners are not so good, and the noise makes conversation difficult. The only trouble is that fish twice a week. We got it tonight so all of us brought ours home and Pop made us all steaks which Zen gave him for his special diet. This was the first time we had dinner in a quiet family group. I am getting quite used to these tin plates and cups. A little girl down the way usually wraps her knives and plates up in a cloth, if handed her, instead of setting a table like all girls usually do. It must be the influence of the environment. With Mom sick, our family unit is slowly drifting apart and nobody pays much attention to Tom and Miyako. Jack usually eats with some girl. Emiko wants to eat with Mike, Bette often eats with some boys, etc. At noon I eat at Mess #2 and Jack and Alice and Emiko eat in the first shift. We haven't all eaten together for quite a while. Our evening snacks, however, have become customary. We are one of the few families allowed to use a hot plate (because of Pop's special diet) and there is an abundance of good food around. People are always bringing something in for us from the outside.

When we first came here, everybody wore jeans and slacks. Now they are all dressing up, especially the girls. Only a few stay in jeans. They have brought their good clothes out of the trunk and are wearing them more often. Almost all of the office workers dress up, at least in good clothes. Only a few of the professional people wear the suits, except on Sundays. The little kids all wear rough clothes and the unskilled workers keep to the jeans.

The laundry situation is pretty good now. People can send their stuff out. Laundries have been built in all districts and there is plenty of hot water. Recently wringers and wash boards have been installed. During the first month not a laundry was ready. The shower rooms are also good now. Compartments have been placed in the women's showers, plus foot baths. A place for germicide to kill athlete's foot has been recently installed. The men's latrines still do not have compartments; but in the women's, plywood separates every two toilets. Outside of the women's latrines, at the end of our barracks, a lot of clothes-lines have been put up.

Our Grant Avenue is no longer a mud hole. It has been leveled off and a gravel walk has been put in. Roads have also been built in the infield. When we first came, there were few houses in the infield, but they were thrown up in a hurry during the first month. Street lights now help the people from getting lost in the pitch darkness. Gardens have sprung up all over the place and vegetables are now ready to eat. A hot house provides flowers for the various flower projects around here. All kinds of baseball, golf, and basketball fields dot the formerly vacant landscape. In front of many barracks are to be seen many fine pieces of architecture.

The moral problems have not increased tremendously on the surface, except from rumors heard. The night police patrol and the lights keep things in good order. But there have been cases of moral problems going on that we don't hear much about. Social outlets that have been developed are primarily for the young Nisei; there is not much available for the older groups and the Kibei. Rumors are still heard of saltpetre in the food and of girls being molested. They don't go out alone at night as they used to. Reports from Santa Anita indicate that the problem is much more acute down there. So far only two engagements have been announced and one marriage performed. All kinds of talk about "professional women" circulate, but I have not been able to trace any of these rumors down to its source. Undoubtedly a lot of it is true.

Gambling developed into a very big problem, but since the recent edicts it has greatly diminished. A lot of money changed hands when it was going full blast. With so many internal police floating around, the big games have been broken up. The professional gamblers are closely watched.

.   .   .   .

The attitudes of the people have settled down in many respects. From fearing and hating everything about the place, many of them have arrived at the point where they like it here and would not mind if they stayed on indefinitely without moving on to a relocation area. Although the older people have a lot of spare time on their hands, they are taking up such things as gardens, sailboats, etc., to fill in. The mothers work as hard as ever with the exception of cooking. The laundry work is probably much harder. The Issei as a whole believe that their status is a result of the war and have accepted it. Social barriers have also broken down and people are on a much more equal footing. Money and former position do not mean so much as they did on the outside.

Our family have also fitted in with this process of adjustment. Alice is set in the supply room and it takes up most of her time. The matter of Pop's diet has been straightened out and it is mere routine for the girls to go get the food. Emiko is an established part of the mimeograph room and she seems content with it although I have told her that she should be thinking more in terms of the future. She is still very much "social"-events minded. Bette is going to school and not getting too much out of it. Lately she has been doing additional study on the side. Her prime concern right now is her boyfriend. Tom and Miyako also go to school. Miyako probably is getting the most out of school. At least she is learning something. She is not completely satisfied with her teachers. She and Tom have probably made the easiest adjustments.

Mom and Pop are apparently resigned to this life and take it as cheerfully as possible. Pop no longer insists about going to work as a barber here. He now considers himself more as a retired person. Mom has been ill for the past month so that the family is not such a close unit as it was when we first arrived (on the surface). Most of the responsibility for the younger children rests with Alice, Jack, and me.

The family scene has changed considerably in the past few years. Pop is now 67 and Mom 52. Their lives have not been dull and completely uneventful as I had formerly thought. They have certainly gone through many periods of change.

August 3, 1942 Monday

Emiko, Alice, Jack, and I went to folk dancing tonight. I had made a first resolution to do some reading and also some writing for Dr. Thomas tomorrow, but people came dropping in and out so that it was impossible to concentrate. I tried to get some cooperation, but when there are nine of us around, we can't all have things to suit ourselves. It is getting so that somebody comes over every evening or else we go out to some event. We will have to make some sort of a plan in the relocation center whereby a certain part of the evening will be reserved for studying, writing letters, reading, or some other very quiet activity. We have little enough privacy as it is and when people drop in evening after evening, it makes our stall that much less of a private place.

C. H. says that the Fellowship of Reconciliation is doing a lot of work to help out the evacuated Japanese. He showed me a bulletin published by them entitled "Behind Barbed Wire: Convicted of No Crime." The group is chiefly interested in the student element. C. H. is a college student, but he thinks nothing can help us now. His father was a merchant, but he lost everything. He thinks that the church groups are too ineffective and that the people that need to be reached are never touched by the churches. He is very bitter and thinks that the churches are capitalizing on the gross injustices done to the evacuees in order to win them over to the church. C. H. does not believe this sort of escapism is any solution to the problems of the group. It tends to make the Nisei more defeatist and they become more willing to sit back and let their friendly "white gods" make a lot of noise for them without putting much effort out in cooperation. He believes that the Japanese here do not need the spiritual leadership of some of the white reverends that come in and act so sympathetic. He would rather have them fighting mad in order to shake the whole group out of its lethargy and for them to make a very positive stand on the war and to hell with hurting the feelings of the Issei any more.

C. H. believes that labor unions could do more for the Nisei in the long run.[66]

August 4, 1942   Tuesday   11:07

The Council worked hard. Toby said that in another month he had hoped to have some measure of democratic self-government by getting the people to participate in it. When this thing burst in their faces,[67] they did not know how to take it. The councilmen said that they all felt tired suddenly and did not care about anything except to rest for a few days.

In reviewing their short-lived five weeks in office they did accomplish a lot in the way of added service to the community. Much credit goes to them for putting so much time and effort into fulfilling their responsibilities. The Administration did not back them as fully as they could have. They helped to settle the maintenance strike. They pushed through the laundry service. They initiated the Committee of seven to prepare an Issei program for Army approval. Radio and watch repairing services were started after the Council pushed them. The shoemakers' program is getting under way as well as the clothing issues. The Council helped by spreading information about the procedures in the clothing and barber service. A movie committee was set up and we will probably get our first full length pictures in the H. S. grandstands, next week. Clarifications on roll calls and transfers were made by the group and funeral services were ar-

[66] C. H.'s perceptions are heavily colored by the political ideology Kikuchi had absorbed less fully. In fact, despite the low valuation placed on their activities by C. H. and others, groups like the Fellowship for Reconciliation and the Fair Play Committee worked persistently if not terribly effectively for the Japanese Americans during the war. Organized labor, on the other hand, was at best mixed and at worst openly hostile to the Japanese Americans.

[67] The previous day the council had received a letter from Davis, quoted by Kikuchi in his diary. "In accordance with supplement 8 to the WCCA Operations Manual of the Western Defense Command and the Fourth Army, WCCA, dated August 1, 1942, and received in this office August 3, 1942, the center Executive Council and the Center Congress as well as any and all other activities of the self-governing organization in this center is hereby declared dissolved. . . . The employment of all assigned evacuee employees in this center will be terminated as of the close of business today." Regulations would permit only an advisory committee, lacking even the pretense of power.

ranged for. They cooperated with the internal police and house managers on such regulations as phonograph record collecting and gambling. Personal adjustments were made in several of the "Social Welfare" cases. They sent letters to the Army to have Japanese books translated and returned if found innocent —nothing was done. They had all the known gamblers come in and promise to behave or else. The traffic regulation of 15 miles per hour was established to protect the people; street light adjustments were also made. The banking facilities were investigated and it was through their efforts that the hours were lengthened. They appointed a committee of house managers to take care of the package deliveries. Most of their time was expended in the formulation of the Constitution and the election of the Congress, all wasted effort now. The Council also worked on the Social Security benefits for old age in order to get those that were eligible informed on the procedures.

Now that the Council has been swept aside, the house managers will no doubt resume their position as the voice of the people, although Speares has them eating out of his hands now. They threw a big party for him last Saturday and paid $1.50 each for the privilege. Everyone realized that we would not have complete self-government here; but nevertheless this blow is a little hard to take. Much hope has been placed in the WRA centers, but I don't count too much on it. Things have a funny way of backfiring and slapping one in the face when least expected. I left the Councilmen to mourn by themselves and went down to see Dr. Thomas on her weekly visit with my stuff after I had taken a note to Davis asking for a typewriter.

Fred and the others were already there, and Fred was a little excited because he had heard that Dr. Thomas was on the "blacklist" at the visitors' gate. Immediately I figured that Kilpatrick had something to do with it and silently I cursed Ernie T. under my breath for messing things up. I went to the visitors' office and got in on the pretense of finding out how many visitors we had in the past month. The Inspector was very nice and I sort of felt guilty for blowing off at him the other day. I casually glanced up at the private notices for Livingston and sure enough, Dr. Thomas' name was on the list along with Helen Gahagan, and a professor from U. C., and some German-sounding names. This was enough to satisfy my curiosity so when Morton Grodzins and Bob Spencer [both of the JERS project staff] came in, I told them about it. M. G. wanted to know if I was positive and I said, "Yes." When we got upstairs we all sat at one of the desks and I just handed him the bulletins and the folder when Greene popped out from nowhere puffing on a cigar and reached over and said, "What is this and who are you?"

M. G. gave his name and he said, "Who are you?" Then Greene started in and said that such a study was unauthorized and that nothing official could go out of here either written or verbally. M. G. answered that the information was public and he did not see how they could possibly control it. Greene said that the Army sent a teletype notice that no written material could go out about the camp and produced the message as proof. M. G., "Is this censorship?" Greene, "Absolutely not! We are only acting for the best interests of the people and if the wrong information gets out, it will hurt them." (You mean you want to protect yourself and the Administration, I was thinking.) Then Greene asked me where I got the bulletins, etc., and I said they were for the paper. This was the only way I could tell him since I did not care to reveal who had given them to me, even though it was no crime. Greene acted as if a crime had been done. The way he kept thumbing through the stuff made my blood rise and I almost spoke my opinion. I just reached over and took my personal notes out. Greene said that he would have to take the folder and since M. G. was handling the situation, I kept quiet. He certainly was cool and calm. He explained the Study to Greene and expressed the opinion that nothing secret was being done, and that he felt certain that things would be straightened out through the proper procedures. Greene backed down and he said that if the proper procedures had been followed, he would be more than glad to cooperate, even going as far as to offer a private room where we could meet in quiet. He said that nothing could go out under the present arrangement. I don't think they can do much about it; there certainly was nothing in the folder that would have been of harm to either the people or the Administration. I pulled the piece about "such men as _____ being at the head of the ship of state around here was an insult to our intelligence." It was the principle of the thing that burned me up. I could feel the blood running to my face, I was so damn mad. What in the hell have they got to be afraid of anyway? All we are doing is to make some sort of honest study about how a group of evacuees adjust themselves to an extraordinary condition. My whole approach is to work for the Americanization of the group. Wang was right when he said that anyone in camp upholding the cause of democracy would be crucified. That is a little heroic, but it hits somewhere near the truth. There are no such things as freedom of the press or speech around here. Everything has to have the "approval" of the Administration. I realize that they have a heavy responsibility, but why can't they start from the assumption that we are average Americans and give us a decent chance instead of being so suspicious about everything that we do. Chas., you are getting excited over something you cannot control!

.   .   .   .

I didn't do a damn thing on the paper today either. Suddenly, the paper is unimportant. I can feel what Taro has been saying for the past couple of weeks now. It's such a waste of time struggling to get the news for the people, yet there is morale-raising value in it, that can't be denied. Most of the Nisei are just starved for news and almost all that I have talked to say that they read the *Totalizer* from cover to cover. This proves that time hangs heavy on their hands!

.   .   .   .

Toby told me confidentially that the visiting system is going to be changed. It will be announced soon. The plan is to have visitors stay in the social hall on one side of the table with us on the other, just like in Prison! No more cakes, pies, or fruit will be allowed in the Center. It is so unnecessary. I know for one thing, it will definitely discourage visiting.

Kenny M. is leaving for Poston this week. It seems that he made the news. The New York daily, *P. M.*, wrote up the story about how the city of Dearborn, Michigan (Safety Commission), refused to let him come. The Mount Olive Methodist Church had planned to bring him there for studies. But the members of the City Safety Commission, led by a member of the Veterans of Foreign Wars, said that the U.S. had been stabbed in the back December 7, by the very ancestors of the people which the clergy wanted to bring to Dearborn. Poor Kenny, the treacherous Jap! Now he has a cause to fight for once more! It was hinted that they already had enough subversive elements in Dearborn. How simply the minds of some people do function!

August 5, 1942   Wednesday   11:30

Mom said that she was worried about her family because she was sick and she did not like to see it all scattered out. She could not cook for us any more so asked if we would not sit together at the Mess Hall. I said I would explain to the others and we would probably cooperate on this. Mom was pleased that the work was all divided up according to a schedule since we didn't have all of those arguments among the girls any more. She said it made her very happy to see all of us getting along together so well and appreciated the fact that we took care of them so well. Tears started to come to her eyes. She said that she should not have scolded Jack the other day about putting a woolen underwear in the Clorox water because she only meant to give him advice and he got fresh. She wanted me to explain the situation to him. I told her that he was an adult and that scolding was not the right method. She answered that she used English so much these days that she could not explain things the way she felt, forgetting that Jack understands Japanese and I'm the only one that doesn't. Pop said that he was proud of the family and did not want anyone to spread gossip about any of the members. Both felt that pressing down of the children by

the Issei was bad, but too much freedom was also bad. Mom
said that Bette used to study all of the time, but doesn't any
more and wondered why she got a "C" in Chemistry and I said
that it was due to the lack of facilities. They wanted Jack and
me to fix up a schedule so that we could have a private home
and not have the same bunch of young boys in day after day
and disrupt family life. I said that we were on the verge of leaving but in the relocation center we would have a definite study
hour to read and write letters. This suited me because then I
would get a chance to do some reading earlier in the evening.
Jack said he wanted to study a little also. It would be good for
the young kids also when the summer is over. Mom thought
that we could fix up a program that would not be too strict or
too loose. She did not care if they went to dances if they came
home at a reasonable hour and got their homework done. She
wondered about Emiko, what she was going to do in the next
three or four years. I said that there was no reason to worry because she would probably pick up some sort of office work to
do. The main thing was to have good cooperation in the family
during the time we were evacuated.[68]

.   .   .   .

I saw Rev. I. in the Administration building and asked him
what ministers were passing out the contraceptives for married
people. He replied that the ministers refused to do it so it looks
like they are passing the buck also. The hospital doesn't want to
do it either and that's where the matter stands right now.

August 6, 1942   Thursday   11:40

I went down to get some sunshine in the grandstand around
10:30 and Fred H. told me that Morton Grodzins' name is also
on the blacklist but not Bob Spencer since they do not know
about him. I decided to go see Greene about the folder he con-

---

[68] Mrs. Kikuchi's condition, to the great relief of the family, had turned out
not to be threatening. She was still weakened, however, which made it necessary
for the family to split up temporarily so that she might further recuperate before removing to Gila.

fiscated from me on Tuesday. As I walked into his office, Ernie T. was anxiously asking Greene how it could be fixed up so that he would not have to go to Poston. He would rather stay here and be "principal" of his grammar school.

I asked Greene if I could have the bulletins and he said absolutely not because I had some highly confidential administrative bulletins and notices in there and he demanded to know how I had gotten hold of them. I said that I did not think I would answer. Greene said that I was a "fool" for being taken in by a group that had no official sanction and who would cut my throat just to serve their selfish interests. I replied that I should be the judge of that myself and I saw nothing wrong in a scientific study in which I could learn methods and techniques. My blood began to rise.

He said that there was no chance of my getting any of the bulletins back and that a full report had been sent to the S. F. offices [of WCCA]. Again he started to patronizingly tell me how immature in mind we were for being victimized by a group that wanted to use us and that I had better be careful or my whole future would be endangered.

I told him that these bulletins were public since they were posted on the boards and what was to prevent a person from taking them down to send out if he desired, or even copying them down. "Honesty of the person," he replied, glaring at me. I said that my conscience was clear and I was doing nothing underhanded.

Greene said that we were too young and had no experience. "Let us with the mature minds do your thinking for you. You people are in a tough spot and the administration here has been picked because we know a little more about life than you do." (WPA!)

He emphasized the point that I could take no written material out of here. "What is to prevent me from mailing it out?" I said, calmly. "I wouldn't try anything like that," he threatened.

Then he went on to say that I acted mighty suspicious when I grabbed some stuff out of the folder. I told him that they were private letters, and that I was not ashamed to show them to him now only it was the principle of the thing that bothered me. I thought it was rude of him to snatch and thumb through the material. Greene said that as a government official he had every right to take the folder and the stuff I took out also but he accepted my word that it was private material. Further, he added, I had no right to show it to an outsider. It was just as bad to steal an army jeep as to take those bulletins which were government property and not for outsiders like Thomas who refused to go through official channels. He added that we had too many theories in our heads and that I should do some re-thinking. I said that if my approach towards greater Americanization of the group was wrong, then let it be so. He said that I was treading on dangerous grounds. I couldn't understand what he meant and he did not make himself clear. He wanted Doris sent up to him so I went and told her to say nothing. M. N. is acting much better these days so I also told her to hide whatever bulletins that she wanted to retain. Told E. the same thing.

Greene is feeling so much on the defensive these days. The *Totalizer* just ignores him so far as the paper is concerned. Greene wants no word to go out about the Administration; and gives the reason of protecting the residents from all of these people who want to "victimize them." Davis evidently must be behind him because he ordered the blacklisting of Thomas and Grodzins. It made me so damn mad to see how fascistic they can act and suppress our basic rights. The Army evidently must be behind a lot of this because since the first of the month stricter rules have come out. No member of the administration can cash checks for us; visiting system is made like a prison setup; self-government denied; etc. What can you do with people who are so restricted? I can't very well buck the Army orders about official news being suppressed.

August 8, 1942   Saturday

It was foggy and misty today; the usual heavy fog which we are all acquainted with. Out in the country it is probably hot as blazes. Jack and I were picking peaches near Yuba City this time last year in a heat about 110°. It doesn't get hot in the S. F. area until around September. I actually felt chilly as I walked across the field. Only a couple of the fellows were around since they worked hard last night. J. Y. came in with some of his friends and we sat around and had a bull session. He said that T. M., the girl known as the prostitute, had applied to move over to Mitch's old place along with Mrs. E. who has a Filipino husband on the outside. She claimed that she was being bothered by too many single men who came to knock on her door.

J. said that a lot of the bachelors sent an unsigned letter to the Administration asking for licensed prostitution here because they "were going nuts." We got to talking about how this problem could be worked out for the evacuees. It was agreed that marriage would solve the problem for only a proportionate few since the Nisei would not marry in droves under such uncertain circumstances. And marriage just for this reason would not be lasting.

All of the fellows said that the Japanese community were not willing to face the problem, closing their eyes to it entirely. They figured that the Japanese had an unusual quality about them which would permit them to solve the sex problem by not thinking about it.

J. thought that the only solution was to put a few of the professional women here on a P. & T. [Professional and Technical] rating by the administration in order to protect the young girls as well as to keep the situation under control. He claimed that promiscuity was growing after only three months here and the young fellows especially were developing a "what the hell" attitude. B. made some exaggerated claim that 300 unmarried girls were pregnant at Santa Anita. S. said that the girl's father over where he lives gives his daughter a loud cross-examination every time she goes out because he is so suspicious. He said that a lot of the Issei parents don't let their daughters go out at all because of all the rumors that they have heard about young girls being raped. T. thought that it was very narrow-minded of the ministers not to hand out the contraceptives to the married couples, and suggested that the *Totalizer* be assigned the task.

J. said that the reason why most of the Nisei would not get married was because they still clung to the idea that we would be out of the camps in a year and "the Japanese in this country are through regardless of who wins the war so why drag somebody else through your miseries. You will have a hard enough time getting your own family back on its feet. In all probability, the Japanese will go back across the tracks once more."

.   .   .   .

I knew what the new visitors' setup would be, but when I actually saw the benches all lined up with visitors on one side and the residents on the other, it got me so damn mad! "What in hell do they think we are, a bunch of prisoners?" I thought. And I was not the only one. I stood by the receptionist's desk and three out of four first reactions were the same. The Nisei were pretty burnt up.

"All they need is to put a screen in now."

"What kind of a prison is this?"

"The nerve of them to do this to us."

George was wandering back and forth to see that no packages or written stuff was passed, but he closed his eyes to most of it. Himeko was on the spot because some of the Nisei accused her of being responsible for this new setup. They said that she requested it. Another report was that the new chief put it into effect because too many people were going into the grounds. J. said it was because of the trouble I had with Greene over the confiscated bulletins. The most likely reason was that the WCCA headquarters in S. F. decided the matter since the new visitor's pass had its letterhead on it. Himeko said that they intended to keep all those under 16 out of the place.

Archie wanted to see Mitch, not knowing that he had left. They told him at the gate and suggested that he should go home. Archie said no, he wanted to see me and so they reluctantly let him in. He said that they take about 45 minutes to get in now and he is under the impression that they wish to discourage visiting. People go by in cars and yell "Jap lovers" at them.

Toby and the old council and the former temporary council talked with some WRA men today about the possibilities for industrialization of this group in the WRA camps. He said that the prospects look pretty good. He and the others, plus some house managers, etc., stopped in the grandstand and we got to talking about the coming elections. Tomoto said the hell with the farce, let Tani and his H. S. kids handle the thing and have some fun. The house managers have a sort of verbal agreement to play the thing down to show the administration that we are not being fooled. They were all agreed that it would be crazy for anyone to take part in it. They were all a little peeved about the wishy-washy church group who accepted the appointment on the election committee. It was Greene's selections and he has a number of Reverends and YMCA people. They play along with the administration and don't mind getting shoved around. The group were irritated that they would even accept the appointment to the election committee, knowing what a farce it was.

The setup now is that each voter will vote for one candidate, each of whom must have 50 names signed to his petition. Those that receive the most votes in the first 27 places will be declared elected to the Panel. Davis will pick his 9 men from this list and they can only meet at his calling. They have no power. Everyone I have talked to is very much disgusted with the whole thing and they say that we are not being given a chance to do anything. Greene's statement that "You should not do any thinking, let us with the mature minds do it," reflects the attitude of the administration. They will be lucky to get 27 persons to run for the panel as each has to have 50 signers to the petition and each voter can sign only one petition. This means that about 1400 people have to sign just to get 27 eligible candidates and a small handful of voters will elect a person. The election will not take place until the 25th of this month and we may be moving out by then.

We started talking about passing visitors until Yus noticed one of the dumb internal police trying to listen in so obviously, so they started to talk Japanese for a while and then broke up because he could misrepresent the whole thing in case he reported it.

August 9, 1942   Sunday   10:30 p.m.

Jack is boning up Tom for the big history test tomorrow. Tom studied for three hours this evening but he was not much interested. He keeps saying that he can't do it. Some of the answers he makes are really dumb. Tom doesn't even read the book and then wonders why he can't answer any of the questions. I think we are going to have quite a problem in getting him to study regularly in the fall, especially with the lack of privacy. He had to contend with the radio, typewriter, visitors, phonograph, and talking tonight and it is no wonder his mind was so distracted. Every few moments he would stop to tell Alice how to work a puzzle.

Emiko made me a little bag tonight to carry my tin dish and cups to the messhalls. This is the latest fad. It is practical since it keeps our dishes from getting so dusty. A few of the mothers are wrapping all of the dishes in a large cloth, but most of them have trays of some kind now. On our side of the messhall, family groupings are keeping more or less together, but the older children go sit together in groups more often.

August 10, 1942   Monday

[The house managers] don't think much of Greene either, as they had some not so complimentary things to say about him. The same steam was blown off about Davis and all of the administrative staff, except a few. The root of these feelings is the recent denial of self-government. The house managers are particularly wrought up about it and a spirit of resentment has been growing. They are in a fix about the coming elections because they will be called upon to whip up interest, but the general opinion of the fellows was that the whole thing was a joke and an insult to the group. So in making messhall announcements, they plan to read it hurriedly in English only and they have quietly been spreading the word around that it doesn't mean a thing. Gandhi was arrested yesterday in India and T. S. said that J. H. should lead the movement for passive resistance here.

The fellows (about 8 of the house managers) were bitter in some of their attitudes. I told them that this was no excuse for just lying down and quitting because we still had a long future to work out. J. H. was of the opinion that we should put up a fight now, but the others told him that he would only be jeopardizing his chances by making a "big noise" here when we were only going to be here for another month or so anyway. J. was not so sure that the WRA would be able to do much because of the financial limitations. I told him that getting all excited about little things was a short-sighted approach. Toby came in and he started to tell us about the meeting with the WRA and how he would try to get a representative committee together to propose plans if Davis would recognize us. If not, he planned to have various people in camp work as individuals.

We got back to attitudes of the Nisei and I questioned if all of them were sincere in their manifestations at the same time expecting all the rights and privileges of a democracy. One fellow made the startling statement that Japan was responsible for our good treatment and we should communicate with the Spanish Embassy.[69] I reminded him that we were Americans and our only recourse was with our government. I did not like the remark that we were Japanese and whatever side won, we were a hopeless case. I told the fellow that now more than ever we should take a positive stand for the U.S. and work for democracy as our only hope. He said that this was a "race war" and that four out of five Nisei would agree with him. This disturbed me: I didn't know what to say. Here, they are taking up the very propaganda of the Axis nations while fighting for their "democratic rights" in these Centers. It would indicate that we are still confused, full of uncertain fears. J. cited the example

[69] For the course of the war the Spanish embassy received messages originating in the United States intended for the Japanese government. Spain and the United States had retained diplomatic ties.

that he had said "good morning" to Mr. D.—and had received a sneering "what of it?" for an answer. This infuriated him. J. T. said that small-minded people existed no matter where we were and we should be intelligent enough not to let emotional experiences of this sort prevent us from thinking clearly.

A more constructive discussion was then entered upon. We said that America was the only answer—right or wrong—and we had to make the best of it. I claimed that all the pro-nationalist Japanese already had returned to Japan, which drew a laugh. John was worried that we may develop inferiority complexes when we go back into the American life. Tomoto said we would either come out fighting and full of guts or else become a weak bunch of sissies, afraid of life and forever expecting handouts from the government. I said that there was a definite chance that we (the children especially) would have "messhall manners"—getting into long lines for everything. The whole group said that this should be prevented at all costs and that the leadership within the group would determine a lot of the attitudes. It was agreed that the sudden release of 120,000 Issei and Nisei into the American community after the war would be tragic. We hoped that the government would carry the program through right to the final resettlement of the people, not forgetting the possibility that many may stay on in the relocation areas if they were made a success. T. said that we would be lucky to make enough for the bare necessities and we could expect many days eating beans. They thought that if the Tanforan group went together progress could be made, but were not so sure about the "backwoods" country people.

August 11, 1942   Tuesday   10:30 P. M.

Dr. Thomas and Morton Grodzins were here today. They got an army "O.K." to come in to make social calls but they could not discuss any of the projects with us. An administrative bulletin has come out saying that all business conducted must be under the supervision of Davis or his representative and he has a right to sit in. No papers may be passed without inspection.

Evidently, the Thomas trouble prompted this announcement.

Thomas said that she had contacted Major —— on our moving and we could expect the order any day now—this week or next week. Tom's name was not included on our half of the family so that she will get this straightened out as soon as she gets to S. F.

I can't describe the funny feeling that came over me when I heard the news. We had been expecting it all along, yet—. Hell, none of us really desire to be separated from friends and be planted in an unknown place, but the decision has been made. Since we have to go eventually it may as well be now. Emiko's face dropped a mile when I told her. Bette was numb for a moment and Tom just came out and said he didn't want to go because he would rather stay and see the free movies every Monday night. But this was only a momentary reaction. Tonight we started to pack a little, but we did not get very far. Gods, what a mess it is going to be. We can take only a total of 150 pounds each with us and the rest will follow by freight. Everything has to be inspected before it goes out. Since Jack and the others will come later, we will try to take as much as we can with us. My books and magazines will be a problem, but I want to take them because reading material will not be so available out there.

I got in a quarrel with Alice about the money division tonight. She wanted to divide the whole thing by seven, and I wanted to take one-half out for the "family pot" and then divide the rest proportionately, with those working getting equal shares. I finally compromised by cutting the "family pot" share down.

August 12, 1942   Wednesday   10:30 P. M.

Most of the house managers as well as residents who have been in contact with the administration are of the opinion that Greene is the "big man" in camp and that he is falling down tremendously on his job. All you have to do to get anything around here is to let Greene know you are a church-goer. Why do you suppose that the Catholic Church here is the only one that has those benches while the others have to use messhall tables? (Greene is Catholic.) A few of the house managers are more calm about the whole thing and are putting their efforts into working on the relocation problems. . . . I went up to the Administration building afterwards and found out that only two nomination petitions had been taken out in the four days in which they have been available. I got one and talked Bette into running. She will get a campaign manager from the H. S. group so that they can take part in this election. We may as well encourage the young kids to get some democratic practice; it will be a good experience for them.

August 13, 1942   Thursday   11:05

After lunch I took a nap and didn't start out for work until after 1:30. Most of my news stories for the week are in anyway. I spotted Yae and her sister having a picnic so I stopped to talk. Kay was drawing some pictures of the barracks. Yae cut art classes this afternoon because she got tired of pencil drawing. She wants me to come over before I leave so that her sis can make a drawing of me so I told her that I would drop by one of these evenings. By the time I left them, it was 3:15 so I had to rush up and finish up the marriage story. Jimmy is working hard on a darn good feature on the hospital and he let the editorial page go so that Taro had to get the material. He wanted me to write up the new student court but I was too lazy. Davis only sent down one stencil so that we have nine to go. We are way behind schedule. Bob wants to revamp our style again and use the last four pages for a summary, but we couldn't decide whether it would be worth the effort to do this for the rest of the time here. We are so short-staffed as it is. Bob will quit the 22nd and I will be going soon. This means that Taro, Jim, and Ben will have to do all of the writing. Bill is not much help. K. I. wanted me to give a big plug to the elections coming up but I wasn't much interested. He claims that we have to get a big vote out because this is no time for the residents to get yellow and lie down just because two of the previous elections were not so successful. There is absolutely no interest at all in the elections. The peak of interest was reached after the council was elected during the time the Constitution was being written. It came up a little for the Congress election, but it was a little forced. With the sweeping aside of self-government, all interest was lost and I think the voting will be very light. I doubt if they get 27 persons even nominated.

Most of this evening was passed in making boxes to pack my books in. My carpentry work was not too bad. There is a scarcity of wooden boxes around the place so Alice had some open let-tuce crates sent down. I cut out cardboard and lined them. I barely got all of my books into one of them so had to make another one for the magazines. We decided to take all of them just in case there is a shortage of reading material there. I even put in their funny books and movie magazines. Now that the books are packed my biggest worry is over. Pop is getting some of the stuff ready. He and Mom keep talking about snakes and boa constrictors in Arizona. I am afraid that I let myself in for it, especially if Tanforan goes to a cool place. Mitch sent a card from Poston and he says that the people are intellectually dead.

The suspense of getting our order is getting me down. I know that it is coming soon, but when? I hope that they will give us two or three days of advance notice so that we can pack the rest of the things leisurely. There is so much junk around; I don't know where it was all accumulated from.

Emiko made a skirt tonight. She has her leg all bandaged up because her ankle hurts. Her arches have probably fallen. She put the bandage up high so that people could see that her ankles were not naturally big. Alice read this evening, and Bette studied for the Chem exam with Yosh. Tom and Miyako lis-tened to the radio. Jack went "wolfing."

August 14, 1942   Friday   9:20

Jack said that one of his 8th-grade pupils had a dream last night about one million Japs invading the U.S. to rescue the Issei in the concentration camps. After they had done this, they lined all of the Nisei up and shot them! Evidently the little boy has been doing some thinking on the subject.

August 15, 1942   Saturday   10:45

Nobby was very proud this afternoon because one of his high school teachers had written an article for *Freedom* magazine (a new one) in which he discussed some hardship cases of evacuees. One of his illustrations was Nobby "who came to high school and was so American in everything he did." Nobby was the water boy for the football team and an enthusiast of American jazz, movies, and comic strips. "When Pearl Harbor came, he became quiet and subdued with a personal sense of tragedy." When Nobby left for camp, his teacher told him that he was a good loyal American and that he should never lose faith in his ideals.

I am afraid that the fellows in the office ribbed him a little too much and deflated his egotist conceit, which has become more and more evident lately. Nobby left us very irritated. I told him that he should not let these little things bother him because he has the possibilities to achieve much in life. Nobby is so advanced for his age that it irritates his high school friends when he consciously attempts to show them up. So he goes around with much older boys, a sort of hanger-on around the fringes. They are inferior to him intellectually, but they jitterbug and make a lot of noise, which is the badge of success for the younger kids. We in the office sort of deflate him at times so that he won't get too objectionable to everyone for his own good. Nobby has not said anything about the progress of his parents' repatriation lately. He has milked the last ounce of sympathy from us on this matter.

. . . .

My arm still hurts from the typhoid shot so I got a couple of girls [to] help me deliver my papers. On the way back, I stopped at the *Sumo* ring and watched the boys perform. Momo, Homako, and Jiro were there so we talked for a while on this sport, but none of them could explain it to me. I suppose it is good exercise, but I did not like the part where they bow down and receive a prize with the announcer saying something in Japanese. I think we could just as well get along without the Japanese customs of this sport. It's a sort of bowing down to superior man. A wrestler with a black belt evidently is in a class by himself, and in Japan this is carried over into civilian life and certain customs have to be observed when he is present.

However, the way that it is done here, the only Japanese aspect of it is the yells and announcing and the receiving of the prize in which the winner bows his head humbly. There really does not seem much to it except an exhibition of brute strength. The object is to throw the other fellow out of the little sand ring. There must be skills and techniques to the sport though, because some of those little fellows were tossing the big ones out regularly.

August 16, 1942   Sunday   10:20

On Sunday afternoons there is usually a lot of activities going on for the young people. From where I was standing in the grandstands I could see about five baseball games in progress. Near the barber shop in the infield a lot of fellows were pitching horseshoes in the newly constructed pits. On the far side of the track a basketball game was in progress. Next to them and out of sight the *Sumo* wrestlers were occupied. About 100 persons were sailing boats on the lake. Great crowds stand around the edge of the lake looking on, especially at the man who gives rides to kids in the boat he has built. Our center probably is the only one that can boast of a lake. (We have two.) The builder of the big sailboat is a former captain of a fishing schooner.

Henry Fujita, the National Flycasting champion, and his son usually come out to the lake on Sunday afternoons to practice. The new lake is more a scenic spot where couples go strolling over the bridge or sit on the benches under the transplanted row of trees around the edge of the lake. A fire tower is being constructed out of eucalyptus limbs near one end of this lake for the firemen to practice on, and also conserve water at the same time by shooting it into the lake instead of out on the track as they do now.

Sunday is also a big day for tennis, two courts have been laid out on the tracks up by the postoffice, and there are always lots of golfers going around the miniature 9-hole golf course on the infield. For those who prefer milder activity, there are the weekly bridge tournaments. The rest of the people go visiting each other or else have visitors in the grandstands. The "prison system" of seeing visitors has been eliminated, but the people have to stay in the social hall to see their friends. Needless to say, the various churches draw capacity crowds on Sundays for those with nothing else to do. Most of the people around here dress up on Sunday now.

I was talking to a friend in the social hall when a Caucasian visitor came up to me and inquired if I worked on the "Tote." I answered in the affirmative and he said "It's a fine paper, shake." I shook hands and he passed a dollar into mine. I asked him what it was for and he told me to use it for postage to send out the "Tote" to various interested people that I wanted to pick out because "this was one way of showing the public how American your group really are." Without saying anything else, he walked off leaving me with a silver dollar in my hand!! We can certainly use it because our exchange and mailing list is growing longer and longer.

August 17, 1942   Monday   8:00

The house is not so noisy for a little while so that I can have a little privacy until the kids come in. I had to wait for Bette because she used the table after I cleared it all off. The girls in her Rec. 8 club have ordered a red jacket and all the girls are embroidering "Tanforettes" on the upper right side. Bette "just had" to get hers done this evening. Now she has gone off to the library and from there she will come back to go to the laundry to iron the wash. Emiko went to take a long shower and wash her hair. Jack is ushering at the movies and "to look over the crop." Tom and Miyako have chased off to catch some kittens for pets. Alice is reading.

Our paper staff has been disrupted all day and we only got a little copy in for McQueen's approval. Mitch is bombarding us with letters for the staff to come to Poston at once. Taro, Yuki, and Bob spent all day writing letters to various WRA officials to get a transfer there. Reactions to these centers are an individual matter. Kido writes hysterical pieces in the *Pacific Citizen* [70] about Poston, while Mitch is full of extravagant praise. It all depends upon the outlook of the person. Taro and Jimmy were after me all day to go to Gila. Bob says to stick around here and go with the group.

Anyway, following are excerpts from Mitch's letter to us: "Kids: Aug. 13.

"The Center Press is not going to be started until all of the evacuees are settled and that will take us until the end of the month. The press is under a funny arrangement here. Under the administration setup the press is in the department of Public Relations. The gee that is the head of this department is a guy named Norris James, a man sent here from Hawaii and who is supposed to keep the press 'in line.' I hear he is a member of the Navy Intelligence.

.   .   .   .

"The administrative staff as far as the cultural and educational aspect of the center is concerned is beyond reproach. The Ed. program has perspective and is going to be rich. It is planned to have courses of Jr. College level. There are at present three seminars on the great books. The teachers are all progressive and very intelligent. Too good for the Japs: they're all Ph.D.'s from small universities like St. John's and the Meikeljohn school in S. F., where progressive education reigns. This guy Powell for whom I work is excellent—a professor of philosophy at Wisconsin and with the Meikeljohn school in S. F. —talks the jargon of the longshoreman and thinks like the *New*

[70] The official newspaper of the Japanese American Citizens League.

Republic—. For Charlie's information—there is a sociological survey being conducted by a Dr. Leighton, a Captain in the Navy, a swell guy who is a social psychiatrist and an anthropologist by profession.[71] His survey is not for history but for use in improving life at Poston. He is trying to get the kids on his staff university credit not only for an A.B. but for Ph.D. Boy that is something—. What a program!!!

"When you guys write the letters to the WRA etc., qualify yourselves not as writers, but as prospective *teachers*. This is very important. Tell every sonofabitch who is a radical to come —we need them—the deadheads are plentiful—. It is still very warm and the food is fair at best, but goddammit we have such a good top that you don't give a damn. . . .

"Charlie! come here rather than to Gila.

"Mitch."

Mitch would make a good press agent and the paper staff has been sold. But I guess I'm stuck with Gila. I can't be deciding at a moment's notice where I want to go; I have a whole family that I am making a decision for. If it were just myself, it would make no difference, but I'll be damned if I am going into a community of Japs without some safety valve which I can fall back upon. Tulare and Turlock [Assembly Centers] are at Gila now —this means that there will be the greatest proportion of rural people there—and more Japanesy. Here I don't notice this element so much because I am with Nisei most of the time and they probably are more advanced in this group.

.   .   .   .

Alice received a letter from an old Caucasian high school friend which expresses the opinion of a lot of well-meaning people:

"When I found out where you were evacuated, I was at first inclined to sympathize a bit with you. But when you think it over, you folks are really better off than we are. Because you will be moved inland and will not be in such danger of bombings as

71 The Leighton group is discussed in the Suggestions for Further Reading.

we are and you do not have to see your loved ones go off to war, perhaps never to return; you are all together and as far as freedom is concerned, we do not have it in the strict sense of the word, either, the rubber and gas shortage, you can bet we don't go any more than necessary. And, although you've heard it before, no doubt, I think you will be thankful that you are a Japanese in America and not an American in Japan. I will try to get down to see you before you move inland."

Even this close friend considers us (the Nisei) as Japanese and not American. The work of educating these people is going to be an immense job. And she is of Jewish extraction at that, several generations removed from Europe!

Tom and I pulled a little joke on Emiko tonight and I think it hurt her feelings. She is very sensitive about her extra avoirdupois and has been trying hard to go on a diet. Tonight, she slipped out and had a box of cheese crackers out of view near her bed. Tom and I found it and while she was out of the room, we put all the crackers into another box and hid them. We left one cracker in the original box with an enclosed note saying: "Remember your Diet! Wise up, Bub!" She came in later munching away on a hamburger sandwich and reading a movie mag. Innocently, she reached for a cheese cracker only to pull out our note. The expression on her face was so funny, a sort of guilty look. Tom and I just howled! She was raging mad, a cover up for her feelings, but we kept laughing and returned her crackers. Finally, she broke down and saw the humor of the whole thing instead of taking it as a personal affront and so she laughed with us. She ate all the cheese crackers by herself afterwards!! Now Tom and I have a secret on her. (Emiko was whispering to Bette: "It is rumored that Mickey Rooney is going to have a baby!")

.   .   .   .

Jack says that he is not banking on the Student Relocation Group but he will go out after Alice [does] as he feels that he can get a job easily enough. I told him that I would stick it out in camp and I didn't know what I would do afterwards because

I could not continue on for a further degree with the family to be considered. There may be the possibility that the draft will include us later on. I think I would just as soon go then. Life is really getting interesting. Sometimes I get overwhelmed with such a lost feeling and then a wave of rage and resentment develops when I think of being concentrated in such a small area. Individual cases don't mean a damn anymore, but principles and ideals are important. And Mary O. thinks that I am a social butterfly around here! I was talking for a while with her in the library at noon time. It's the third time I have seen her since coming here. Used to see her quite a bit on the campus. Mary plans to go on with the library work in the relocation center. They have a fair collection of books now. Certainly is an increase over the 40 I gave them when they started out! They must have 4 or 5,000 volumes now. A lot of young children come in regularly and they are keeping up with their reading interests. Most of them speak surprisingly good English.

Today was one of my very good days. Nothing disturbed me much and I made several pleasant contacts. There are so many interesting people in camp. They are Americans! Sometimes they may say things that arise out of their bewildered feelings, but they can't throw off the environmental effects of the American way of life which is ingrained in them. The injustices of evacuation will some day come to light. It is a blot upon our national life—like the Negro problem, the way labor gets kicked around, the unequal distribution of wealth, the sad plight of the farmers, the slums of our large cities, and a multitude of things. It would make me dizzy just to think about them now.

August 18, 1942   Tuesday   10:30 P. M.

The movies were scheduled for eight o'clock and the place was not supposed to be open until 7:30, but the 1500 people were in line by 6:35. It extended all the way down past the postoffice in three columns. The shows are given every Monday, Tuesday, Friday, and Saturday night with 1500 people attending each showing. Only the first 7 or 800 to get in can see the picture very well. This week a lot of blankets were put up against the windows to darken the place and two loudspeakers have been installed on the girders crossing the large room.

The Issei are as bad as the kids when it comes to pushing and crowding in. They just come and plop down on any space that is even left slightly open. And they take their shoes off! Seeing a show is a form of self torture. One sits on the floor and the cushions do not eliminate the hardness of the boards. Soon your back gets tired and the feet cramped. You shuffle around to get an easier position and step on somebody's hand. The owner of the hand turns around and gives you a dirty look. About half way through the picture, your neck gets awfully stiff from looking up at an angle. With people pressing in on you from both sides, you feel suffocated. And to add further torture the sound is not very clear. But in spite of all this, everyone that can walk to the grandstands comes for the show. This week Abbott and Costello in "Hold That Ghost" was playing. The audience really seemed to enjoy the picture, but I thought it was a bit corny. But why should I be an old wet blanket?

The film scheduled for next week was "Citizen Kane" but Yoshio K. told me that he had to cancel it upon the request of Mr. Thompson of the Rec. Department, who claimed that the picture would be too deep for 80% of the audience and he thought that comedies should be shown.

August 19, 1942   Wednesday

Nominations for the Advisory Panel elections were closed yesterday and only two petitions were handed in: Rev. T. Goto and Bette's!! The election committee met with Davis and this morning K. T. came up to tell me that the elections were off and that Davis would appoint his nine men for the advisory committee.

T. was very disappointed with the attitude of the people. "Certain groups are against everything. They feel that they are not appreciated for what they have done around here so they push down everything. They have given up." He evidently meant the house managers, but the general lack of interest is camp-wide as far as the elections are concerned. Besides being a farce, most of the residents are concerned primarily with relocation and they feel that the time left here will be short.

Bob Tsuda is definitely set on quitting the paper this Saturday and the staff has been trying to coax him to stay on. But Bob claims that we will be going to Utah for sure by the 15th and he wants to get a little rest before the mad rush. "Where are we going" is the chief topic of conversation every place and the people will be greatly surprised if it is not Utah. They seem to have the idea that the climate there will be much more agreeable than in Arizona. Many of the people want to go to Wyoming, and Bob tells me that the former San Franciscans in Santa Anita will be given a chance to join this group.

Pop has the packing fever now. He doesn't know whether to board the things up or not. Chief White says that all the baggage will have to be inspected so Alice is trying to have them send someone down here to look over the things before we tie them up. Some of the people who have left here forgot to leave the keys to their baggage and they will not send the stuff until the owners send the keys back so that they can open up the trunks. This means that they will not get their baggage for several weeks. They go through everything very thoroughly; but when all the people start to move, the inspection will probably be very hasty.

. . . .

Alice still has not done anything about her situation. She gets so much on the defensive every time Jack and I talk to her that it is no use. We just want to help her, but she has the idea that we look down on Angelo or something. She just can't make the break yet and she feels that she is indispensable to the family and fiercely clings to this belief. This is probably one of the reasons why she unconsciously resents Jack and me because she feels that her place in the family status has been usurped. She made the remark this afternoon that one of the reasons why she did not go was because there would be nobody to look after

Mom and the laundry if half of us went to Gila. I said that
Jack could do it and that it would only be for a couple of weeks
anyway before we were rejoined.

Alice is going through a struggle in her mind. She is set on
marrying Angelo, but doesn't know whether to do it before he
joins the Army. It is up to us to leave her alone and think it
out for herself. She might as well make the plunge; it's her happiness and she can't keep postponing it forever. This is war now,
but afterwards there will also be a severe period of readjust-
ment. Because of her present uncertainties, she is very touchy
and would probably "blow off" if we even attempted to give her
any advice. I think she realizes that we are not trying to get rid
of her, only thinking of her best welfare. She has had four
months of secretarial experience and could undoubtedly get
some sort of office work if she went to Chicago and joined
Mariko. This would be the easiest way for her to get out of the
camp. Then she could do what she pleased. Angelo is leaving
for the middle west next week. He is going to deliver a car to
some Nisei in the Army and all his expenses will be paid. He
will stay out there so that it is unlikely that Alice will be making
up her mind very shortly. This time I think she will make the
break.

.   .   .   .

Miss Masken of the U. C. Social Welfare Department wrote
today to ask me if I am still interested in the possibility of a
scholarship. Pauline Sifton's sister is doing some work with the
Friends Society about scholarships and she is sending me an
application form. They think that there may be a chance for the
U. of Chicago, as Miss Abbott, Dean of the Social Service
School, is a Quaker and would be interested in taking in students.

I hate to turn down this offer, but I just can't see going on to
school at this time. This is about the third offer with which I
have been tempted, but I have to get to a relocation center to
try my luck first and I can't see my way clear on doing more
graduate work. All available Nisei will be needed in these

centers and it may be the opportunity which we have been looking for. However, I have been doing a little thinking lately and
have arrived at the conclusion that I will never be happy in a
wholly Japanese community. There is something about it which
raises resentment. My only hope is to get into Civil Service and
the prospects are not so good right now.

August 20, 1942   Thursday   10:40

Irene urges me to fill out the application form which Pauline
Sifton is sending me because she feels that a scholarship would
definitely be given—the chances are so good. My mind is fairly
well made up; I just don't see the purposes of going on right
now. I still haven't had the "chance" for work that I want and
I am set on going to the relocation center to see if things will
not work out. An additional year at school will be an opportunity missed at this time. I don't think I will regret my decision,
but I may.

I told Mom about it this morning and she wants me to get
another "degree" because the Japanese will look up to it. I said
that this was silly—a man should not be judged on how many
degrees he holds, but on what he does. That is the trouble with
the Japanese—they are always bowing down to a person who
they think is superior. The only reason that Mom would like
me to get an additional degree is that it would add to her prestige. The Issei never did get to achieve what they wanted and
they try to foster their frustrations on the children. They keep
pushing and pushing them just so they can have a son or
daughter who is a college graduate. They often do not stop to
consider that a lot of these people are not fitted or ready for a
college education and consequently they drift through without
a goal or a purpose. When they get out they have nothing. This
is one of the reasons why so many of the A.B.'s went back to
farm work, plus the lack of economic opportunities.

I have made up my mind that if I ever go to school again, it
will be because I have a definite purpose and goal. I can't see it
right now. School at this time would merely be an escape from

the realities of our present problems for me. Later on I may
want to go on, I think.

.   .   .   .

Bill H. went to the Rec staff meeting this morning. They
are planning a big three-day celebration for over the Labor Day
holidays with huge programs that will give all the talent in
camp an opportunity to show their stuff. But Ernie T. and
others in the Ed. Department are raising a big squabble and
are opposed to such a lengthy celebration. The Ed. Department
said that this would disrupt the school schedule and the pupils
would not settle down and get back to their studies for several
days afterwards. The Ed. Department feels that it has grown up
now and they implied that the promotions for many of the students, who left in the middle of the term, would depend upon
the grades that they received here. In other words, the Ed.
Department now considers itself as a formal school. Shojo told
me this afternoon that all of the teachers were competent and
able to take the same status as any high school faculty and that
the only difficulty was in facilities! He wanted me to give a
lecture for the "Contemporary World and Its News" class, but
I begged off because of the uncertainty of my leaving and the
"heavy burden" of the paper work. He wanted me to speak on
the future work opportunities of the Nisei and I did not feel
qualified enough to talk on the subject.

Sammy and I had a silly discussion today. He maintained
that the students who went to U. C. were smarter and had a
higher I. Q. than those that went to a small college. I maintained that the intelligence curve would be almost equal and
that there would not be that great difference since a larger
college would also have a greater proportion of not so smart
people, making the curve bell shaped in both instances. He
claimed that any person with a B average at Cal. in the liberal
arts college would get an A average at a small college by doing
the same amount of work. I claimed that this was too broad a
generalization. Sammy is a Phi Bete. He also went on to claim
that the Japanese were intellectually superior to the white race

and I accused him of accepting Hitler doctrines. Sammy has a definite class consciousness. He comes from a family economically well off, but since he has been associated with us, a lot of his dogmatic opinions have been discarded. Today he admitted that a Phi Bete key was not the ultimate of success in life. I pointed out that the reason why so many Nisei got good grades was because they escaped into studies and did not develop a well-rounded personality. I elaborated that the grading system was actually harmful for a person desiring education because it tended to make him lose sight of the real purpose of education. He tried to say that the students at Tanfo had a higher I. Q. curve than an average Caucasian school. According to what some of the teachers say, this is not true. They are definitely backward in all English courses. It seems to me that any differences that do exist are largely due to environmental circumstances. It is just as silly to say that all Japanese are imitative. They would be just as inventive if the circumstances demanded it. We call Sammy the "Fascist Republican," but actually he is open-minded and wants to learn. He hasn't any social consciousness because he has taken too many math courses at college and does not have the background. Here he is out of college and he has never heard of the Sacco-Vanzetti case. He is a believer in rugged individualism and is of the opinion that any person can be a success regardless of the environmental obstacles. We have been giving him the works lately and he is doing a lot of reading on social problems and developing rapidly. By the time he gets out of our clutches, we will make a radical out of him. He is one nice kid who hasn't ever faced the reality of life, but is still in the shadows of the Ivory Tower. He is going on to school to be an engineer.

August 21, 1942   Friday   8:00

Jack came in . . . to tell me that Mrs. Adamic had written him a letter saying that there was a possibility of getting him a factory job in Cleveland with one of her friends. At the same time Jack could attend Western Reserve University for his med course. She wanted to know whether he wished to work full time and attend evening school part time or vice versa. Jack is going to write and tell her that he wants to work full time at first. Alice is also going to leave. She says that her mind is made up now and she has written Mariko a letter asking for her to look around for a job for her. She has also written to Washington, D.C., for a job. It is her plan to get out of the camp and then get married. When Angelo goes into the Army, Alice intends to keep working. We were talking about it today and Alice feels that she must make the break at this time. Emiko will probably take over a lot of the family responsibility if she is given the chance. Up to now, Alice sort of gave her the feeling that she was not capable of it and Emiko resented this greatly.

.   .   .   .

Mom is getting better these days and has been on her feet much more. She can straighten up now. I was surprised to see that she was actually getting fat. Pop has been feeding her so well. They have continued to get along well and appear fairly well adjusted to this life at Tanforan. Now they are doing a lot of unnecessary worrying about Gila. Pop has been getting more of his things packed up for us to take along. Both Mom and Pop have been taking it easy. They sit around most of the day listening to news reports. Pop has started to make a big boat for Tom and he has been working on it a little the past few days. Pop has one objectionable habit which he has developed in the past few months. Somehow or other he has the idea that garlic is good for his health. So he eats them by the dozens. Now he smells like a regular garlic factory and it smells his side of the house all up.

Davis came into the office about 4:30 today to tell us that we could publish the news that the relocation of this center would take place between the 15th and the 30th of September. Taro was in the process of cutting the heads for the news page so that we had to make a completely new dummy and throw out a couple of the less important stories. This was the first time that he has ever given us advance news of any sort. Davis said that no family or community groups would be separated in the relocation, but he would not disclose the exact place to which this camp would go because this information is classified as confidential military information and he could not release it at the present time.

Davis said to make a note of the fact that any resident who fails to cooperate for the general benefit of the entire center or who was a "disturbing influence" in the center in the preparation for relocation would be subject to immediate relocation, with the possibility that he would be separated from his community group and even from his family group.

He said that instructions concerning the exact days on which individuals would be relocated, plus other detailed information, would be posted on official bulletin boards. He wanted us to ask the residents to cooperate in preserving the orderly routine of center operations prior to relocation.

We felt that this was a big "scoop" so got the stencil ready in a hurry and we all came up here this evening to get the thing run off. Everyone got here early, but our spirits were dashed when Davis came in and said that we could not print the news because the Army would not give clearance. So another stencil had to be cut.

August 22, 1942   Saturday

Davis finally decided that it would be too much bother to put the information about moving into an extra so Emiko just ran off the mimeograph bulletin to be posted with the information that Davis had previously given us.

Everyone around the camp already knows the news now because we passed it on. Only the story has grown to the belief that Utah has definitely been announced and that Mess 8 would go first, followed by 15 and 2. A section of the fence is being taken down and made into a gate behind our barracks and people will go from there. A platform is to be constructed for the baggage since the train goes right past the back of the camp. This morning people were running around grabbing what boxes they could in order to get started with their packing.

There seems to be a general relaxation of the tension which has been building up, although the place of relocation is not announced yet.

The Relocation committee met in the grandstands this morning and Tad asked me to come so I left the staff to staple the papers without my aid. I wasn't doing anything anyway, except to heckle Taro about his love life.

This committee is greatly concerned about setting up some sort of organization as soon as the new camp is reached. They were a little uncertain about the type of administration which would prevail there so I tried to tell them what little I knew about the policy of the WRA as compared to the WCCA. I did not think that there would be a chance of many of the WCCA people getting into the relocation program. The committee has given up this idea and they were writing letters to see if they can get some sort of recognition from the WRA so that when they get to the new center, they can help avoid some of the confusions we had around here when we first entered.

*   *   *   *

The question arose as to whether the people in the new community would recognize them. Babe thought that we would not get the same reaction as was directed against the Temporary Council, who were made the scapegoats for all the confusion at first. John Yoshino was appointed to talk to key men of the Church, Cooperative, and Issei groups and try to work with them so that a unified front could be presented.

Babe and I thought that the Issei must recognize the fact that this was principally the Nisei future and that they should not try to dominate the picture. About 100 Nisei are taking cooperative classes now with the idea of taking over the relocation. One of them made the remark to Frank: "Let the Issei handle this matter." Babe is opposed to having the Issei in the picture. "It's about time they realized that we can't always be bowing to their wishes. Some of us are getting to be 35 and 40 years old and why should we not try to develop the responsibility? The Issei as a group are too old and it will be the Nisei who are going to support them after the war. I was in business with an Issei and just because he was older he wanted to run everything his own way. He didn't want to keep books, but I made him. It was a good thing because when December 7 came around everything was in order. Otherwise he would have had a lot of embarrassing questions to answer and he would have been sunk. It's the same thing here. Sure, they are older, but they don't know any more about this new problem than we do. We are the ones to do the work and they must recognize the fact that we have to take a firm stand in this whole business. A lot of the Issei have the idea that we are all going to Japan after the war and they want to lead us in the 'right direction.' They say that our citizenship is no good, etc., and that we should listen to them. I am not condemning the whole Issei group, but the ones who want to get into control are often the more pro-Nationalistic ones. We don't want that."

Toby: "The Issei power is hard to buck. You know how it is. I remember when the war broke out, I was on the Board of Governors of the Golden Gate Institute (Japanese language school) but I never had a say. Well, when war broke out, they shoved the whole thing on us and told us to settle everything. Now they are complaining that we did not do things right and that we are not experienced enough to handle these problems so they want to lead us. How to break down this attitude and yet not cast them aside? A lot of the feeling is defensive. They have been pushed aside here as far as self-government was concerned and they don't like it. I can't blame them for that but that should not be the basis for saying that they must get into control or everything will be a failure. We have to work out something so that we can get the greatest degree of cooperation."

Ernie did not believe that it was a matter of Issei-Nisei conflict. He thought that the greatest trouble would come from the church groups. They would try to control the co-ops. If this happened there would be lack of cooperation by the various church factions in this center. Ernie said that the co-op idea would be a failure from the beginning if the Issei were not allowed an equal vote. The church attitude was not practical, he thought, because they believed too much in turning the other cheek, regardless of what happened.

It was agreed by all that the greatest problem would be to coordinate all the interest groups as much as possible so that a good start would be made.

.   .   .   .

Miss Masken of the Social Welfare Department at U. C. came with Miss Printemps of the U.S. Children's Bureau of New Orleans to visit me. We had quite a long discussion on the social problems around here and how a social worker could fit into the program. She asked me again if I were interested in a fellowship at U. of Chicago and I gave her my point of view on the setup. I told her that I was desperately anxious to go to the relocation center just to see if I could be of some good in fitting into the picture. I felt that I would never have another opportunity to get an experience like this and I go into it with my eyes wide open. Later on I could continue school for a further advanced degree but I would never get a chance like this again. I hold a lot of high hopes and think that something good can be developed out of it in spite of the fact that it is no choice of mine to be put in a concentration camp. I still feel that this is a part of the whole phase of the wider minority problem of America and of the world. Miss Masken saw this point and she said that if I decided to reconsider at any time, she was sure that some arrangements could be made. She brought me some books, magazines, and fruit. It makes one feel good inside to have friends who are interested in one's welfare. Miss Masken may do some teaching of social case work at Manzanar on the weekends, flying down on Friday evening. I have been sending the department papers and occasional letters to keep them aware of the fact that this is a social problem which needs all the skills and abilities of social agencies and individual social workers.

August 25, 1942

Dr. Thomas and Mr. Grodzins were in again today. They are only supposed to make social calls with us so we can't discuss the project. Dr. Thomas does not know when our orders will come although it has been moved to the top of the list. Dysentery is very prevalent in the Southwest so that she has consulted one of the leading dietitians in the country on what to eat. On her advice Dr. Thomas has sent down a supply of fruit juices, [and] a bottle of Galen B concentrate ($5.00 a pint) as a supplement to our diet. She said that we should avoid bulky foods—fibrous fruits, cabbage, and especially sweets and milk. We should concentrate on meats, cheese, crackers, and fruit juices and Vitamin B. Mr. Grodzins mentioned that we were to get a raise, lord knows for what. The others in the study must really be producing valuable data. This sort of hasty emptying of my mind is so illogical that it doesn't make sense. Fred amused me today by his fawning over Prof. Obata, whom he introduced to Dr. Thomas. Fred should be a press agent for this place, he likes it so much. These Church people certainly must have a lot of faith in God, but I don't think they are practical enough in many instances. The church people around here get along so palsy-walsy with the administration—they get slapped down and then come back with the other cheek turned. As long as they don't try to solve this whole problem by religion they will get along in their little sphere. The trouble is that they try to include everyone. Nobu N. is going into a seminary because he thinks that religion is the only way that the Nisei can carry their future heavy burdens.

Tom was busy all evening pounding away on some boards to make a floor seat for Emiko to sit in at the movies. Emiko was still in bed. The chair did not come out right so he got mad and broke it up. We said that he should not give up so easily so he went to work and built another one. Bette spent most of the evening writing a composition on the challenge of relocation. Later on she went to the laundry to help Alice iron.

We had some lousy fish tonight and it was so bad that we did not eat it. We brought all of the rice home and then fried it with some eggs and meat. I am afraid that we will really miss the food around here. It was cold this evening so we had to eat something hot in order to keep our blood circulating. Well, in a few days now we will be headed for the hot country and we can say, "Move over Gila Monsters, here we come."

August 26, 1942   Wednesday   8:45

After lunch I was lying around when T. K. knocked on the door. He had a message from Mr. Gunder telling me to come up right away.

"This time is it," I thought. It was almost a feeling of relief. I went up there and the first thing Gunder said was: "Casa Grande." "What's that?" I asked. "Arizona," said he, digging his fat nose into the papers.

So I asked him a lot of detailed questions. We are leaving next Tuesday at 6:45 in the morning. The train will leave at 3:15 from San Francisco. I asked him whether we would have any time to stop over in the city. Gunder tried to give me a scare story about how the Daylight Limited did not want any Japanese and that they were going to shoot us right on the train. It will take 24 hours to get to Gila. There will be a one-hour stopover in Los Angeles and we will arrive about 8:40 on Wednesday. It will probably be hot as blazes.

Four meals will be provided at 75¢ each. We will be limited to 150 pounds of personal luggage, anything more will have to be paid for by us. All of the rest of the stuff will be sent on later. Blankets will be included as part of our personal luggage. The inspector will come down on Monday to look through our stuff.

It is hard to describe my feelings. I just don't feel anything. It's another move, only this time there is a lot more packing to do. Everyone took it rather calmly. Emiko started her packing and Bette waited around for a trunk. I made a box for Emiko's records. Pop has been busy all evening getting out essential things for us to take. He got an old tea kettle out and gave me detailed instructions on how to boil water in Arizona so that the water won't make us sick. Tom got a lot of cardboard boxes and the place is now a mess.

.   .   .   .

Jack seems to have run into a little difficulty with the FBI. For the Junior H. S., the kids picked the school colors of red and white. Jack used the Vallejo Junior High school song and just substituted the red and white colors in the place of the Vallejo colors. Today an FBI man came around and asked about the song. He thought that it was subversive because the colors are the same as the Japanese flag. Jack said that the man was going to investigate his background. He told Jack not to tell the kids about the song and he will observe them on September 11 when they have a school party to see if they sing it with extra emotion.

Bette went to a party this afternoon given by some of the girls who are giving her a sendoff when she leaves. She did not eat much dinner. We just had rice and some pork. All of us decided to bring it home and cut the meat up and mix it in with eggs and the rice. Pop fixed it up for us. I took an extra portion and left it on the bureau. Alice came in to pick up all the dishes to wash. When she picked up mine I told her to save it. Jack said, "throw it out," so I repeated for her to save it. Evidently she did not hear me. Afterwards we started to pack a little and Alice fixed her jacket. This sort of infuriated me (evacuation nerves) but I did not say anything. Earlier in the day I had an argument with her about some mineral oil which was labeled for internal use. I said that I was going to use it for hair oil (as most of the pharmacists had suggested) and she said that I could not because it was for internal use. Then yesterday, Jack and I were peeved at her because she had turned in some of our spoons as Federal property.

Anyway, I went to get my meat and rice later around 9:30 but it was not there. Mom and Alice had thrown it out. I asked Alice, "What's the idea, I told you to save it."

"You did not, you said throw it out."

"God damn it, I said for you to save it. I told you twice."

Bette: "I remember him saying it."

Emiko: "No, he said throw it out."

Alice: "Quit yelling, you know you said throw it out."

I almost broke a blood vessel. It was the first time I had ever gotten so darn mad, especially when Alice sat there looking so righteous. Jack kept egging both of us on. She made only one more remark about it so I got exasperated and slapped her for the first time in my life. It was the first time I have ever slapped any girl. Alice: "You coward, hitting a girl with glasses." Then she kicked at me so I slapped her again. I felt so repentant immediately. Pop came in and bawled her out. Mom came in to bawl me out. We kicked them both out of the room and told them not to interfere. Alice went out in the cold wind in a rage. Emiko and Jack laughed because they thought it was so funny arguing over whether Alice did or did not hear me say "save it." Only Alice said that I told her to throw it out. I don't know what made me so irritated. Perhaps the impending move, nerves on edge for the long wait although I had not realized it. Anyway, I felt so sorry and like a heel afterwards so I went out to look for Alice. I could not find her so dropped over to Jimmy's place for a while to pick up the ironing board which I had loaned him about three months ago. It was 11:30 before I got home.

I went in at 12:30 and woke her to apologize to her. I guess it's all "ok" now. And all over a measly dish of rice—Jap food at that! Maybe we will have a whole series of family squabbles before we leave. One of the things which has been disturbing me, I think, is the fact that I am taking the responsibility of taking the family to Arizona and it will be hard for them there and I know that they may think it is my fault if the weather gets extra hot while the weather at Utah is good. Well, the die is cast now and there is not much I can do about it.

August 27, 1942 Thursday

The diarrhea epidemic which has been sweeping our district caught up to me. About the middle of the night I got a sharp pain in my stomach which grew in intensity. By morning I felt weak, with a headache and backache added. I went to the shower room and took a very hot shower, but it did not help much. I went up to the paper office and got a few stories. We are way behind this week. Cutting the paper down to six pages did not help much—instead of working ahead, we have been taking it easy, except Taro. I have almost finished up the two pages of "Your Opinion" and two pages of employment interviews of workers for the final edition and Bob is cutting them down. He showed up today. Jim has been practically useless as he is preoccupied with his card game—says he won $12.00 in the last session. It's the same bunch which we used to have up in the grandstands for our games. Alex is now on the payroll—they transferred him from the messhall and he will work on some features and take my place in getting the news when I leave. Bill Hata has come around in the last couple of days. He had to get his sports stuff in by today. Taro was a little irritated because it was late in coming in and he has to rewrite it anyway.

Davis still will not give us clearance on publishing the date for relocation. He says that the Army will not give the "ok."

. . . . .

The group around here interested in relocation today had a meeting in the Council chamber. A lot of the former Issei businessmen were there and they wanted to make sure that they will have a strong say in the cooperatives. The whole bunch (Toby, K., & Co.) want to get the thing all set up so that they can take control. Ernie has sort of dropped out from this former council group and their cohorts. He is more interested in the wider issues. The Comrades are circulating a petition to ask the WRA to have only strong anti-Fascists, those who have taken a firm stand, be eligible for "key" positions in the WRA centers.

This will not be restricted to citizens only, but to those that hold strong democratic beliefs. I signed the petition yesterday as well as all of the staff present. Toby and K. were discussing it this afternoon and they made the statement that they would have to kill this movement because you could not penalize the residents this way. Toby claimed that anyone advocating such a thing was intolerant himself and dangerous for the group. Toby and Ernie fundamentally are poles apart. Toby clings to a lot of conservative ideas and tends to cater to the Issei. But, he cannot be branded as a conservative because a lot of his ideas are also progressive. The only thing wrong with him is that his social vision is not as broad as Ernie's. The same goes for K. But they are good men to have and potential leaders. The people seem to have confidence in them. Maybe the group needs more of these practical men.

August 28, 1942

The rumors are growing in number again now that relocation is impending. One of the wildest stories sweeping the camp is about the murder of Walter Isukamoto up at Tule. I heard it at least five times today. Bob Iki was in to find out all the details this afternoon. Tom Y., our house manager, says that all of the Issei are passing the story around. Mr. S. even came over this evening to tell Pop all about it. Tom F. even believes that it is true. The story goes that the *Totalizer* got telegrams today saying that Isukamoto was murdered because he was too pro-America. Tom says that many Issei and Nisei are just holding back until they get to the relocation camp and then they are going to get all of the guys who are advocating Japan's belief. He says that they even got the guys [to admit] that there was no basis for such a story and furthermore it was about time that the Nisei took a definite stand.

Mom has been listening to too many of these stories. She says that this is the only way that she can get the news of what is going on. It got pretty bad when she went into the back room today just to listen to the neighbors gossiping so we ganged up on her and concocted a wild story about Mitch and Ann. I told her that Ann was very anxious about her baggage not arriving, so that she went to the postoffice at Poston to make inquiries. Mitch waited around at home for an hour and when she did not return, he got a little worried so that he walked down to the postoffice. Nobody was in sight so he started to look around. Suddenly he was shocked to see a huge boa constrictor crawling along with what looked like a human form in its belly.

Mitch whipped out his knife and running up to it, he slit its stomach open. Horrified, he jumped back. Who but Ann rolled out almost smothered to death. She opened her eyes and whispered, "I couldn't find our baggage," and passed out. Mitch rushed her to a hospital and Ann is now in serious condition with a broken arm and internal injuries. But she will recover.

Mom turned white as the story was being told and when I finished, she exclaimed: "I don't want to go to Arizona." It was so funny that we all began to laugh. Then Mom made out that she was wise all the time and she said that she made the remark in order to make the story better. This made us laugh all the more. We told her that this should be a lesson to her to discount all rumors she heard from now on.

.   .   .   .

Pop was quite worried today. Now he has the idea that he does not want to be left behind because we won't know how to take care of ourselves in the desert. Then he figures that it will be dangerous to remain down here after all of the other people are moved out. He thinks that bad men will come over the fence and harm the scattered few left behind. Jack told him not to worry, he would shoot anybody that attacked our house. Pop then got all excited and worried because he thought that Jack really had a gun! He has been puttering around all day lining the crate boxes with paper so that we can stuff our junk in. Nobody has gotten the ambition up to do any serious packing. There is an awful lot to be done and tomorrow we will have to tackle it in earnest.

Tom had his fun today also. He told Pop and Mom that we

would not have to worry about the Indians in Arizona, but we would have to be very careful about the Pueblo Indians since they are on the war path with all the Japanese moving onto their reservations.

August 29, 1942   Saturday

After lunch I packed a little. We are only going to take eight pieces of essential luggage with us and the rest will be sent by freight. The big problem was to decide just what to take. Emiko and Bette were having a big problem about their clothes. They had nothing big enough to put them in so I gave them one of my trunks. I think this was a big mistake because now I have to shift my things around in order to get them to fit into my remaining grips.

By the time it was 3:00 o'clock we really got going in earnest. Jack and I fixed up a lot of the boxes. Pop was in and out bringing me all sorts of things that he did not want me to forget. He was very helpful. We took apart the benches, tables, and desk and also the shelves. Any piece of lumber that we have is going with us. We sent Tom out to take nails out of all the boards. I never knew we had so much junk. The house was a regular madhouse with everybody running around and getting in the way. We still have a lot of packing to do tomorrow. Already we have about twenty boxes ready for inspection and shipment.

Mom came in and said that Emiko and Bette were getting too fresh. They disturbed Mom while she was talking to Mr. S., arguing [with] her to tell him about the "snake swallowing story." Mom said that they copied me too much and that I was "too much against the Issei." So we stopped packing for about five minutes to have a little debate and patch things up. Then we went back to work. By 8:00 o'clock things were in fair shape so Ernie and I left them with the mess to go to see "Elephant Boy" at the show. Jack wanted us to get a couple more of the ropes from the flagpoles by the South Hall. The picture was very dull. Emiko felt the call of nature afterwards so I led her into the men's latrine in the grandstand and stood guard so that no men would wander in.

With the Army blanket slung over my shoulders, I walked down to the social hall to accomplish our deed. There were a lot of "wolves" peeping in the window and I could not get any privacy while I cut down the ropes and pulled them down. Emiko is sure one heck of an accomplice. I told her to stand guard and give me a warning when anyone approached. Every time I pulled on the rope and it squeaked a bit, she started to giggle like anything, attracting the attention of the "wolves." Finally I had to bribe her—I told her that I would take her into the dance if she would not giggle so much. She agreed and I got two long ropes down without any further difficulty.

However, when I got inside I got my revenge. Everyone was there in ties and sport clothes. I had a dirty pair of jeans and a T-shirt on. When they played a real fast music, I took her right out to the middle of the floor and danced very slowly. The people all started to drop out, except about four couples who were jitterbugging and us. Emiko got so embarrassed that she walked off the floor leaving me flat! I wasn't embarrassed in the least since I knew a lot of the small crowd present. Everyone is busy packing these days or else having small parties in their barracks.

. . . .

I caused a sensation this morning by actually getting up for breakfast! It was an accident. I looked at my watch and I thought it said 8:15 so I got up and dressed. But I was griped no end when I found out that it was only 7:15. So I went around awakening everyone up to let them know that I was going to breakfast for the third time in the four months I have been in camp.

. . . .

We got a huge quantity of weenies and potato salad for the party tonight. After lunch we did some more packing. Jack knocked the furniture apart and wrapped it up. Emiko spent

most of the afternoon trying to figure out what clothes she
would need immediately. This is the third day she has been on
this. It must be quite a problem for girls to take the right
clothes no matter what destination. Emiko was helpful today
though, since she took an inventory of all the things we are
going to take and typed out triplicate copies so that we will
know if anything is missing. She also made out some tags for our
baggage. Bette scraped all the Japanese travel seals from our
luggage and finally found a place for her clothes. We are taking
quite a bit of lumber with us so that we can build some shelves,
etc., when we get there. There have been many letters coming
into camp from the various relocation centers telling how scarce
wood is to find. Since we are not to pay for the freight anyway,
we may as well take what we can in order to make our new
home more livable. After all we didn't ask to be evacuated. We
got most of the packing done today and it was one terrific job.
Alice wasn't of much use this time. Usually she is in the thick of
things trying to direct all. Now she is busy trying to get out of
camp so she can go marry Angelo. That has been settled between them. But she may have to come to relocation camp
before she can get a release.

August 31, 1942   Monday

After lunch Bette and Emiko went up to get their free scrip
tickets. Jack and I waited around for the Inspector to come, but
after an hour of waiting, Jack went up to the grandstands to
play out the final Junior High School party. Tom stayed here to
run for him when the Inspector came. Around 2:00 o'clock the
fellow came down. The truck backed up to our door, he stepped
out and asked: "Have you any contraband like Japanese records
or any Army blankets?" I said "no." "OK, nail them up and
load them on the truck, boys," he says and that was that. Jack,
Pop, and I nailed them all up and tied them up. Jack ordered
me not to nail up the bureau because I would mess things up.
I went ahead and drove the nails through the sides, only I forgot
to leave it out a little so that it is going to be a very hard job to

pull the nail out. Curious people gathered around to watch. The Inspector said: "I'll be damned if I'm going through all that stuff. I'll take your word." He seems to be a simple but a good-hearted fellow. He is going to ride down with us and be our "traveling guard."

.   .   .   .

Mr. I. gave me a carton of cigarettes for a going-away present and Mr. S. gave me 8 packs. I now have about 6 cartons to smoke. I hear that cigarettes are 18¢ a pack in Arizona. I have been saying "good bye" to so many people today that it is getting automatic. "I hear you are leaving?" is the standard question and then I have to go into the details.

After dinner we rushed around again to get our personal grips all fixed up. Bette and Emiko still were at their trunks. This time the problem was to get the dishes and cups in. We ended up by taking another small grip.

Then the people started to come in. Alice counted over 35. A whole mob of H. S. kids came to see Bette off. I didn't think Emiko and Bette wanted to leave, but would rather stay here. It won't make any difference to them in the Relocation Center— just another camp. We let Tom go to the movies tonight for the last time. Mom and Pop were busy all evening taking care of all the details and making sandwiches so that we would not get hungry on the train. Naturally they are quite worried about us leaving. Pop just came in to give me a few last-minute instructions to look over the floor when I get there so that snakes could not crawl in.

Everyone in the family is under a nervous tension, although tempers did not flare today. There were many instances during the day, however, when one or the other of us were on the verge. Bette probably was the touchiest. She would become furious at a moment's notice. This is no doubt due to the fact that she was just establishing a circle of friends and now she has to leave them without the prospects of seeing them again for a long time.

Now that the time for leaving has almost arrived, I feel a little uneasy about taking the kids down there. It would be all my responsibility if anything should happen to any of them. I don't have any fear of the place, but things are not going to be easy. And the rest of the family may end up in Utah and there will be the problem of getting reunited. This will make Mom and Pop worry like anything.

In reviewing the four months here, the chief value I got out of this forced evacuation was the strengthening of the family bonds. I never knew my family before this and this was the first chance that I have had to really get acquainted. There is something wholesome about it and with the unity which it presents, one does not feel alone, knowing that there are some who will back one up in moments of crisis. It sort of binds strength to an individual thrown into a completely strange group. We have had our arguments and bickerings, but this has been a normal process which only lasts for a little while. This family is composed of very strong individualists, but the right of the individual in the family is respected by the others if it does not conflict with the whole group and is [not] harmful to it.

Because the older children are around, the family is more advanced as far as Americanization is concerned. We were pretty far advanced even before our arrival in Tanforan in this respect, coming from a community where there were very few Japanese.

I don't quite know how to explain the growth of family unity rather than disorganization. One thing may be that it never was an economic bond since we never did have much money. Mom and Pop have conceded a lot to their children and they don't expect us to be anything else but American. The personalities of all the family are good. I certainly was not that way when I was of high-school age. Even now, the majority of the young Nisei that I see around seem rather reserved. It must be due to their wider contacts with Caucasian children. Emiko and Bette are much maturer than most of the other Nisei girls their age in this camp.

Pop and Mom have come through a difficult adjustment period. Now I believe that they actually like it here since they don't have any economic worries. Mom still has not realized that the children have grown up, but she is strongly aware of it. Most of the family decisions are now made by the older children. They [Mom and Pop] are naturally consulted and an effort is made to believe that it came from them.

Of course, we have only had four months of this life and things may be different after we have been in a camp for a much longer period. But we always manage to get along in a fair way. I wonder what will happen if we all suddenly rebelled against this kind of living? The postwar period is going to be trying no matter which way we look at it. I may do further graduate work or else try to get into Civil Service. The latter is the only future for me that I can see at this time.

Well, the new chapter starts tomorrow. I don't feel up to the effort to attempt a review of the camp now. I'm sleepy and I have to get up at 3 o'clock!

Notes on the Author and the Editor

Charles Kikuchi, an American-born son of Japanese parents, was interned with his family at the relocation center at Tanforan Race Track south of San Francisco in 1942. When World War II broke out, Kikuchi was a twenty-six-year-old graduate student in social welfare at the University of California. He recorded his experiences and observations in his diary, kept from December 7, 1941, to September, 1942, when the family was moved to another center. After the war Kikuchi completed his studies and worked for twenty-five years as a counselor in a Veterans' Administration hospital. He remained politically active until his death in 1988.

John Modell is professor in the Department of History at Carnegie-Mellon University. His publications include *The Economics and Politics of Racial Accommodation: The Japanese of Los Angeles, 1900–1942, Into One's Own: From Youth to Adulthood in the United States, 1920–1975,* and, with Edna Bonacich, *The Economic Basis of Ethnic Solidarity.*

PS 76

Alice
Jack
Emiko
Bette